Rust Essentials

Safe and Fast Programming

AF808156

Contents

Introduction

Rust is a modern systems programming language that places a premium on both safety and performance. It is engineered to ensure that developers can write fast, reliable, and efficient software without compromising on maintainability and robustness. This balance is struck through Rust's novel ownership system, which enforces strict rules that prevent many common programming errors at compile time. The language's syntax and semantics are meticulously designed to help developers achieve memory safety and thread safety with minimal runtime overhead.

Rust was developed by Mozilla Research and first appeared in 2010. Since then, it has grown in popularity and maturity, backed by an ever-increasing number of production applications, developer tools, and learning resources. The language was conceived to address the deficiencies in other systems programming languages such as C and C++. It aims to eliminate entire classes of bugs, particularly those related to memory management, which are notorious for being sources of security vulnerabilities and system crashes.

One of Rust's core principles is its concept of ownership. Ownership is a powerful feature that ensures memory safety without the need for a garbage collector. By encoding ownership rules into the type system, Rust allows the compiler to enforce memory safety guarantees statically, thereby preventing bugs related to dangling pointers, double frees, and data races. Borrowing and lifetimes further refine ownership rules by allowing flexible, safe references to data.

Rust is not just a language for systems programmers; it has a wide range of applications, from web development and network programming to game development and compiling other programming languages. The ecosystem around Rust is facilitated by Cargo, its integrated build system and package manager, which simplifies the process of managing dependencies, building projects, and distributing libraries.

A distinguishing feature of Rust is its focus on fearless concurrency. It provides robust abstractions for concurrent programming, leveraging its ownership system to statically prevent data races. The language's constructs for thread and memory management allow developers to write concurrent code that is both efficient and safe.

Learning Rust requires a shift in thinking, especially for those accustomed to other programming paradigms. However, the investment is well worth the effort, as it leads to more robust and maintainable codebases. This book is designed to introduce you to Rust's fundamental concepts and guide you through its essential features and libraries. Through carefully curated examples and exercises, you will gain practical experience that will enable you to harness the full potential of Rust in your projects.

As we embark on this exploration of Rust, you will encounter its core principles and features, from basic syntax and control structures to advanced topics like smart pointers and concurrency. Whether you are a seasoned programmer looking to add another tool to your toolkit or a newcomer eager to learn a modern, safe programming language, this book aims to provide you with the knowledge and confidence to excel in Rust programming.

Chapter 1

Introduction to Rust

This chapter provides an overview of Rust, including its origins, guiding principles, and the unique features that make it stand out in the landscape of modern programming languages. It introduces the core concepts of ownership, borrowing, and lifetimes, which are critical to Rust's memory safety guarantees. Additionally, this chapter covers the initial setup of a Rust development environment and guides the reader through writing their first Rust program, offering insight into Rust's syntax, conventions, and the broader ecosystem, including key resources and community involvement.

1.1 Welcome to Rust

Rust is a systems programming language designed for safety, speed, and concurrency. Introduced by Graydon Hoare while working at Mozilla Research, Rust has rapidly grown in popularity due to its unique combination of features that address common issues in other programming languages. At its core, Rust aims to eliminate entire classes of bugs, particularly related to memory safety and concurrency, making it an exceptional choice for system-level programming.

One of Rust's most distinguished features is its emphasis on memory safety without sacrificing performance. Unlike traditional languages such as C and C++, Rust enforces strict rules around memory allocation, deallocation, and access to prevent common errors like null pointer dereferencing, buffer overflows, and use-after-free bugs. These issues are mitigated by Rust's ownership model, which is a novel approach to managing memory and other resources.

Ownership in Rust revolves around three key concepts:

- Ownership
- Borrowing
- Lifetimes

These concepts dictate how memory is managed and ensure that programs are memory-safe.

Rust's ownership model assigns a single "owner" to each piece of data. The owner is responsible for cleaning up the data when it is no longer needed. This approach avoids the need for garbage collection, which can introduce latency and overhead in other programming languages. Here is a basic example of ownership in Rust:

```
fn main() {
    let s = String::from("hello"); // 's' comes into scope
    takes_ownership(s); // 's''s value moves into the function...
    // ... and so is no longer valid here
    // println!("{}", s); // this would cause a compile-time error
}

fn takes_ownership(some_string: String) { // 'some_string' comes into scope
    println!("{}", some_string);
} // Here, 'some_string' goes out of scope and 'drop' is called.
```

In the example above, the takes_ownership function takes ownership of the String. After the function call, the original s variable is no longer valid.

Borrowing allows a function to access data without taking ownership. This is useful when you want to read or modify data temporarily. Rust enforces borrowing rules to ensure memory safety. Here is an example:

```
fn main() {
    let s = String::from("hello"); // 's' comes into scope
    let len = calculate_length(&s); // 's' is borrowed here
    // 's' is still valid here and can be used
    println!("The length of '{}' is {}.", s, len);
}

fn calculate_length(s: &String) -> usize { // 's' is a reference to the 'String'
    s.len()
} // 's' goes out of scope, but since it does not have ownership of what it refers to,
    nothing happens.
```

Lifetimes in Rust ensure that references are always valid. They provide a way to specify that with certain references, the referenced data must outlive the reference. Lifetimes are usually implicit and inferable by Rust's compiler, but they can be explicitly annotated when necessary.

Rust also brings strong type safety to the table, leveraging a powerful type system that prevents many bugs and enhances code clarity and maintainability. Traits, Rust's feature for defining shared behavior, allow for ad-hoc polymorphism, offering flexibility and the ability to define methods for types, ensuring consistency across the codebase.

Concurrency in Rust is managed through "fearless concurrency," where the type system ensures safe access to data by multiple threads. Unlike in traditional languages where concurrent programming can be fraught with data races and other issues, Rust provides compile-time guarantees of safety. Here's an example of spawning a new thread in Rust:

```
use std::thread;

fn main() {
    let handle = thread::spawn(|| {
        for i in 1..10 {
            println!("hi number {} from the spawned thread!", i);
        }
    });

    for i in 1..5 {
        println!("hi number {} from the main thread!", i);
    }

    handle.join().unwrap(); // Ensure the spawned thread completes before main thread
        ends
}
```

This code creates a new thread using thread::spawn and ensures it completes using handle.join(). Rust's type system ensures that data shared across threads is safely accessed, avoiding common concurrency pitfalls.

Rust's compiler plays a crucial role in enforcing these strict rules. The compiler actively checks for violations of ownership, borrowing, and lifetimes, catching potential bugs at compile time rather than runtime. This proactive error-checking leads to more robust code and shifts the focus from debugging to writing correct code from the beginning.

Moreover, Rust embraces modern development practices such as modularity, with a strong emphasis on package management and dependency resolution through Cargo, its package manager and build system. Cargo simplifies the process of managing external libraries and ensures that all dependencies are appropriately versioned and resolved.

A basic Cargo project structure looks like this:

```
my_project/
  Cargo.toml
  src/
     main.rs
```

In Cargo.toml, dependencies are listed, and metadata about the project is stored, making it straightforward to manage larger projects and their dependencies.

By embracing safety principles without compromising on performance, Rust sets a new standard in systems programming. Its growing ecosystem and community support, coupled with its capabilities for writing reliable and efficient code, make Rust an attractive language for both beginners and experienced programmers.

1.2 Why Rust?

When selecting a programming language for system-level work or performance-critical applications, several factors come into play, including performance, safety, concurrency, and ecosystem support. Rust meets and often exceeds these criteria, positioning itself as a superior choice for a broad range of applications. Here, we will delve into the specific reasons Rust is preferred by many developers and organizations for developing safe and fast software.

Rust is celebrated for its unique approach to memory safety. Unlike other systems programming languages like C and C++ which rely heavily on manual memory management, Rust leverages a system of ownership with rules that the compiler checks at compile time. This system is designed to prevent common programming errors such as null pointer dereferencing, dangling pointers, and buffer overflows. By ensuring that such errors are caught during compilation, Rust significantly improves the reliability and robustness of the code.

Furthermore, Rust achieves impressive performance by performing zero-cost abstractions. This means that Rust's abstractions are designed to have no runtime overhead, optimizing performance without sacrificing safety or expressiveness. It produces binaries that are highly efficient, matching the performance of code written in traditional systems languages. Thus, developers can write high-level, readable code without compromising on execution speed.

Concurrency in Rust is handled in an innovative way. Rust's concurrency model is built on the same ownership principles, making data races virtually impossible. Data races are a common and hard-to-detect problem in concurrent programming, occurring when two or more threads access shared data simultaneously, and at least one of the accesses is a write. Rust's ownership system, alongside its borrowing mechanism, ensures that data is shared safely among threads, enabling the development of concurrent programs that are both efficient and free of data races.

Rust's ecosystem is robust and rapidly growing. The package manager and build system, Cargo, makes dependency management and project compilation straightforward. Cargo also facilitates the integration of external libraries through crates.io, Rust's package registry. This repository is filled with numerous well-maintained libraries that accelerate development by providing essential functionality and optimizing common tasks.

Let us examine a basic Rust program to demonstrate some of these features:

```
fn main() {
    let numbers = vec![1, 2, 3];
    for number in &numbers {
        println!("The number is {}", number);
    }
}
```

This program first initializes a vector of integers using the vec! macro, then iterates over each integer in the vector, printing it out. The use of the &numbers syntax indicates borrowing the vector, ensuring no ownership is transferred, which allows safe read-only access to its content within the loop. The Rust compiler will enforce the borrowing rules, preventing unsafe interactions or modifications of numbers during iteration.

Another significant advantage of Rust is its vibrant and supportive community. Resources such as the Rust Book, official documentation, and numerous online forums provide extensive learning materials and community support, aiding new developers in their journey with Rust. The Rust community adheres to the values of inclusivity and friendliness, often emphasizing helpfulness and approachability, which contributes to a positive developer experience.

Incorporating these elements, one can appreciate why major corporations, including Mozilla, Dropbox, and Microsoft, have adopted Rust for numerous critical projects. The language's ability to combine performance and safety seamlessly has also made it an attractive option for startups and solo developers alike. It has grown to be a keystone in the programming landscape, well-suited for everything from embedded systems to web assembly.

Therefore, Rust's ownership system, its performance, concurrency model, robust package management, and supportive community make it an exceptional choice for developing reliable, efficient, and maintainable software. Implementing Rust in projects is an investment in code quality and efficiency, providing benefits that resonate throughout the entire software development lifecycle.

1.3 History and Development of Rust

The Rust programming language has a rich history and distinct development path that contributes significantly to its current features and strengths. This section delves into the origins, evolution, and key milestones in the development of Rust.

Rust was originally designed by Graydon Hoare in 2006 as a personal project aimed at creating a 'safe, concurrent, practical' language. Hoare's motivation stemmed from his experience with existing programming languages and the frequent occurrence of segmentation faults and data races. The development took place at Mozilla Research, and by 2009, it attracted widespread interest within the Mozilla organization. This growing interest was primarily due to Rust's promise of guaranteeing memory safety without needing a garbage collector, which was particularly appealing for system-level programming.

Mozilla officially sponsored the Rust project in 2009, which accelerated its development. The sponsorship provided the resources necessary for a dedicated team, and the Rust project saw its first major release with version 0.1 in January 2012. Rust's early releases were integral in refining its core principles, particularly the ownership system, which remains a cornerstone of Rust's memory safety guarantees.

In 2013, the language gained full-time developers, and the team worked intensively on the stability and performance of Rust. The following year, in 2014, marked several critical developments. One such milestone was the replacement of the original object system with traits, inspired by Haskell's typeclasses. This change underscored Rust's focus on zero-cost abstractions and ensured better performance while maintaining flexibility and expressiveness in type design.

Rust 1.0, the first stable release, was launched on May 15, 2015. This version was a significant milestone because it established a commitment to stability and backward compatibility, ensuring that code written in Rust 1.0 would remain compatible with future versions. The Rust team introduced a rigorous six-week release cycle, which balanced the need for innovation with the assurance of a dependable development environment.

One of Rust's pioneering features that emerged during this period was its pervasive use of the ownership system, which consists of the following core principles: ownership, borrowing, and lifetimes. These principles are key to managing memory safety and concurrency without a garbage collector. Ownership dictates that each value in Rust has a single owner, preventing data races by design. Borrowing enables references to data without taking ownership, providing a way to access data safely and ensuring that references remain valid through the use of lifetimes.

The ecosystem around Rust continued to evolve rapidly, supported by a growing and vibrant community. Cargo, Rust's package manager, played a vital role by simplifying dependency management and building processes, fostering open-source contributions and collaboration. Cargo's integration into the language from the early stages was a strategic move that ensured coherence and efficiency in Rust project workflows.

In subsequent years, Rust's community and contributions expanded significantly. The 'Rust RFC (Request for Comments)' process was established to manage and moderate the inclusion of new features and changes. This process involves comprehensive discussion and review, ensuring that every modification aligns with Rust's philosophy and long-term vision.

In 2016, Rust received recognition as the 'most loved' language in the Stack Overflow Developer Survey, a testament to its growing popularity and the satisfaction of developers who adopted it. This accolade has been repeated in multiple subsequent years, further solidifying Rust's position in the programming landscape.

From a technical perspective, the evolution of Rust's toolchain and compiler has been noteworthy. The Rust compiler, 'rustc', has seen numerous optimizations over the years, contributing to faster compile times and more efficient runtime performance. Additionally, the introduction of the 'Rust Language Server (RLS)' enhanced development by providing features like auto-completion, goto definition, and inline error messages, significantly improving developer productivity.

Rust has also been influential in various domains such as WebAssembly, with 'wasm-bindgen' enabling Rust to be used for web applications by facilitating interactions between Rust and JavaScript. This adaptability demonstrates Rust's versatility across different platforms and its capability to interoperate with other languages and technologies seamlessly.

As Rust continues to develop, the core team remains dedicated to upholding the principles of safety, concurrency, and practicality. The language has expanded its reach across diverse application areas, including web development, embedded systems, and operating system development, reflecting its robustness and flexibility. Continuous advancements in the 'async' programming model and improvements in the ergonomics of the language further attest to its evolving nature in addressing modern programming needs.

Rust's development journey, marked by strategic decisions and community collaboration, has created a reliable and powerful programming language. Its commitment to memory safety, zero-cost abstractions, and concurrency ensures that it remains a formidable tool for developers building reliable and efficient software. The ongoing contributions from its community and the structured approach to feature enhancements promise a promising trajectory for Rust in the years to come.

1.4 Rust's Core Principles

Rust's design is heavily influenced by several core principles that underpin the language's unique position within the programming landscape. Among these, three principles—ownership, borrowing, and lifetimes—are central to Rust's approach to memory management and safety. Understanding these principles is crucial for mastering Rust and leveraging its full potential.

Ownership is a mechanism that ensures memory safety without a garbage collector by enforcing strict rules about how memory is managed. Every value in Rust has a variable that is called its owner. The key rules of ownership are:

- Each value in Rust has a single owner.
- When the owner goes out of scope, the value will be dropped.

- Values can be passed to other variables, but this transfers ownership.

Consider the following example:

```
fn main() {
    let s1 = String::from("hello");
    let s2 = s1;
    println!("{}", s1); // This line will cause a compile error
}
```

In this example, s1 owns the string "hello". When s2 is assigned the value of s1, ownership is transferred to s2. As a result, s1 is no longer valid and trying to use it will cause a compile-time error.

Building on ownership, **borrowing** lets a value be referenced without transferring ownership. There are two types of borrowing: immutable and mutable. Immutable references allow reading data without modifying it, whereas mutable references allow data modification. However, Rust enforces strict borrowing rules:

- Any number of immutable references are allowed.
- Only one mutable reference is allowed at a time.
- References must always be valid, ensuring there are no dangling pointers.

Example of immutable and mutable references:

```
fn main() {
    let mut s = String::from("hello");

    // Immutable borrow
    let r1 = &s;
    let r2 = &s;
    println!("{} and {}", r1, r2);

    // Mutable borrow
    let r3 = &mut s;
    r3.push_str(", world!");
    println!("{}", r3);

    // The following line would cause a compile error due to simultaneous
    // immutable and mutable borrows:
    // println!("{} and {}", r1, r3);
}
```

This program demonstrates borrowing where r1 and r2 hold immutable references to s, allowing read-only access. A mutable reference r3 later allows modification but cannot coexist with immutable references.

Finally, **lifetimes** are annotations that connect borrowing with the scope in which references are valid. Lifetimes prevent dangling references by ensuring all references are valid for as long as they're needed, and no longer. Rust's compiler can often infer lifetimes, but explicit specification may be required in more complex scenarios. Lifetimes use a tick notation, e.g., 'a:

```
fn longest<'a>(x: &'a str, y: &'a str) -> &'a str {
    if x.len() > y.len() {
        x
    } else {
        y
    }
}

fn main() {
    let string1 = String::from("long string is long");
    let string2 = String::from("xyz");

    let result = longest(string1.as_str(), string2.as_str());
    println!("The longest string is {}", result);
}
```

In this function, 'a defines a lifetime that is shared across the function parameters and return value. This specification ensures that the returned reference is valid as long as either of the input references.

These core principles together ensure that Rust programs are memory safe, preventing common issues like null pointer dereferencing, buffer overflows, and use-after-free errors. As we continue exploring Rust, these principles will remain foundational to understanding more advanced concepts and writing effective, efficient, and safe code.

1.5 Setting Up Your Development Environment

To effectively work with Rust, setting up a robust development environment is crucial. This section provides detailed instructions for installing Rust, using the Rust package manager cargo, integrating development tools, and configuring your IDE for optimal productivity.

Installing Rust

The recommended way to install Rust is via rustup, a command-line tool that manages Rust versions and toolchains. To install rustup, execute the following command in your terminal:

```
curl --proto '=https' --tlsv1.2 -sSf https://sh.rustup.rs | sh
```

Follow the on-screen instructions to complete the installation. Once installed, verify that Rust and cargo are correctly installed by running:

```
rustc --version
cargo --version
```

You should see output similar to:

```
rustc 1.55.0 (c8dfcfe04 2021-09-06)
cargo 1.55.0 (32da73ab1 2021-08-23)
```

Setting Up the Toolchain

Rust is continuously evolving, and managing different versions can be crucial for various projects. rustup allows installing and configuring multiple toolchains:

```
rustup install stable
rustup install nightly
rustup default stable
```

The above commands install both the stable and nightly versions of Rust and set the stable version as the default toolchain.

Using cargo

cargo is Rust's package manager and build system, streamlining the process of managing dependencies, running tests, and building projects. To create a new Rust project, use:

```
cargo new my_project
cd my_project
```

This creates a new directory called my_project with a basic Rust project structure. To build and run the project, use:

```
cargo build
cargo run
```

cargo also manages dependencies through the Cargo.toml file. Adding dependencies is as simple as including them in this file under the *[dependencies]* section.

Configuring Your Development Environment

While you can write Rust code in any text editor, integrating with an IDE can significantly improve your productivity. Popular IDEs and editors that support Rust include Visual Studio Code, IntelliJ IDEA, Eclipse, and more.

Visual Studio Code

To set up Visual Studio Code for Rust development:

- Install Visual Studio Code from https://code.visualstudio.com/.
- Add the rust-analyzer extension from the Extensions Marketplace.

Once installed, rust-analyzer provides features like code completion, inline documentation, syntax highlighting, diagnostics, and more.

IntelliJ IDEA

For JetBrains users, the IntelliJ Rust plugin is a robust choice:

- Download and install IntelliJ IDEA from https://www.jetbrains.com/idea/download/.
- Navigate to File > Settings > Plugins and search for Rust, then install it.

The plugin offers comprehensive support, including a smart editor, Cargo integration, and debugging tools.

Further Configuration

To optimize your Rust setup, several additional tools and configurations can enhance your development experience:

- **Clippy:** A Rust linter that helps catch common mistakes and improve your code. Install it with:

  ```
  rustup component add clippy
  cargo clippy
  ```

- **Rustfmt:** A tool for auto-formatting your Rust code according to style guidelines. Install it using:

  ```
  rustup component add rustfmt
  cargo fmt
  ```

Taking these steps ensures that your development environment is well-equipped for both learning and professional development, enabling you to leverage the full power and potential of Rust in an efficient manner.

1.6 Your First Rust Program

To create your first Rust program, you need to follow a series of steps, from setting up your development environment to compiling and running your code. This section will guide you meticulously through this process.

First, ensure that you have Rust installed on your system. Rust provides a tool called rustup, an installer for the Rust programming language, which can be used to manage Rust versions and associated tools. To install rustup, open your terminal and type the following command:

```
curl --proto '=https' --tlsv1.2 -sSf https://sh.rustup.rs | sh
```

This command downloads and runs the rustup-init script, which installs rustup along with the latest stable version of Rust. Follow the on-screen prompts to complete the installation. Afterward, ensure that your system's path is correctly set up by restarting your terminal or running:

```
source $HOME/.cargo/env
```

Verify the installation by checking the version of Rust:

```
rustc --version
```

A successful installation will display the version number, e.g., rustc 1.55.0 (c8dfcfe04 2021-09-06).

Next, create a new directory for your project and navigate into it:

```
mkdir hello_rust
cd hello_rust
```

Within this directory, create a new Rust project using cargo, Rust's build system and package manager:

```
cargo new hello_world
cd hello_world
```

The cargo new command generates a new directory named hello_world with the following structure:

```
hello_world
  Cargo.toml
  src
     main.rs
```

The Cargo.toml file is the manifest file for Rust's package manager,

Cargo. It contains metadata about your project, including its name, version, and dependencies. The src/main.rs file is where you'll write your Rust code.

Open src/main.rs in your preferred text editor. You will find the following code pre-generated:

```
fn main() {
    println!("Hello, world!");
}
```

This small program defines a main function, which is the entry point for Rust programs. Inside the main function, it calls the println! macro to print the message "Hello, world!" to the console.

To compile and run your program, use Cargo:

```
cargo run
```

You should see the following output in your terminal:

```
   Compiling hello_world v0.1.0 (path/to/hello_rust/hello_world)
    Finished dev [unoptimized + debuginfo] target(s) in 1.40s
     Running `target/debug/hello_world`
Hello, world!
```

The cargo run command performs several actions:

- **Compiles your code:** Cargo invokes the Rust compiler, rustc, to compile main.rs into a binary executable.
- **Builds dependencies:** If your project has dependencies listed in Cargo.toml, Cargo fetches and builds them.
- **Runs the output:** After compilation, Cargo executes the resulting binary.

If you prefer to compile your code without running it immediately, you can use:

```
cargo build
```

This command compiles your code, generating an executable in the target/debug directory. To run the compiled program manually, use:

```
./target/debug/hello_world
```

Let's modify the program slightly to understand more aspects of Rust. Edit src/main.rs to include a variable:

```
fn main() {
    let name = "Rustacean";
    println!("Hello, {}!", name);
}
```

In this modified program:

- The let keyword introduces a variable name, which is bound to the string "Rustacean".
- The println! macro is used to print the greeting, but this time with a placeholder {} that is replaced by the variable name.

Run the updated program with:

```
cargo run
```

The output will be:

```
   Compiling hello_world v0.1.0 (path/to/hello_rust/hello_world)
    Finished dev [unoptimized + debuginfo] target(s) in 0.89s
     Running `target/debug/hello_world`
Hello, Rustacean!
```

This example demonstrates variable binding and string interpolation in Rust. Rust's variables are immutable by default, but you can make them mutable using the mut keyword.

Further enhancements can be made by adding more complex functionality. Consider adding a function to the program:

```
fn main() {
    let name = "Rustacean";
    greet(name);
}

fn greet(name: &str) {
    println!("Hello, {}!", name);
}
```

In this updated program:

- A function greet is defined, which takes a single parameter name of type &str.
- The main function now calls greet, passing the variable name as an argument.

Running cargo run again will produce the same output but demonstrates how to define and use functions in Rust. The function greet takes a string slice &str, which is a reference to a string. This is related to Rust's references and borrowing principles.

By following these steps, you should now have a clear understanding of creating, compiling, and running a basic Rust program, along with foundational knowledge of variables and functions in Rust.

1.7 Understanding Rust's Syntax and Conventions

Rust, as a system programming language, offers a syntax that, while unique in several respects, draws familiarity from languages like C++ and Python. A precise understanding of its syntax and conventions is crucial for writing effective and idiomatic Rust code. This section delves into key syntactical elements and conventions in Rust, providing examples to illustrate their usage.

Variable Bindings and Mutability

In Rust, variable bindings are immutable by default. This ensures safety and reduces bugs due to unintended changes of values. However, variables can be made mutable using the mut keyword. Consider the following examples:

```
let x = 5; // Immutable binding
let mut y = 10; // Mutable binding
y = 15; // Valid, as y is mutable
```

To underline this, attempting to change an immutable variable will result in a compile-time error.

Data Types and Type Inference

Rust is statically typed, requiring that the type of each variable be known at compile time. However, Rust's compiler can often infer the type based on the context, making declarations concise. Explicit type annotations are optional but sometimes necessary for clarity or complex expressions.

```
let a = 42; // Type inferred as i32
let b: f64 = 3.14; // Type explicitly specified
```

Functions and Methods

Functions in Rust are declared using the fn keyword. Methods, which are associated with object-like structures, follow a similar syntax but are defined within impl blocks. Here is a simple function declaration:

```
fn add(x: i32, y: i32) -> i32 {
    x + y
}
```

The -> symbol indicates the return type of the function. Returning values can be done implicitly by omitting the semicolon at the end of the return expression.

Control Flow

Rust supports traditional control flow constructs such as if, else, and else if. Additionally, loop constructs include loop, while, and for. Here's how they are expressed:

```
let number = 7;

if number < 5 {
    println!("Less than five");
} else if number == 5 {
    println!("Equal to five");
} else {
    println!("Greater than five");
}
```

```
let array = [10, 20, 30, 40];

for element in array.iter() {
    println!("Element: {}", element);
}
```

Pattern Matching

Pattern matching, facilitated by the match keyword, is a powerful feature in Rust. It allows for concise handling of various conditional branches. Consider the following usage:

```
let number = 2;

match number {
    1 => println!("One"),
    2 => println!("Two"),
    3 => println!("Three"),
    _ => println!("Something else"), // The underscore is a catch-all pattern
}
```

Ownership, Borrowing, and Lifetimes

Key to understanding Rust's memory safety features are the concepts of ownership, borrowing, and lifetimes. Each value in Rust has a single owner, and when the owner goes out of scope, the value is dropped. Borrowing allows references to a value without taking ownership.

```
let s1 = String::from("hello");
let s2 = &s1; // Borrowing s1
```

The concept of lifetimes denotes the scope for which a reference is valid. This is often annotated in function signatures to ensure references do not outlive their data.

Structs and Enums

Structured data types in Rust are defined using structs and enums. Structs are typically used to group related data together.

```
struct Point {
    x: i32,
    y: i32,
}

let origin = Point { x: 0, y: 0 };
```

Enums are used to define a type by enumerating its possible variants.

```
enum Direction {
    North,
    South,
    East,
    West,
}

let dir = Direction::North;
```

Traits

Traits in Rust are similar to interfaces in other languages. They define shared behavior that types can implement. Rust's standard library includes many useful traits like Clone, Debug, and PartialEq.

```
trait Greet {
    fn greeting(&self) -> String;
}

struct Person {
    name: String,
}

impl Greet for Person {
    fn greeting(&self) -> String {
        format!("Hello, my name is {}", self.name)
    }
}

let p = Person { name: String::from("Alice") };
println!("{}", p.greeting());
```

Adhering to these syntactical rules and conventions not only helps in writing safe and efficient code but also makes your code more readable and maintainable for others working within the Rust ecosystem.

1.8 Exploring the Rust Ecosystem

The Rust ecosystem encompasses a wide array of tools, libraries, and frameworks designed to support developers in creating high-performance and safe applications. This section explores the pivotal components of the Rust ecosystem, focusing on the package manager *Cargo*, the official package registry *crates.io*, and automated documentation generation with *rustdoc*. Attention to these elements will provide a comprehensive understanding of the productivity tools central to Rust development.

Cargo: The Rust Package Manager

Cargo, Rust's package manager, simplifies the process of managing dependencies, compiling code, running tests, and generating documentation. It is installed alongside Rust, making it readily available to developers. A typical Rust project structure includes a Cargo.toml file, which outlines the project's configuration and dependencies.

To create a new Rust project using Cargo, use the command:

```
$ cargo new project_name
```

This command initializes a new directory with the project's name, containing the fundamental structure:

```
project_name/
  Cargo.toml
  src
    main.rs
```

The Cargo.toml file sets the project's metadata and dependencies in the following format:

```
[package]
name = "project_name"
version = "0.1.0"
authors = ["Your Name <email@example.com>"]
edition = "2021"

[dependencies]
```

To add a dependency, such as the rand crate, include it under the [dependencies] section:

```
[dependencies]
rand = "0.8"
```

Run the command cargo build to download the dependencies, compile the project, and create an executable in the target/debug/ directory. Developers can further utilize:

- cargo run – to compile and execute the project.
- cargo test – to run unit and integration tests.
- cargo doc – to generate documentation.

Crates.io: The Official Package Registry

Crates.io is Rust's official package registry, where developers can publish, discover, and share libraries for reuse. Accessing crates.io enables developers to browse available packages, download dependencies, and view documentation and source code.

To include a crate from crates.io in a Rust project, specify its name and version in the Cargo.toml file. For example:

```
[dependencies]
serde = "1.0"
```

The serde crate, a popular serialization framework, will then be fetched and integrated into the project upon executing cargo build or cargo update.

To publish a crate, first ensure the Cargo.toml file contains all necessary fields, and run:

```
$ cargo login
$ cargo publish
```

Successful publication will make the crate available on crates.io, simplifying its inclusion in other projects.

Rustdoc: Automated Documentation Generation

Rust provides *rustdoc*, a tool to generate HTML documentation directly from the source code. It extracts comments and annotations, creating robust and navigable documentation. Rust supports Markdown within comments, facilitating the inclusion of rich text elements.

To document a function, use triple slashes /// for brief descriptions, or the block comment form /** ... */ for more detailed explanations:

```
/// Adds two numbers together.
///
/// # Examples
///
/// ```
/// let result = add(2, 3);
/// assert_eq!(result, 5);
/// ```
fn add(a: i32, b: i32) -> i32 {
    a + b
}
```

Running cargo doc generates documentation for the entire project, allowing access via target/doc/ index.html. This generated documentation includes not only user-written comments but also API documentation derived from the source code.

Together, Cargo, crates.io, and rustdoc provide a cohesive development environment, enhancing productivity and encouraging the reuse of reliable components. Understanding these tools enriches the development experience and aligns with Rust's philosophy of safety, concurrency, and speed.

1.9 Community and Resources

The Rust programming language boasts a vibrant and supportive community, which serves as an invaluable resource for both novice and experienced programmers. This section explores various facets of the Rust community and provides detailed information on the resources available to help you navigate and leverage the ecosystem effectively.

Rust Users Forum

The Rust Users Forum is one of the primary destinations for seeking help, sharing knowledge, and discussing ideas related to Rust development. The forum can be accessed at https://users.rust-lang.org/. It is an inclusive platform where users of all skill levels can pose questions, answer queries, and engage in discussions about projects, careers, and language features.

Rust Internals Forum

For those interested in the more technical aspects of Rust, including compiler development and language design, the Rust Internals Forum is the go-to place. Found at https://internals.rust-lang.org/, it caters to contributors who wish to delve deeper into the language's internals and engage in discussions about its evolution.

Rust Language Team and Governance

The Rust language is maintained and steered by a team of dedicated contributors from across the globe. The Rust core team is responsible for the overall direction of the language, while several sub-teams focus on specific areas like libraries, compiler, language design, and tooling. Information about the various teams and their roles can be found on the official Rust governance page: https://www.rust-lang.org/governance.

Official Documentation

The official Rust documentation is a comprehensive resource that covers every aspect of the language. The primary documentation can be accessed at https://doc.rust-lang.org/, and it includes sections such as:

- The Rust Programming Language (also known as "The Book") - A detailed guide that introduces Rust's syntax and features progressively.
- Rust by Example - A hands-on approach that provides examples and exercises for learning Rust concepts.
- Rust Reference - An exhaustive reference detailing the complete specification of the Rust language.
- The Rust Standard Library - Documentation of the standard library API, covering all the essential modules and functions.

Crates.io and Cargo

Crates.io is the official Rust package registry, where developers can publish and share their Rust libraries and applications. It is accessible at https://crates.io/. Cargo, Rust's package manager and build system, integrates seamlessly with Crates.io to simplify the process of dependency management and project compilation.

To illustrate how to use Cargo and Crates.io, consider a scenario where you need to add a dependency to your project. This can be done by editing the Cargo.toml file and specifying the desired crate:

```
[dependencies]
serde = "1.0"
```

By running the command cargo build, Cargo automatically fetches the specified crate and its dependencies, making them available for use in your project.

Rust Playground

The Rust Playground is an online editor that allows you to write, compile, and run Rust code directly in your browser. It is particularly useful for experimenting with code snippets and sharing them with others. Access the Rust Playground at https://play.rust-lang.org/.

Rustaceans on Social Media

The Rust community extends to various social media platforms, providing avenues for informal interaction, announcements, and networking. Notable platforms include:

- Twitter - Follow @rustlang for official updates and join the conversation using the hashtag #rustlang.
- Reddit - The r/rust subreddit is an active community where users share articles, ask questions, and discuss Rust-related topics.
- Discord - The Rust Community Discord server offers chatrooms for real-time discussions and support.

Rust Conferences and Meetups

Rust developers frequently organize conferences and meetups, providing opportunities for in-person connections, learning, and collaboration. Prominent conferences include RustConf, RustFest, and local RustBridge workshops. Information about upcoming events can often be found on the official Rust website or community forums.

Learning and Mentoring Programs

The Rust community is dedicated to fostering growth and inclusivity. Programs such as "RustBridge" offer workshops aimed at introducing underrepresented groups to Rust, while the "Rust Mentorship Program" pairs experienced developers with newcomers to provide guidance and support.

Books and Guides

Several high-quality books and guides complement the official documentation, catering to different learning styles and levels of expertise. Noteworthy titles include:

- "Programming Rust" by Jim Blandy and Jason Orendorff

- "The Rust Programming Language" by Steve Klabnik and Carol Nichols
- "Rust in Action" by Tim McNamara

Engaging with the vibrant Rust community and utilizing the wide array of available resources can significantly enhance your learning experience and proficiency with the language. The collaborative and supportive nature of the Rust community is one of its greatest strengths, providing a fertile ground for both personal and professional growth within the ecosystem.

Chapter 2

Getting Started with Rust

This chapter focuses on the practical steps to begin programming in Rust. It details the installation process, introduces Cargo as Rust's build system and package manager, and walks through the creation and configuration of a new Rust project. Readers will learn basic Rust syntax and structure, how to use external crates and modules, and the importance of Rust documentation. Additionally, the chapter covers version control, debugging techniques, and the steps required to build and release a Rust project.

2.1 Installing Rust

Before diving into Rust programming, it is imperative to set up the development environment. The installation process for Rust is straightforward and well-supported across various operating systems. Rust utilizes a command-line tool called rustup to manage the Rust installation and provide seamless updates. The following steps outline the process to install Rust on different operating systems: Windows, macOS, and Linux.

Windows:

- Download and run the rustup-init.exe installer from the official Rust website (https://www.rust-lang.org/tools/install).
- Follow the on-screen instructions provided by the installer. The default installation options are recommended for most users.

- After the installation completes, verify the installation by checking the Rust and Cargo versions:

```
$ rustc --version
$ cargo --version
```

  The output should display the installed versions of rustc (the Rust compiler) and cargo (the Rust package manager).

macOS:

- Open the Terminal application.
- Execute the following command to download and run the rustup installer script:

```
$ curl --proto '=https' --tlsv1.2 -sSf https://sh.rustup.rs | sh
```

- Follow the on-screen prompts. The default installation options are suitable for most users.
- Once the installation is finished, confirm the installation by checking the Rust and Cargo versions:

```
$ rustc --version
$ cargo --version
```

  The output will show the installed versions of rustc and cargo.

Linux:

- Launch the terminal window.
- To download and execute the rustup installer, run the following command:

```
$ curl --proto '=https' --tlsv1.2 -sSf https://sh.rustup.rs | sh
```

- Follow the prompts in the terminal. The default options are recommended for a standard installation.
- Verify the successful installation by checking the Rust and Cargo versions:

```
$ rustc --version
$ cargo --version
```

The displayed versions provide information about the installed rustc and cargo versions.

Updating Rust:

- Use rustup to update the Rust toolchain:

```
$ rustup update
```

- This command ensures that both rustc and cargo are up to date with the latest stable releases.

Uninstalling Rust:

- If you need to uninstall Rust for any reason, use the following command:

```
$ rustup self uninstall
```

- This command will remove Rust and the rustup toolchain manager from your system.

Verifying the Installation: To ensure that the Rust installation is correctly configured, you can compile and run a simple Rust program. Create a new file called main.rs with the following contents:

```
fn main() {
    println!("Hello, Rust!");
}
```

Compile the program with the Rust compiler:

```
$ rustc main.rs
```

Execute the compiled binary:

```
$ ./main
Hello, Rust!
```

The output Hello, Rust! indicates that Rust is installed correctly and the compiler is functioning as expected.

Rust installation through rustup not only installs the necessary components but also facilitates managing different Rust versions and toolchains, ensuring a flexible development environment tailored to specific project needs or development stages.

2.2 Understanding Cargo: Rust's Build System and Package Manager

Cargo is Rust's integrated build system and package manager. It streamlines the process of managing Rust dependencies, compiling projects, running tests, and building packages. By automating these tasks, Cargo allows developers to focus on writing code rather than worrying about build configurations and dependency management.

Installing and Running Cargo. Cargo is bundled with the standard Rust installation, so there is no need to install it separately. Verify the installation by running the following command in your terminal:

```
$ cargo --version
```

The output should display the installed version of Cargo, similar to the following:

```
cargo 1.55.0 (32da0a45 2021-08-23)
```

Creating a New Rust Project. Cargo simplifies project creation with the cargo new command. For instance, to create a new Rust project named hello_world, execute:

```
$ cargo new hello_world --bin
```

The –bin flag indicates that this is an executable project. Cargo creates a directory named hello_world with the following structure:

```
hello_world/
  Cargo.toml
  src
     main.rs
```

Understanding the Cargo.toml File. The Cargo.toml file contains project metadata and dependencies. This file uses the TOML (Tom's Obvious, Minimal Language) format. Here is an example of the initial Cargo.toml created by Cargo:

```
[package]
name = "hello_world"
version = "0.1.0"
authors = ["Your Name <youremail@example.com>"]
edition = "2018"

[dependencies]
```

The [package] section includes metadata such as the project name, version, authors, and Rust edition. The [dependencies] section is initialized empty, where you will add external crates required by the project.

Building and Running a Project with Cargo. To build the project, navigate to the project directory and run:

```
$ cargo build
```

Cargo compiles the project and stores the output in the target/debug directory. To run the project, use:

```
$ cargo run
```

This command compiles the project (if necessary) and runs the resulting executable. The output should be:

```
   Compiling hello_world v0.1.0 (/path/to/hello_world)
    Finished dev [unoptimized + debuginfo] target(s) in 0.87s
     Running 'target/debug/hello_world'
Hello, world!
```

Adding Dependencies. To include external libraries, or crates, specify them in the [dependencies] section of the Cargo.toml file. For example, to add the rand crate for random number generation, modify Cargo.toml as follows:

```
[dependencies]
rand = "0.8"
```

Next, update the dependencies and build the project:

```
$ cargo build
```

Cargo fetches the rand crate and its dependencies, compiles them, and incorporates them into the project.

Using Cargo with Existing Projects. For projects not initially created with Cargo, initialize Cargo support using:

```
$ cargo init
```

This command creates a Cargo.toml file in the current directory, transforming it into a Cargo-managed project.

Organizing Project Workflows with Cargo. Define additional configurations, scripts, and workflows in the Cargo.toml file. These configurations streamline tasks such as running tests, checking code coverage, and deploying applications.

Running Tests with Cargo. To execute tests, ensure your project includes test functions annotated with ##[cfg(test)]. Run tests using:

```
$ cargo test
```

Cargo discovers and runs tests automatically, displaying the results.

For example, in a project with passing and failing tests:

```
running 2 tests
test tests::test_success ... ok
test tests::test_failure ... FAILED

failures:

---- tests::test_failure stdout ----
thread 'tests::test_failure' panicked at 'assertion failed: `(left == right)`
  left: `2`,
 right: `1`', src/lib.rs:10:9
note: run with `RUST_BACKTRACE=1` environment variable to display a backtrace

failures:
    tests::test_failure

test result: FAILED. 1 passed; 1 failed; 0 ignored; 0 measured; 0 filtered out; finished in 0.01s

error: test failed, to rerun pass '--lib'
```

Building and Publishing Crates. For publishing libraries or executables to the Rust community, create an account at crates.io. Configure Cargo with your API token using:

```
$ cargo login <your_crates_io_token>
```

Then publish your crate:

```
$ cargo publish
```

Cargo verifies your crate configuration and uploads it to crates.io, making it available to other developers. Implement Cargo best practices to ensure smooth management and integration of Rust projects effectively.

2.3 Creating and Configuring a New Rust Project

To create and configure a new Rust project, engage the Cargo build system and package manager, which simplifies the process of initializing, building, and managing project dependencies.

First, create a new project using Cargo. Open a terminal and execute the following command:

```
cargo new my_project
```

This command generates a new directory named my_project containing a basic Rust project structure. Navigate into this directory:

```
cd my_project
```

Within the project directory, observe the following structure:

```
my_project/
  Cargo.toml
  src
    main.rs
```

The Cargo.toml file is the project's manifest file, specifying the project's metadata and dependencies. It contains sections such as [package] for project metadata and [dependencies] for external crate dependencies.

Open Cargo.toml to see the following default contents:

```
[package]
name = "my_project"
version = "0.1.0"
edition = "2021"

[dependencies]
```

[package] includes the project's name, version, and edition, typically set to the most recent stable edition, ensuring your project adheres to the latest language features and conventions.

Next, examine the src/main.rs file. By default, it contains a simple Hello, world! program:

```
//! Main entry point of the application

fn main() {
    println!("Hello, world!");
}
```

To build and run this project, execute:

```
cargo run
```

The command compiles the program and runs the resulting executable, producing:

```
   Compiling my_project v0.1.0 (~/my_project)
    Finished dev [unoptimized + debuginfo] target(s) in 2.15s
     Running `target/debug/my_project`
Hello, world!
```

Modify the program in src/main.rs to display a custom message:

```
fn main() {
    println!("Welcome to my Rust project!");
}
```

Run the project again with cargo run to see the updated output:

```
    Compiling my_project v0.1.0 (~/my_project)
     Finished dev [unoptimized + debuginfo] target(s) in 0.26s
      Running ‘target/debug/my_project‘
Welcome to my Rust project!
```

To add a dependency, edit the [dependencies] section in Cargo.toml. For example, to include the rand crate for random number generation:

```
[dependencies]
rand = "0.8.4"
```

Save Cargo.toml and execute:

```
cargo build
```

Cargo downloads and compiles the rand crate along with your project. Utilizing this dependency, enhance src/main.rs:

```
use rand::Rng;

fn main() {
    let mut rng = rand::thread_rng();
    let n: u32 = rng.gen_range(1..101);
    println!("Random number between 1 and 100: {}", n);
}
```

Run the program with cargo run:

```
    Compiling my_project v0.1.0 (~/my_project)
     Finished dev [unoptimized + debuginfo] target(s) in 1.47s
      Running ‘target/debug/my_project‘
Random number between 1 and 100: 42
```

Configuring a project involves managing different build profiles. By default, Cargo includes two profiles: dev for development and release for optimized releases. Adjust these profiles in Cargo.toml:

```
[profile.dev]
opt-level = 0

[profile.release]
opt-level = 3
```

opt-level specifies the optimization level. Dev profile (opt-level = 0) focuses on fast compilation, while release profile (opt-level = 3) prioritizes runtime performance.

Finally, ensure your project is documented. Rustdoc, Rust's documentation generator, processes inline documentation to create comprehensive project documentation. Annotate code with comments and documentation:

```
/// Generates a random number between 1 and 100.
///
/// # Returns
```

```
///
/// A random 'u32' between 1 and 100.
fn generate_random_number() -> u32 {
    let mut rng = rand::thread_rng();
    rng.gen_range(1..101)
}

fn main() {
    let n = generate_random_number();
    println!("Random number between 1 and 100: {}", n);
}
```

To create documentation, use Cargo:

```
cargo doc --open
```

This command compiles the documentation and opens it in a web browser, providing a user interface to explore the project's functions and modules.

2.4 Writing and Running Your First Rust Program

Writing and running your first Rust program involves creating a simple "Hello, World!" application, which is the canonical first program for most programming languages. This section guides you through each step needed to successfully write, compile, and execute your initial Rust code.

First, let's create a new Rust project using Cargo. Open your terminal and type the following command:

```
cargo new hello_world --bin
```

The cargo new command creates a new directory named hello_world and initializes it as a new Rust project. The -bin flag specifies that this project is a binary crate, which is an executable program as opposed to a library.

Navigate into the newly created hello_world directory:

```
cd hello_world
```

Inside the hello_world directory, Cargo generates the necessary files and directories for a basic Rust project. The default structure looks like this:

```
hello_world
  src
    main.rs
  Cargo.toml
```

The src/main.rs file is where you will write your Rust code. Open this file in your preferred text editor. By default, main.rs contains a simple program that prints "Hello, world!" to the console:

```
fn main() {
    println!("Hello, world!");
}
```

The fn keyword declares a new function named main. In Rust, the main function is the entry point of every executable program. The println!("Hello, world!"); line calls a macro that prints the string "Hello, world!" to the console.

To compile and run your program, use the cargo run command in your terminal:

```
cargo run
```

Cargo will compile your project and run the resulting executable. The output should be:

```
  Compiling hello_world v0.1.0 (file:///path/to/hello_world)
   Finished dev [unoptimized + debuginfo] target(s) in 1.34s
    Running 'target/debug/hello_world'
Hello, world!
```

Cargo performs several tasks when you execute the cargo run command:

- Compiles your project: Converts your Rust code into machine code.
- Creates an executable: Generates an executable binary file in the target/debug/ directory.
- Executes the binary: Runs the executable, producing the output of your program.

Examining the Cargo.toml file, you will notice it contains metadata about your project and its dependencies. The default content looks like this:

```
[package]
name = "hello_world"
version = "0.1.0"
authors = ["Author Name <email@example.com>"]
edition = "2021"

[dependencies]
```

The Cargo.toml file uses TOML (Tom's Obvious, Minimal Language) format. The [package] section holds information about your package, like its name, version, and the authors. The [dependencies] section is where you would list any external libraries your project depends on.

The Rust compiler, rustc, can also be used directly to compile Rust programs, although Cargo is generally preferred for its additional functionality. To use rustc, navigate to the src directory and execute:

```
rustc main.rs
```

This command generates an executable named main. Run it directly from the terminal:

```
./main
```

You should see:

```
Hello, world!
```

Using Cargo simplifies project management by handling dependencies, compilation, and execution in one streamlined process. This is why it is recommended for most Rust development tasks.

Understanding the nuances of Cargo and Rust's compilation process is essential as you build more complex projects. Exploring the combinations of Cargo commands and Rust syntax will greatly enhance your productivity and mastery of Rust.

By comprehending this foundational example, you are now equipped to dive deeper into Rust programming, exploring sophisticated constructs and advanced modules while effectively managing your projects with Cargo.

2.5 Rust's Basic Syntax and Structure

Rust's syntax and structure are designed to facilitate safe and efficient programming. Understanding these fundamentals is essential to coding effectively in Rust. We will examine variable bindings, data types, control structures, functions, and error handling.

let is used to bind variables in Rust. Variable bindings are immutable by default, meaning the value cannot be changed once assigned:

```
let x = 5;
```

To create mutable variables, use the mut keyword:

```
let mut y = 5;
y = 6;
```

Rust uses four primary scalar types: integers, floating-point numbers, booleans, and characters. Integers can be signed (e.g., i32) or unsigned (e.g., u32). Floating-point types include f32 and f64.

```
let int_var: i32 = 42;
let float_var: f64 = 3.14;
let bool_var: bool = true;
let char_var: char = 'R';
```

Compound types include tuples and arrays. Tuples group multiple values of different types:

```
let tuple: (i32, f64, u8) = (500, 6.4, 1);
let (x, y, z) = tuple;
```

Arrays have elements of the same type and fixed length:

```
let array: [i32; 5] = [1, 2, 3, 4, 5];
```

Control structures in Rust include conditional statements and loops. The if expression checks conditions:

```
if x < 10 {
    println!("x is less than 10");
} else {
    println!("x is 10 or greater");
}
```

The loop, while, and for keywords facilitate looping:

```
let mut counter = 0;

loop {
    counter += 1;
    if counter == 5 {
        break;
    }
}

while counter < 10 {
    counter += 1;
}

for number in array.iter() {
    println!("{}", number);
}
```

Functions in Rust are defined using the fn keyword. They can take parameters and return a type:

```
fn add(a: i32, b: i32) -> i32 {
    a + b
}
let result = add(2, 3);
```

Rust's error handling can be accomplished with the Result type and the panic! macro. The Result type is an enum with Ok(T) and Err(E) variants:

```
fn divide(a: f64, b: f64) -> Result<f64, String> {
    if b == 0.0 {
        Err(String::from("Division by zero!"))
    } else {
        Ok(a / b)
    }
}

match divide(10.0, 2.0) {
    Ok(result) => println!("Result: {}", result),
    Err(e) => println!("Error: {}", e),
}
```

The panic! macro causes a program to terminate when an unrecoverable error occurs:

```
fn access_element(array: &[i32], index: usize) {
    if index >= array.len() {
        panic!("Index out of bounds");
    } else {
        println!("{}", array[index]);
    }
}
```

Understanding these core aspects of Rust's syntax and structure will allow you to write more effective and reliable Rust programs. As you progress, incorporating advanced features like ownership, borrowing, and lifetimes will further enhance your Rust programming capabilities.

2.6 Using External Crates and Modules

To enhance the functionality of Rust applications, developers often rely on external crates and modules. Crates are the fundamental compilation units in Rust, akin to libraries or packages in other programming languages. Modules, on the other hand, provide a way to organize and encapsulate code within a crate. This section elucidates the process of including and utilizing external crates and organizing code with modules in a Rust project.

Adding External Crates

Rust's package manager, Cargo, simplifies the inclusion of external crates through the Cargo.toml file. This file, located in the root directory of a Rust project, specifies the package dependencies required for the project.

To include an external crate, add a [dependencies] section to your Cargo.toml file with the desired crate and its version number. For instance, to include the serde crate for serialization and deserialization, the Cargo.toml file should be modified as follows:

```
[package]
name = "my_project"
version = "0.1.0"
authors = ["Author Name <email@example.com>"]
edition = "2018"

[dependencies]
serde = "1.0"
```

After updating the Cargo.toml file, run cargo build to download and compile the specified crate. Cargo handles the fetching of the crate from the crates.io repository and ensures all dependencies are resolved.

Using External Crates

Once the crate is added to the project, its functionalities can be utilized by importing the crate into your Rust code. This is done using the extern crate declaration. However, with the 2018 edition of Rust, explicit declaration with extern crate is often unnecessary. Instead, developers can import the desired components directly with use statements.

For example, after adding the serde crate, you can import it and use it in your main Rust file as follows:

```
use serde::{Serialize, Deserialize};

#[derive(Serialize, Deserialize)]
struct MyStruct {
    field1: String,
    field2: i32,
}

fn main() {
    let instance = MyStruct {
        field1: String::from("example"),
        field2: 42,
    };

    // Serialization and deserialization logic here
}
```

This example demonstrates the use of serde to derive the Serialize and

Deserialize traits for a custom data structure, allowing for easy serialization to formats such as JSON.

Organizing Code with Modules

Modules in Rust provide a way to organize code within a crate, promoting modularity and reusability. A module is declared using the mod keyword, followed by the module name. Modules can be nested and can reside in separate files.

A simple module can be declared in the main Rust file (main.rs) as follows:

```
mod my_module {
    pub fn my_function() {
        println!("Hello from my_module!");
    }
}

fn main() {
    my_module::my_function();
}
```

The pub keyword makes the function my_function publicly accessible outside of the module. The function can then be called using the module path my_module::my_function.

For larger projects, placing modules in separate files enhances code organization. Consider the following directory structure:

```
my_project/
  src/
     main.rs
     my_module.rs
```

The main file (main.rs) would declare the module as:

```
mod my_module;

fn main() {
    my_module::my_function();
}
```

And the module file (my_module.rs) would contain the implementation:

```
pub fn my_function() {
    println!("Hello from my_module!");
}
```

Modules can be nested by creating subdirectories. For instance, to create a nested module sub_module within my_module, the directory structure would be:

```
my_project/
  src/
     main.rs
     my_module/
        mod.rs
        sub_module.rs
```

The mod.rs file serves as the root of the my_module module, declaring the nested sub_module:

```
pub mod sub_module;
```

The sub_module.rs file contains the implementation:

```
pub fn sub_function() {
    println!("Hello from sub_module!");
}
```

Finally, the main file includes the nested modules:

```
mod my_module;

fn main() {
    my_module::sub_module::sub_function();
}
```

This approach encourages a clean separation of concerns and maintains the project structure. Rust's module system and Cargo's dependency management together provide robust tools for building and maintaining scalable and organized codebases.

2.7 Understanding Rust Documentation

Effective use of documentation is a critical skill for any programmer. Rust provides comprehensive and elaborate documentation tools to facilitate this process. In this section, we will examine how to access and utilize Rust documentation, the structure of Rust documentation, writing documentation comments, and generating documentation through Rust's inherent tools.

Rust documentation can be found at https://doc.rust-lang.org. This official resource includes the Rust Programming Language book, standard library API documentation, and other guides. To dive into the core concepts of Rust, this site is invaluable.

Rust's documentation consists of several key components:

- The Rust Programming Language book (often called the Rust

Book)

- Rust by Example (RBE)
- The Rust Standard Library API
- Rust compiler (rustc) documentation
- Cargo, Rust's package manager, documentation

The Rust Book and Rust by Example offer an in-depth introduction to Rust and various tutorials. The Standard Library API provides a detailed description of the library functions and modules available in Rust.

Documentation comments in Rust are written using three slashes (///). These comments precede the code elements they document, such as functions, structs, modules, or traits. To illustrate:

```
/// Adds two integers.
///
/// # Arguments
///
/// * `a` - The first integer
/// * `b` - The second integer
///
/// # Examples
///
/// ```
/// let result = add(2, 3);
/// assert_eq!(result, 5);
/// ```
fn add(a: i32, b: i32) -> i32 {
    a + b
}
```

In the above example, /// is used to write documentation for the add function. The # Arguments section describes the function parameters, and the # Examples section demonstrates its usage. These sections help provide necessary context to the function, enhancing its usability and maintainability.

Rust provides the rustdoc tool to generate HTML documentation from these comments. Run the following command in the terminal to generate documentation for a crate:

```
cargo doc --open
```

This command compiles the documentation and opens it in a web browser. cargo doc examines the documentation comments in your code and creates a user-friendly, HTML-formatted document.

The Rust Standard Library API features comprehensive documentation, generated using rustdoc, exemplary for learning documentation practices. Let's explore a struct example with inline documentation:

```
/// A struct that represents a rectangle.
///
/// # Fields
///
/// * `width` - The width of the rectangle
/// * `height` - The height of the rectangle
struct Rectangle {
    width: u32,
    height: u32,
}
impl Rectangle {
    /// Calculates the area of the rectangle.
    ///
    /// # Examples
    ///
    /// ```
    /// let rect = Rectangle { width: 10, height: 20 };
    /// assert_eq!(rect.area(), 200);
    /// ```
    fn area(&self) -> u32 {
        self.width * self.height
    }
}
```

Here, the Rectangle struct is documented along with its fields. The 'impl' block includes the area method, also properly documented.

The documentation can further use markups such as:

- # Panics - Information about when a function might panic.
- # Errors - Details on possible errors a function might return.
- # Safety - Unsafe code remarks.

Example:

```
/// Finds an element in a slice.
///
/// # Panics
///
/// Panics if the index is out of bounds.
///
/// # Examples
///
/// ```
/// let v = vec![1, 2, 3];
/// assert_eq!(find_element(&v, 1), Some(&2));
/// ```
fn find_element(v: &[i32], index: usize) -> Option<&i32> {
    if index < v.len() {
        Some(&v[index])
```

```
    } else {
        None
    }
}
```

Rust automatically tests the code snippets within /// comments during cargo test. This feature ensures the examples in the documentation remain accurate and functional with ongoing code changes.

Using markdown within documentation comments allows for enhanced readability. This includes creating links, headers, lists, bold, and italic text. Rust's documentation tends to follow these conventions for clarity and coherence.

Moreover, documentation can be enriched by adding explanations of algorithms, complex logic, and usage scenarios, invoking a more profound understanding for future maintainers or users. Hence, when writing documentation, consider elaborating on the design decisions and operational constraints.

Finally, all projects should incorporate proper inline documentation to foster an environment of clarity and maintainability. Rust, by leveraging its robust documentation tooling, sets a high standard, facilitating comprehensive understanding and fostering an ecosystem where documentation is effortlessly integrated with the development workflow, maintaining a dynamic and insightful coding tradition.

2.8 Version Control with Rust

Version control systems (VCS) are crucial for maintaining and tracking changes in software projects over time. Rust projects benefit significantly from using a VCS, and Git is one of the most popular choices in the software development community. This section provides a detailed understanding of integrating Git with Rust projects, covering commands, practices, and methods to ensure effective version control.

Installing Git: Ensure that Git is installed on your system. On Debian-based systems, you can install Git using the following command:

```
sudo apt-get install git
```

On macOS, you can use Homebrew:

```
brew install git
```

Initializing a Git Repository: Navigate to your Rust project directory and initialize a Git repository. This can be achieved using the following command:

```
git init
```

This command creates a .git directory inside your project, which contains all the necessary metadata for the repository.

Basic Git Commands: Familiarize yourself with several essential Git commands to manage your repository efficiently.

- git add <file>: Stages changes for the next commit.
- git commit -m "commit message": Commits the staged changes with a commit message.

```
git add .
git commit -m "Initial commit"
```

- git status: Displays the status of the working directory and the staging area.
- git log: Shows the commit history of the repository.
- git diff: Compares the changes in the working directory against the last commit.

Managing Remote Repositories: Git allows you to work with remote repositories, typically hosted on platforms like GitHub, GitLab, or Bitbucket. To add a remote repository, use:

```
git remote add origin <remote-url>
```

To push changes to the remote repository:

```
git push -u origin master
```

If you've cloned a repository, you can fetch the changes from the remote using:

```
git pull origin master
```

Using .gitignore: It's often necessary to exclude certain files or directories from being version-controlled, such as build outputs or dependencies. Create a .gitignore file in your project's root directory and list paths or file patterns to be ignored. For Rust projects, a typical .gitignore file includes:

```
# Rust specific files #
# Generated by Cargo #
target/

# Remove Cargo.lock from version control if you're building an open source project #
# Cargo creates it, but you don't want to add it to your VCS #
Cargo.lock

# Ignore IDE specific files #
.idea/
.vscode/
```

Branching and Merging: Git utilizes branches to allow concurrent development. To create a new branch:

```
git checkout -b new-feature
```

To switch between branches:

```
git checkout master
```

Merge changes from one branch to another:

```
git merge new-feature
```

Best Practices for Commits and Branching: Effective version control practices contribute to better project management. Here are some best practices:

- Make frequent, small commits with clear, descriptive messages.
- Use branches for different features or bug fixes to isolate development efforts.
- Regularly merge feature branches to avoid large, difficult-to-resolve merge conflicts.
- Rebase feature branches before merging to maintain a linear project history:

  ```
  git checkout feature-branch
  git fetch origin
  git rebase origin/master
  ```

Collaboration and Pull Requests: When collaborating with others, pull requests (PRs) facilitate code review and discussion before merging changes. Platforms like GitHub provide user-friendly interfaces to create, review, and merge PRs.

To create a PR:

- Push the feature branch to the remote repository.
- Navigate to the repository on GitHub.
- Click on New pull request and select the base and compare branches.
- Add a descriptive title and detailed comment, then click Create pull request.

The review process ensures high code quality and collective ownership of the codebase.

Tagging Releases: Tags in Git are useful for marking specific points in the repository's history, such as releases. To create a tag:

```
git tag -a v1.0 -m "Initial release"
```

Push tags to the remote repository:

```
git push origin v1.0
```

This allows others to easily checkout and reference specific versions of the project.

```
Build ID: 12345

Building version 1.0
Successfully built version 1.0
```

Integrating Git into your Rust projects enhances collaboration, maintains historical context, and facilitates the release process. By adhering to these practices and utilizing Git's powerful features, developers can manage and scale their Rust projects effectively.

2.9 Debugging Rust Programs

Effective debugging is essential to developing reliable and efficient software. Rust provides several tools and techniques to aid in identifying and resolving bugs. This section covers the use of common debugging tools, strategies to isolate and fix bugs, and practices to prevent them.

Debugging Tools in Rust

Rust supports various debugging tools, notably the gdb and lldb debuggers. To use these tools, ensure you have the necessary dependencies:

```
sudo apt-get install gdb
sudo apt-get install lldb
```

rust-gdb and rust-lldb are wrapper scripts provided by the Rust toolchain to configure these debuggers with the correct settings. These can be invoked with:

```
rust-gdb target/debug/<your_program>
rust-lldb target/debug/<your_program>
```

Setting Up Debug Symbols

For optimal debugging, including symbols in the build is essential. When compiling your Rust program, use the –debug flag or ensure the Cargo.toml file is configured appropriately. In the Cargo.toml file, ensure the following configuration under the [profile.dev] section:

```
[profile.dev]
debug = true
```

Breakpoints and Stepping Through Code

Setting breakpoints allows you to pause the program execution at specific points to inspect the state. In gdb or lldb, you can set breakpoints using the break command followed by the function name or line number. For example:

```
(gdb) break main
(gdb) break src/main.rs:42
```

Once the breakpoints are set, run the program in the debugger:

```
(gdb) run
```

When execution pauses at a breakpoint, you can inspect variables, view the call stack, and step through code line by line. The following commands are essential:

- next (n) - Executes the next line of code.
- step (s) - Steps into functions.
- continue (c) - Continues execution until the next breakpoint.
- print (p) - Prints the value of a variable.

For example, printing a variable and stepping to the next line:

```
(gdb) print my_variable
$1 = 42
(gdb) next
```

Using Logging for Debugging

Rust's println! macro can be utilized for basic logging purposes. For more advanced logging, the log crate is recommended. Add log to your Cargo.toml dependencies:

```
[dependencies]
log = "0.4"
```

Configure a logger, such as env_logger, in your src/main.rs:

```
extern crate log;
extern crate env_logger;

use log::{info, warn, error};

fn main() {
    env_logger::init();

    info!("Rust program started.");
    warn!("This is a warning message.");
    error!("This represents an error.");
}
```

Run your program with RUST_LOG environment variable to filter log levels:

```
RUST_LOG=info cargo run
```

```
INFO  main: Rust program started.
WARN  main: This is a warning message.
ERROR main: This represents an error.
```

Panic Messages and Backtraces

When a Rust program encounters an unrecoverable error, it panics. Enable full backtraces by setting the RUST_BACKTRACE environment variable:

```
RUST_BACKTRACE=1 cargo run
```

A full backtrace reveals the sequence of function calls leading to the panic, aiding in identifying the root cause.

Unit Testing and Debugging

Proper unit testing helps in catching bugs early. To write unit tests, use the #[cfg(test)] attribute and test module in src/lib.rs:

```
#[cfg(test)]
mod tests {
    #[test]
    fn test_addition() {
        assert_eq!(2 + 2, 4);
    }
}
```

Run tests with:

```
cargo test
```

To debug a specific test, run:

```
cargo test --test <test_name> -- --nocapture
```

–nocapture ensures test output is displayed in the terminal.

This detailed walkthrough should provide a comprehensive foundation for effective debugging in Rust. Employ these techniques to enhance the reliability and performance of your Rust applications.

2.10 Building and Releasing Rust Projects

Building and releasing a Rust project involves several critical steps that ensure the code is compiled efficiently, dependencies are managed correctly, and the final product is ready for deployment. This section delves into these processes, highlighting key commands and techniques using Cargo, Rust's build system and package manager.

To begin, let's revisit the Cargo.toml file, a central piece in any Rust project. This file specifies various dependencies, build scripts, and metadata about the project. Here is an example of a basic Cargo.toml:

```
[package]
name = "example_project"
version = "0.1.0"
authors = ["Author Name <email@example.com>"]
edition = "2021"

[dependencies]
serde = "1.0"
```

In this file, the [package] section contains metadata about the project, while the [dependencies] section lists external crates that the project depends on.

After setting up the Cargo.toml file, the next step is to build the project. The most common command to compile a Rust project is:

```
cargo build
```

Executing cargo build compiles the project in debug mode, which is suitable for development and testing. It generates an executable in the target/debug directory. To optimize the build for release, use the following command:

```
cargo build --release
```

This command compiles the project in release mode, applying various optimizations. The resulting executable can be found in the target/release directory. Release mode builds are typically faster and smaller, making them ideal for deployment.

To run the compiled project, simply use:

```
cargo run
```

For release mode:

```
cargo run --release
```

Running these commands executes the compiled binary, providing immediate feedback on the program's behavior.

Packaging and Distributing the Project

Cargo simplifies the process of packaging and distributing Rust projects. To publish a crate to the crates.io registry, ensure that the Cargo.toml file contains the necessary metadata fields such as license, description, and repository. Here is an expanded version of Cargo.toml:

```
[package]
name = "example_project"
version = "0.1.0"
authors = ["Author Name <email@example.com>"]
edition = "2021"
license = "MIT"
description = "An example project demonstrating Rust packaging"
repository = "https://github.com/username/example_project"

[dependencies]
serde = "1.0"
```

Before publishing, it is crucial to run tests to ensure that the project behaves as expected:

```
cargo test
```

This command runs all tests defined in the project, providing detailed output on the results. If all tests pass, the project is ready for publishing:

```
cargo publish
```

Once executed, Cargo packages the project and uploads it to the crates.io registry. Note that publishing a crate for the first time requires authentication. Cargo prompts for a token, which can be obtained by signing in to crates.io and navigating to the Account Settings.

Continuous Integration and Deployment

Integrating Continuous Integration (CI) and Continuous Deployment (CD) services ensures the reliability and stability of a Rust project. Commonly used CI/CD services like Travis CI, GitHub Actions, and GitLab CI support Rust out of the box.

Here is an example configuration for GitHub Actions, stored in .github/workflows/rust.yml:

```
name: Rust

on: [push, pull_request]

jobs:
  build:

    runs-on: ubuntu-latest

    steps:
    - uses: actions/checkout@v2
    - name: Install Rust
      uses: actions-rs/toolchain@v1
      with:
        toolchain: stable
    - name: Build
      run: cargo build --verbose
    - name: Run tests
      run: cargo test --verbose
```

This configuration file defines a workflow that triggers on every push and pull request. It sets up an Ubuntu environment, checks out the code, installs the Rust toolchain, builds the project, and runs the tests.

By implementing CI/CD pipelines, developers ensure that every change is automatically tested, and potential issues are identified early in the development process.

To conclude, building and releasing Rust projects involves setting up the Cargo.toml file, compiling the code in both debug and release modes, and packaging the project for distribution. Integrating CI/CD pipelines further enhances the reliability and stability of the project, facilitating seamless deployment.

Chapter 3

Understanding Ownership and Borrowing

This chapter delves into the fundamental concepts of ownership and borrowing that underpin memory safety in Rust. It explains the rules of ownership and how references and borrowing work within these constraints. Topics include mutability and borrowing, the use of slices for partial data, and the prevention of dangling references through lifetimes and lifetime annotations. The chapter also explores common and advanced patterns in ownership and borrowing, offering best practices for writing efficient and safe Rust code.

3.1 The Concept of Ownership

Ownership is a central feature in Rust, crucial for ensuring memory safety without needing a garbage collector. Ownership defines how memory is managed and how the Rust compiler enforces rules to prevent data races, null pointer dereferencing, and other memory management issues.

When a variable owns a value, it has several responsibilities and constraints. These ensure that once a value is no longer needed, its memory can be safely deallocated without any risk of memory leaks or undefined behavior. Rust's ownership system is built upon three main rules:

- Each value in Rust has a single owner.
- Value's ownership can only be transferred from one variable to another.
- When the owner goes out of scope, the value is dropped, and its memory is freed.

To understand ownership, consider the following Rust code:

```
fn main() {
    let x = String::from("Hello, World!");
    println!("{}", x);
}
```

Here, x owns the String value "Hello, World!". When x goes out of scope at the end of main, Rust automatically calls the drop function to free the memory.

Ownership transfer, or *moving*, occurs when you assign a value to another variable. Examine this additional code example:

```
fn main() {
    let a = String::from("Ownership");
    let b = a;
    println!("{}", b);
}
```

In this example, a owns the String "Ownership". When b is assigned a, the ownership of the String is transferred to b. After this move, a no longer owns the String, and it cannot be used. If you attempt to use a, the compiler will generate an error since b is now the rightful owner.

```
fn main() {
    let a = String::from("Ownership");
    let b = a;
    println!("{}", a); // Error: value borrowed here after move
}
```

Rust's compiler will report:

```
error[E0382]: borrow of moved value: `a`
 --> src/main.rs:4:20
  |
2 |     let a = String::from("Ownership");
  |         - move occurs because `a` has type `String`, which does not implement the `Copy` trait
3 |     let b = a;
  |             - value moved here
4 |     println!("{}", a);
  |                    ^ value borrowed here after move
```

The compiler error message indicates that a was moved to b and hence cannot be used after the move.

Ownership plays a vital role in function calls and return values. When passing a value to a function, ownership can either be transferred (moved), or the value can be passed via a reference (borrowed). The transfer of ownership during function calls looks like this:

```
fn takes_ownership(s: String) {
    println!("{}", s);
}

fn main() {
    let s = String::from("Ownership");
    takes_ownership(s);
    // println!("{}", s); // Error: value borrowed here after move
}
```

In the above code, the function takes_ownership takes ownership of the parameter s. After the function call, s in main cannot be used anymore because its ownership has been transferred to the function.

Conversely, when a function returns a value, the caller gains ownership of that value, as illustrated below:

```
fn gives_ownership() -> String {
    let s = String::from("Ownership");
    s
}

fn main() {
    let s = gives_ownership();
    println!("{}", s);
}
```

In this instance, gives_ownership creates a String and transfers its ownership to the caller when it returns. main now owns the returned String, and it can be used without issues.

Rust's ownership system significantly impacts memory management and safety disciplines. It ensures that each piece of memory is cleaned up appropriately when it is no longer needed, through a methodology where ownership is distinctly defined and tracked. The upcoming sections will explore how Rust handles borrowing and references, adding further dimensions to memory safety outside the ownership model.

3.2 Understanding Borrowing

In Rust, borrowing allows functions to access data without taking ownership. This mechanism ensures memory safety and prevents data races by enabling references to data. Rust enforces strict borrowing rules to uphold its guarantees. We will explore borrowing, references, and the constraints and benefits they offer.

Borrowing divides into two categories: immutable and mutable borrowing. Each type comes with specific rules to maintain safety.

Immutable Borrowing

Immutable borrowing allows multiple references to a piece of data without giving them the capability to modify it. This is accomplished via the & operator. Here is an example to illustrate immutable borrowing:

```
fn main() {
    let x = 5;
    let y = &x;
    println!("The value of x is: {}", x);
    println!("The referenced value of y is: {}", y);
}
```

In this example, the variable x is defined and initialized to 5. The reference y borrows the value of x immutably. Both x and y can be used to access the value, preserving Rust's safety guarantees. Immutable borrowing ensures x remains unmodified by any reference.

Mutable Borrowing

Mutable borrowing allows exactly one reference to modify the data. This borrow occurs through the &mut operator. Below is an example of mutable borrowing:

```
fn main() {
    let mut x = 5;
    let y = &mut x;
    *y += 1;
    println!("The modified value of x is: {}", x);
}
```

In this scenario, the variable x is mutable. The reference y borrows x mutably. Using *y, the dereferenced value of y is incremented by 1. After the modification, printing x confirms its value has changed.

Rules of Borrowing

To ensure memory safety, Rust enforces strict borrowing rules:

- Only one mutable reference at a time or any number of immutable references.
- References must always be valid.

Single Mutable or Multiple Immutable References

Rust permits either multiple immutable references or a single mutable reference, never both simultaneously. The following example demonstrates a violation:

```
fn main() {
    let mut x = 5;
    let y = &x;
    let z = &mut x; // Error!
}
```

Rust's compiler will raise an error because z attempts to borrow x mutably while y holds an immutable reference.

Reference Validity

References must always point to valid data. Consider the following:

```
fn main() {
    let r;
    {
        let x = 5;
        r = &x; // Error!
    }
    // x goes out of scope here, making r a dangling reference
    println!("r: {}", r);
}
```

The variable x goes out of scope at the end of the inner block, making r a dangling reference. Rust prevents this compilation by ensuring all references remain valid throughout their usage.

Using Borrowing in Functions

Functions often leverage borrowing to improve flexibility and safety, passing references instead of ownership. Immutable references are common when functions only need to read data:

```
fn calculate_length(s: &String) -> usize {
    s.len()
}

fn main() {
    let s1 = String::from("hello");
    let len = calculate_length(&s1);
    println!("The length of '{}' is {}.", s1, len);
}
```

In this example, calculate_length borrows s1 immutably. The function reads length without taking ownership, which allows s1 to be accessible in the main function.

Mutable references pass data for modification:

```
fn add_one(x: &mut i32) {
    *x += 1;
}

fn main() {
    let mut a = 10;
    add_one(&mut a);
    println!("The value of a is: {}", a);
}
```

Here, add_one accepts a mutable reference, modifying a within the function. This pattern enables controlled data mutation without transferring ownership.

Borrowing and Aliasing

Alias analysis ensures that when mutable borrowing ensues, no other references can alias the same data. Rust's borrow checker enforces the rule to eliminate data races, enhancing concurrency safety. Consider:

```
fn main() {
    let mut data = vec![1, 2, 3];
    let ref1 = &data[0];
    let ref2 = &mut data[0]; // Error: Cannot borrow as mutable since it is also
        borrowed as immutable
    println!("ref1: {}", ref1);
}
```

Attempting to borrow data[0] mutably while it is borrowed immutably breaks Rust's borrowing rules. The compiler catches this and prevents unsafe code execution.

Understanding borrowing in Rust requires careful attention to these rules. By adhering to these principles, developers can write robust, safe, and efficient code, leveraging the power of Rust's ownership model.

3.3 The Rules of Ownership

The ownership system in Rust is designed to ensure memory safety without a garbage collector. This system revolves around three key rules of ownership, which are critical for managing memory and ensuring thread safety. These rules are:

- Each value in Rust has a variable that is its owner.
- There can only be one owner at a time.
- When the owner goes out of scope, the value will be dropped.

To illustrate these rules, consider the following piece of Rust code:

```
fn main() {
    let s = String::from("hello"); // s is the owner of the String
    takes_ownership(s); // s is moved here, and can no longer be used
}

fn takes_ownership(some_string: String) { // some_string becomes the owner
    println!("{}", some_string);
} // some_string goes out of scope and the String is dropped
```

In this example, the s variable owns the String. When takes_ownership is called, the ownership of the String is transferred to some_string. After the function takes_ownership finishes execution, some_string goes out of scope, and the String is dropped. The variable s is thus invalidated after it is passed to takes_ownership, adhering to the rule that there can only be one owner at a time.

A crucial aspect of Rust's ownership system is the way values are passed to functions. When a non-copy type is passed to a function, ownership of the value is transferred to the function parameter. This is depicted in our example where the ownership of the String is moved to the takes_ownership function.

To further clarify the rules of ownership, consider another example demonstrating the concept of borrowing alongside ownership:

```
fn main() {
    let s1 = String::from("hello");
    let s2 = s1; // s2 now owns the String, and s1 is invalidated

    // println!("{}", s1); // this would cause a compile-time error
    println!("{}", s2);
}
```

In this code snippet, the ownership of the String is moved from s1 to s2. Attempting to use s1 after transferring ownership would lead to a compile-time error, as shown by the commented-out line. This ensures there are no dangling references or memory leaks because only one variable can own a particular piece of data at any given time.

Rust offers a mechanism called borrowing, which allows functions to use values without taking ownership. Borrowing is achieved using references. A reference to a value does not transfer ownership, thereby enabling safe and shared access to data. Consider the following example:

```
fn main() {
    let s = String::from("hello");
    let len = calculate_length(&s);
    println!("The length of '{}' is {}.", s, len);
}

fn calculate_length(s: &String) -> usize {
    s.len()
}
```

In this code, the calculate_length function takes a reference to a String, denoted by &String. This function does not take ownership of the String. Consequently, the String is not dropped when the function exits. Therefore, we can still use s in the main function after calling calculate_-length.

Returning data ownership from functions is another critical aspect of ownership rules. When a function passes ownership of a value back to the caller, it prevents the data from being prematurely dropped. Here is an example that demonstrates this:

```
fn main() {
    let s1 = gives_ownership(); // gives_ownership moves its return value into s1
    let s2 = String::from("hello");
    let s3 = takes_and_gives_back(s2); // s2 moves into takes_and_gives_back,
        which also moves its return value into s3
}

fn gives_ownership() -> String {
    let some_string = String::from("yours");
    some_string // some_string is returned and moves out to the calling function
}

fn takes_and_gives_back(a_string: String) -> String {
    a_string // a_string is returned and moves out to the calling function
}
```

In this code, gives_ownership function transfers ownership of its return value to s1. The takes_and_gives_back function takes ownership of s2 and then returns it, transferring ownership to s3.

Rust's ownership rules ensure memory safety and prevent data races by enforcing strict ownership and borrowing constraints. Understanding these fundamental principles is essential for writing robust and efficient Rust code. The rules prevent issues such as double-free errors, dangling pointers, and memory leaks, making Rust a reliable choice for system-level programming. Mastery of these concepts enables developers to write code that is both safe and performant, adhering to Rust's promise of zero-cost abstractions.

3.4 References and Borrowing

Understanding references and borrowing is essential for mastering Rust's memory safety guarantees. A reference in Rust, denoted by the & symbol, provides access to an object without taking ownership of it. This allows you to read or modify data without transferring ownership, which facilitates safe memory access patterns. There are two types of references: immutable references and mutable references. Let's explore these in detail.

To create an immutable reference, use the & symbol followed by the variable name.

```
fn main() {
    let x = 5;
    let y = &x; // Immutable reference to x
    println!("x: {}, y: {}", x, y);
}
```

An immutable reference to x is created and bound to y. This allows y to read the value of x without owning it. Because y does not take ownership, x remains valid for use after y has been created.

A key aspect of immutable references is that you can have multiple immutable references to the same data simultaneously.

```
fn main() {
    let x = 10;
    let a = &x;
    let b = &x;
    let c = &x;
    println!("x: {}, a: {}, b: {}, c: {}", x, a, b, c);
}
```

In this example, a, b, and c are all immutable references to x. They can coexist because they do not modify the referenced data. However, Rust's borrowing rules prevent having a mutable reference while any immutable references exist:

To create a mutable reference, use &mut followed by the variable name.

```
fn main() {
    let mut val = 42;
    let val_ref = &mut val; // Mutable reference to val
    *val_ref += 10; // Dereferencing and modifying val via the mutable reference
    println!("New val: {}", val);
```

```
}
```

Here, val is declared mutable with the mut keyword. val_ref is a mutable reference to val, allowing it to modify val's value.

Rust enforces strict rules regarding mutable references. Only one mutable reference to a particular piece of data is allowed at any time. This rule avoids data races at compile time, contributing to the language's strong guarantees around memory safety. Violating this rule results in a compile-time error.

```
fn main() {
    let mut x = 5;
    let y = &x;
    let z = &mut x; // Error: cannot borrow 'x' as mutable because it is also borrowed
        as immutable
    println!("y: {}", y);
    println!("z: {}", z);
}
```

In this scenario, the compiler throws an error because x is already borrowed immutably by y. Attempting to create a mutable reference z leads to a compile-time conflict.

To safely manage references, one must adhere to the following rules:

- You can have either one mutable reference or any number of immutable references at a time.
- References must always be valid.

Rust avoids dangling references through its ownership system and borrowing rules. A reference should always point to a valid object. The following example demonstrates a scenario where a reference becomes invalid.

```
fn main() {
    let y: &i32;
    {
        let x = 5;
        y = &x; // Error: 'x' does not live long enough
    }
    println!("y: {}", y);
}
```

In this case, x goes out of scope before y is used, leading to a dangling reference. Rust's borrow checker detects this and prevents the code from compiling.

Understanding scopes and lifetimes is crucial for managing references.

Each reference must not outlive its referent. This principle ensures that all references are valid when used.

The interaction between mutable and immutable references, alongside Rust's strict borrowing rules, protects against a wide array of memory safety issues. This mechanism prevents data races, use-after-free errors, and various other concurrency pitfalls without needing a garbage collector.

Both immutable and mutable references play a vital role in Rust's borrowing system. They maintain memory safety and concurrency guarantees while allowing flexible and efficient access patterns to data. It is essential to understand and correctly apply these rules to leverage Rust's full potential in producing safe and high-performance code.

3.5 Mutability and Borrowing

In Rust, managing how variables can change and how they are accessed is essential for safe and efficient memory management. A critical concept underlying this management is "mutability," which dictates whether a variable's value can be changed after it is initialized. Borrowing is the mechanism through which one part of the code can access the data owned by another part without taking ownership. Understanding the interplay between mutability and borrowing is crucial for taking full advantage of Rust's safety guarantees.

Mutability in Rust is explicit: a variable must be marked as mutable using the mut keyword to allow its value to change after it is bound. For example:

```
// Declare a mutable variable
let mut x = 5;
x = 6; // Valid, as x is mutable
```

If x had not been declared with mut, attempting to modify it would result in a compilation error. The explicit marking of mutable variables minimizes unintended side-effects, enhancing code predictability and maintainability.

Borrowing in Rust is categorized into two types: immutable borrowing and mutable borrowing. When a function or part of the code borrows a variable, it does not take ownership but is granted access to the original owner's data.

An immutable borrow occurs when a variable is borrowed without the intention to modify it. This is done using the & operator:

```
// Immutable borrowing
let y = 10;
let z = &y; // z is an immutable reference to y
// y and z can be used concurrently since y is not modified
println!("y: {}, z: {}", y, z);
```

While y is immutable in this example, z can still access its value without changing it. Rust allows multiple immutable borrows to coexist, but it enforces that there are no mutable borrows active during immutable borrowing, maintaining data integrity through compile-time checks.

For mutable borrowing, the &mut operator is used:

```
// Mutable borrowing
let mut a = 15;
let b = &mut a; // b is a mutable reference to a
*b += 1; // modify value through mutable reference
println!("a: {}", a); // Output will be "a: 16"
```

When a variable is mutably borrowed, Rust ensures that no other references to that variable are allowed until the mutable borrow goes out of scope. This prevents data races, ensuring that only one part of the code can modify the value at any time. Hence, it enforces the rule that either one mutable reference or any number of immutable references are allowed, but not both simultaneously.

Let us encapsulate and illustrate these points through a more complex example involving function calls:

```
fn add_one(x: &mut i32) {
    *x += 1;
}

fn main() {
    let mut y = 5;
    add_one(&mut y);
    println!("y: {}", y); // y: 6
}
```

In this example, add_one takes a mutable reference to an i32 and increments its value. The main function mutably borrows y to add_one, leading to a modification of y.

Splitting borrows, also known as aliasing, describes a scenario where a mutable reference's interior is divided into immutable parts. This is allowed since the individual parts are not being modified, though the entire structure can still only have one mutable or multiple immutable references. This is often seen in data structures like vectors:

```
fn main() {
```

```
    let mut v = vec![1, 2, 3];
    let first = &v[0]; // Immutable borrow of an element
    // let mutable_reference = &mut v[1]; // This would cause a borrow error
    println!("First element is: {}", first);
}
```

Attempting to mutably borrow a different element of the vector when an immutable borrow exists would cause a compilation error, as Rust strictly enforces borrowing rules to prevent data races.

Understanding these distinctions and rules helps us write safe Rust code that leverages the borrow checker to prevent concurrency issues. These properties collectively enhance Rust's primary objective: ensuring memory safety and preventing undefined behavior without the need for a garbage collector.

3.6 Slices: Borrowing Parts of Data

In Rust, slices are a powerful tool that enable you to reference a contiguous sequence of elements within a data structure without taking ownership of the data itself. This feature is particularly useful when working with collections like arrays or vectors, allowing you to operate on parts of these collections efficiently and safely.

Slices fundamentally consist of a pointer to the first element and a length, encapsulating the start and end of the segment within the collection. They do not own the data they point to; instead, they borrow it, adhering to Rust's borrowing rules to ensure memory safety and avoid issues such as dangling references.

To illustrate the concept of slices, consider the following example where we want to access and manipulate a segment of an array:

```
// Full array of integers
let arr = [1, 2, 3, 4, 5];

// Borrow a slice of the array
let slice = &arr[1..4];

// Print the slice
println!("Array slice: {:?}", slice);
```

```
Output:
Array slice: [2, 3, 4]
```

In this example, slice borrows the elements from index 1 to index 3 (4 is excluded) from arr. The slice itself neither owns the borrowed elements nor changes the original array. By leveraging slices, you access a portion of an array without creating a new array, hence minimizing overhead.

Slices are versatile and can be mutable or immutable, dictated by the context of borrowing. If you need to modify the borrowed part of a data structure, you can borrow it mutably. For instance:

```
// Full array of integers
let mut arr = [1, 2, 3, 4, 5];

// Borrow a mutable slice of the array
let slice = &mut arr[1..4];

// Modify the elements in the slice
slice[0] = 10;
slice[2] = 40;

// Print the entire array to show changes
println!("Modified array: {:?}", arr);
```

```
Output:
Modified array: [1, 10, 3, 40, 5]
```

Here, slice mutably borrows elements from index 1 to index 3 of arr, allowing modifications within that segment. After altering elements slice[0] and slice[2], the changes reflect in arr, demonstrating how slices facilitate efficient in-place updates.

Rust enforces borrowing rules to prevent data races and ensure memory consistency. Consequently, while borrowing a mutable slice, the compiler prevents other mutable or immutable borrows of the same data segment. For example, the following code generates a compilation error:

```
// Full array of integers
let mut arr = [1, 2, 3, 4, 5];

// Borrow a mutable slice of the array
let slice = &mut arr[1..4];

// Attempt to also borrow an immutable slice
let another_slice = &arr[1..4];

println!("Slice: {:?}", slice);
println!("Another slice: {:?}", another_slice);
```

The Rust compiler will output an error like this:

```
error[E0502]: cannot borrow `arr` as immutable because it is also borrowed as mutable
 --> src/main.rs:10:23
  |
8 | let slice = &mut arr[1..4];
  |             ------------ mutable borrow occurs here
10 | let another_slice = &arr[1..4];
  |                     ^^^^ immutable borrow occurs here
```

This error demonstrates Rust's borrowing rules at work, ensuring that we do not simultaneously hold mutable and immutable references to the same data, thereby preventing undefined behavior.

Slices are not limited to arrays; they can also be applied to vectors and strings. For example, slicing a vector looks like this:

```
// Vector of integers
let vec = vec![10, 20, 30, 40, 50];

// Borrow a slice of the vector
let slice = &vec[1..4];

println!("Vector slice: {:?}", slice);
```

```
Output:
Vector slice: [20, 30, 40]
```

Similarly, string slices work on UTF-8 encoded strings, allowing efficient substring operations without copying data:

```
// String
let s = String::from("Hello, Rust!");

// Borrow a slice of the string
let slice = &s[7..11]; // "Rust"

// Print the slice
println!("String slice: {}", slice);
```

```
Output:
String slice: Rust
```

Working with string slices entails respecting UTF-8 boundaries, as slicing within characters can cause runtime panics:

```
// String containing Unicode characters
let s = String::from(" ");

// Attempt to slice part of a multi-byte character, causing a panic
let slice = &s[0..1];
println!("String slice: {}", slice);
```

The above code will result in a panic because the character ' ' spans more bytes than being sliced. Thus, always ensure valid UTF-8 boundaries when slicing strings.

Slices enhance code readability and efficiency by allowing operations on subset data without unnecessary cloning or copying. Utilizing slices effectively enables you to leverage Rust's memory safety guarantees while performing complex data manipulation tasks.

3.7 Lifetimes: Preventing Dangling References

In Rust, lifetimes are critical for ensuring memory safety by preventing dangling references. Dangling references occur when a program references memory that has been deallocated, leading to undefined behavior. Lifetimes, a form of static analysis, allow Rust to enforce that references are always valid.

A lifetime is a construct the Rust compiler (borrow checker) uses to track how long references are valid. Instead of the programmer explicitly managing the memory, Rust uses lifetimes to ensure references do not outlive the data they point to.

When writing functions that accept references as parameters, you need to specify the lifetimes of these references. This is done using lifetime annotations. For example, consider a simple function that returns a reference to the first element of a slice:

```
fn first<'a>(slice: &'a [i32]) -> &'a i32 {
    &slice[0]
}
```

In this example, 'a is a lifetime parameter. The annotation <'a> after the fn keyword indicates that 'a is a lifetime, and it is used to link the lifetime of the input reference to the lifetime of the output reference. The function signature ensures that the reference to the first element of the slice cannot outlive the slice itself.

Attempting to write a function that can return a dangling reference will result in a compile-time error. For instance, consider the following incorrect function:

```
fn erroneous<'a>() -> &'a str {
    let s = String::from("example");
    &s
}
```

This function cannot compile because s goes out of scope and gets deallocated at the end of the function, making the reference to s invalid. Rust detects this and produces an error, preventing the creation of a dangling reference.

To understand how the borrow checker uses lifetimes, let's look at another example involving multiple references:

```
fn longest<'a>(x: &'a str, y: &'a str) -> &'a str {
```

```
    if x.len() > y.len() {
        x
    } else {
        y
    }
}
```

In this function, both input parameters and the return value are annotated with the same lifetime 'a. This expresses that the output reference will be valid as long as both input references are valid. The borrow checker enforces these rules at compile time, ensuring that no dangling references can be created.

Lifetimes can get more complex, especially when dealing with structs. Consider a struct holding a reference:

```
struct ImportantExcerpt<'a> {
    part: &'a str,
}
```

Here, 'a is a lifetime parameter for the struct. This means that an instance of ImportantExcerpt cannot outlive the reference part. You can then implement methods for this struct that also involve lifetimes:

```
impl<'a> ImportantExcerpt<'a> {
    fn level(&self) -> i32 {
        3
    }

    fn announce_and_return_part(&self, announcement: &str) -> &str {
        println!("Attention please: {}", announcement);
        self.part
    }
}
```

In the method announce_and_return_part, the lifetime of self and the return reference are implied to be the same, adhering to implicit lifetime elision rules. Rust uses three rules to infer lifetimes in functions and methods:

- Each parameter that is a reference gets its own lifetime parameter.
- If there is exactly one input lifetime parameter, that lifetime is assigned to all output lifetime parameters.
- If there are multiple input lifetime parameters, but one of them is &self or &mut self, the lifetime of self is assigned to all output lifetime parameters.

Lifetimes are a powerful feature that help ensure references do not outlive the data they point to. When functions, structs, and methods involve references, the Rust compiler's borrow checker enforces correct lifetimes, preventing dangling references and ensuring memory safety. Understanding and using lifetimes correctly is essential for robust and error-free Rust programs.

3.8 Lifetime Annotations in Function Signatures

In Rust, lifetimes are an essential part of ensuring memory safety by preventing dangling references. When writing functions that deal with references, it is sometimes necessary to explicitly annotate lifetimes to inform the compiler about how the lifetimes of various references relate to each other. This section explores the syntax and practical usage of lifetime annotations in function signatures.

Lifetime annotations allow the developer to specify the scope for which a reference is valid. These annotations are indicated using an apostrophe followed by a name, such as 'a or 'b. The names are arbitrary but follow the Rust style convention of using short, descriptive names.

Consider a function that returns a reference to the longest of two string slices provided as inputs. Without lifetime annotations, the compiler cannot determine the relationship between the lifetimes of the input references and the output reference. Consequently, you would encounter a compilation error due to missing lifetime specifications.

Here is a function that correctly uses lifetime annotations:

```
fn longest<'a>(x: &'a str, y: &'a str) -> &'a str {
    if x.len() > y.len() {
        x
    } else {
        y
    }
}
```

In this function signature, 'a is the lifetime parameter. It indicates that both input references, x and y, as well as the returned reference, are all valid for the same lifetime 'a. This informs the Rust compiler that the returned reference is guaranteed to be valid as long as both input references are.

If the lifetimes of the references were not properly related, attempting to compile the function would result in an error. For example, calling longest with references that do not live long enough would produce a compilation error.

Let's consider a more complex example involving structures. Suppose we have a struct that holds a reference to a string slice:

```
struct ImportantExcerpt<'a> {
    part: &'a str,
}
```

The struct ImportantExcerpt contains a field part which is a reference with the lifetime 'a. A function that takes an instance of ImportantExcerpt and returns the referenced string slice will also need lifetime annotations to ensure proper lifetime tracking:

```
impl<'a> ImportantExcerpt<'a> {
    fn level(&self) -> &str {
        self.part
    }
}
```

Here, the method level returns a reference to self.part. The annotation <'a> on the impl block and the reference in self ensures that the returned reference has the same lifetime as self.

Lifetimes can also be used to ensure that a function maintains proper relationships among multiple reference parameters. For example, consider a function that takes two string slices and returns a result indicating whether both strings are equal. We can annotate the function so that both references have the same lifetime:

```
fn are_equal<'a>(x: &'a str, y: &'a str) -> bool {
    x == y
}
```

In practice, Rust often can infer lifetimes without explicit annotations due to its powerful borrow checker and default lifetime elision rules. For example, consider the following functions:

```
fn first_word(s: &str) -> &str {
    let bytes = s.as_bytes();

    for (i, &item) in bytes.iter().enumerate() {
        if item == b' ' {
            return &s[0..i];
        }
    }
    &s[..]
}
```

In the function first_word, Rust can elide lifetimes based on a set of rules because there is a single input reference and a single output reference. However, in more complex scenarios where the relationships between lifetimes are not straightforward, using explicit lifetime annotations is necessary to convey the correct lifetimes to the compiler.

Understanding and using lifetime annotations efficiently requires practice and familiarity with Rust's borrowing rules. By ensuring correct and consistent use of lifetime annotations, developers can leverage Rust's guarantees on memory safety, producing code that is both safe and performant.

3.9 Common Ownership and Borrowing Patterns

In Rust, mastering common ownership and borrowing patterns is essential for writing efficient and safe code. Patterns provide a reliable structure for managing memory and resources, adhering to Rust's guarantees of safety and concurrency without data races. Below, we explore key idiomatic patterns, highlighting their utility and implementation.

Pattern 1: Ownership with Functions

Passing ownership to functions is a straightforward way to transfer the control of a variable to another scope. When a function takes ownership of a variable, it is responsible for its drop when it goes out of scope.

```
fn take_ownership(some_string: String) {
    println!("{}", some_string);
} // some_string goes out of scope and 'drop' is called

let my_string = String::from("hello");
take_ownership(my_string); // my_string's value moves into the function
// my_string is no longer valid here
```

This pattern is efficient when a large data structure needs to be processed by a function and the original variable is no longer needed afterward.

Pattern 2: Mutable and Immutable Borrowing with Functions

Rather than taking ownership, functions can borrow variables, thus maintaining the original variable's validity after the function call. This is accomplished via references:

```
fn calculate_length(s: &String) -> usize {
    s.len()
} // s goes out of scope, but because it does not have ownership, nothing happens.

let my_string = String::from("hello");
```

```
let length = calculate_length(&my_string); // my_string is passed by reference
println!("The length of '{}' is {}.", my_string, length);
// my_string is still valid here
```

For mutable borrowing, functions can modify the variable through a mutable reference:

```
fn change(some_string: &mut String) {
    some_string.push_str(", world");
}

let mut my_string = String::from("hello");
change(&mut my_string);
println!("{}", my_string); // Outputs: hello, world
```

Pattern 3: Borrowing in Loops

In loops, borrowed references are common, particularly when iterating over data without taking ownership. This pattern is beneficial for read-only operations where data integrity must be preserved.

```
let vec = vec![1, 2, 3];
for val in &vec {
    println!("{}", val); // Borrowing each element immutably
}
// vec is still valid after the loop
```

Mutable borrowing can be applied within loops when modifications to the iterated collection are required.

```
let mut vec = vec![1, 2, 3];
for val in &mut vec {
    *val += 1;
}
// vec now contains [2, 3, 4]
```

Pattern 4: Structs and Methods with Borrowing

Struct implementations often make use of borrowing to provide methods that do not take ownership of the struct's fields. This pattern is particularly useful in method definitions where field values need to be readable or modifiable without consuming the struct instance.

```
struct Rectangle {
    width: u32,
    height: u32,
}

impl Rectangle {
    fn area(&self) -> u32 {
        self.width * self.height
    }

    fn increase_width(&mut self, increment: u32) {
        self.width += increment;
```

```
    }
}

let rect = Rectangle { width: 30, height: 50 };
println!("The area of the rectangle is {} square pixels.", rect.area());

let mut rect_mutable = Rectangle { width: 30, height: 50 };
rect_mutable.increase_width(10);
println!("The new width of the rectangle is {} pixels.", rect_mutable.width);
```

Methods using &self borrow the struct immutably, while &mut self allows for mutable access to its fields.

Pattern 5: Slices for Partial Data Borrowing

Slices provide an efficient way to borrow a portion of data without transferring ownership. They are particularly useful for working with sequences, such as arrays and strings.

```
let arr = [1, 2, 3, 4, 5];
let slice = &arr[1..4]; // Borrowing a section of the array
for val in slice {
    println!("{}", val); // Outputs: 2 3 4
}
```

Slicing strings also allows for partial borrowing:

```
let my_string = String::from("hello world");
let hello = &my_string[0..5]; // Borrowing the first five characters
let world = &my_string[6..]; // Borrowing from the sixth character to the end
println!("{} {}", hello, world); // Outputs: hello world
```

Slices preserve the integrity and ownership of the original data structure while enabling efficient access to subsets.

Pattern 6: Lifetime Annotations for Complex Borrowing Relationships

Lifetimes ensure that references are valid as long as necessary and no longer, preventing dangling references. In functions, explicit lifetime annotations may be required when references interact in complex ways.

```
fn longest<'a>(x: &'a str, y: &'a str) -> &'a str {
    if x.len() > y.len() {
        x
    } else {
        y
    }
}

let string1 = String::from("long string is long");
let string2 = "xyz";

let result = longest(string1.as_str(), string2);
```

```
println!("The longest string is {}", result);
```

Here, the lifetime 'a ensures that the returned reference is valid as long as both inputs are valid, enforcing compile-time guarantees about reference lifetimes.

Understanding and employing these common ownership and borrowing patterns enhances the safety and performance of Rust applications. These patterns are idiomatic and leverage Rust's strict compile-time checks to prevent common programming errors, such as use-after-free and data races, promoting robust and efficient code design.

3.10 Advanced Ownership and Borrowing Scenarios

In this section, we will explore advanced scenarios in ownership and borrowing, crucial for mastering Rust's memory safety model. These scenarios often involve combining multiple ownership rules and borrowing patterns to solve complex programming tasks efficiently and safely.

Interior Mutability: One of the core tenets of Rust's ownership model is ensuring that mutable and immutable references adhere to strict borrowing rules. However, certain situations require internal data to be mutable even when it is held behind an immutable reference. This is where the concept of interior mutability comes into play. The standard library provides types such as Cell<T> and RefCell<T> that allow mutable access to data even when these types themselves are immutable. Here's how RefCell<T> is utilized:

```
use std::cell::RefCell;

struct Example {
    value: RefCell<i32>,
}

fn main() {
    let example = Example { value: RefCell::new(0) };

    {
        let mut value_ref = example.value.borrow_mut();
        *value_ref += 1;
    }

    println!("Value: {}", example.value.borrow());
}
```

In the example above, RefCell<T> enforces Rust's borrowing rules at runtime instead of compile-time. The borrow_mut method allows mutable access while keeping the outer structure immutable.

Rc<T> and Arc<T>: Rc, or Reference Counting, is employed when multiple parts of a program need to own a value. For concurrent scenarios, Arc (Atomic Reference Counting) is used for thread-safe reference counting.

```
use std::rc::Rc;

struct Owner {
    name: String,
}

// Heap allocated data holding the Owner.
let heap_owner = Rc::new(Owner { name: String::from("Alice") });

// Clone Rc to increase the reference count.
// Now both rc1 and rc2 own the same data on the heap.
let rc1 = Rc::clone(&heap_owner);
let rc2 = Rc::clone(&heap_owner);

println!("Name: {}", rc1.name);
println!("Name: {}", rc2.name);
```

In the above example, Rc<T> manages the reference count automatically. When an Rc<T> variable goes out of scope, the count decreases, and when it reaches zero, the value is deallocated.

Weak References: Using Rc<T> or Arc<T>, we can introduce a potential for reference cycles, where two Rc<T> instances refer to each other, causing memory leaks. To prevent this, Rust offers Weak<T>, a non-owning reference that doesn't affect the reference count.

```
use std::rc::{Rc, Weak};

struct Node {
    value: i32,
    next: Option<Rc<Node>>,
    prev: Option<Weak<Node>>,
}

fn main() {
    let first = Rc::new(Node { value: 1, next: None, prev: None });
    let second = Rc::new(Node { value: 2, next: None, prev: Some(Rc::downgrade(&first
        )) });

    if let Some(ref prev) = second.prev {
        if let Some(prev_node) = prev.upgrade() {
            println!("Previous node value: {}", prev_node.value);
        }
    }
}
```

Here, Weak<Node> is used for the prev field to break potential cycles, ensuring memory is properly freed.

Static Lifetime: Static lifetime 'static is a special lifetime that signifies the entire duration of the program. Variables with a static lifetime can be useful in scenarios involving global data or long-lived resources.

```
static HELLO: &str = "Hello, world!";

fn main() {
    println!("{}", HELLO);
}
```

In this example, HELLO has a 'static lifetime, meaning it will be available throughout the program's execution.

Lifetime Elision: In more complex function signatures, Rust employs lifetime elision rules to simplify explicit lifetime annotations. When the borrow checker can infer lifetimes, it eases function usage:

```
fn first_word(s: &str) -> &str {
    let bytes = s.as_bytes();

    for (i, &item) in bytes.iter().enumerate() {
        if item == b' ' {
            return &s[0..i];
        }
    }

    &s[..]
}
```

In this function, Rust infers that the output lifetime is tied to the input reference &str.

Understanding these advanced ownership and borrowing scenarios enables writing robust, efficient, and safe Rust code capable of tackling more complex and demanding projects.

3.11 Best Practices for Ownership and Borrowing

Understanding and effectively applying the principles of ownership and borrowing is crucial for writing safe and efficient Rust code. This section compiles best practices for navigating ownership and borrowing, crystallizing the theoretical discussions into actionable guidelines.

First and foremost, follow the Ownership Rules rigorously. Recall the three main rules:

- Each value in Rust has a variable that's called its owner.
- There can only be one owner at a time.
- When the owner goes out of scope, the value will be dropped.

Violating these rules results in compile-time errors, preventing potential memory safety issues.

Effective use of borrowing can significantly minimize unnecessary data duplication and maximize efficiency. When borrowing, utilize references to allow multiple parts of your program to access data concurrently without taking ownership. The following example demonstrates correct usage of immutable and mutable borrowings:

```
let s = String::from("hello");

// Immutable reference
let r1 = &s;
let r2 = &s;
println!("{}, {}", r1, r2);

// Mutable reference
let mut s2 = String::from("hello");
let r3 = &mut s2;
r3.push_str(", world");
println!("{}", r3);
```

```
hello, hello
hello, world
```

Observe the constraint that allows only one mutable reference or any number of immutable references at any point in time. This ensures data consistency and prevents race conditions.

Pay attention to function signatures concerning borrowing. Functions should accept references whenever possible to avoid unnecessary ownership transfers and cloning of large datasets. The following function signature exemplifies borrowing:

```
fn calculate_length(s: &String) -> usize {
    s.len()
}

let s1 = String::from("hello");
let len = calculate_length(&s1);
println!("The length of '{}' is {}.", s1, len);
```

```
The length of 'hello' is 5.
```

In the above code, calculate_length borrows s1, so s1 retains its ownership and can be used after the function call.

When dealing with complex data structures, consider the implications of borrowing and ownership on performance and maintainability. Utilize slices to borrow parts of collections:

```
let numbers = vec![1, 2, 3, 4, 5];
let slice = &numbers[1..3]; // This is a slice, not an array
println!("{:?}", slice);
```

```
[2, 3]
```

Slices are a form of borrowing and are particularly useful for referencing subsets of a collection without unnecessary copying.

To prevent dangling references and lifetime issues, ensure proper use of lifetimes in struct definitions and function signatures. As a reminder, lifetimes explicitly denote the scope for which a reference is valid. This helps the Rust compiler ensure that the references do not outlive the data they point to. A function signature with lifetime annotations is shown below:

```
fn longest<'a>(x: &'a str, y: &'a str) -> &'a str {
    if x.len() > y.len() {
        x
    } else {
        y
    }
}

let string1 = String::from("abcd");
let string2 = "xyz";

let result = longest(string1.as_str(), string2);
println!("The longest string is '{}'", result);
```

```
The longest string is 'abcd'
```

The lifetime `'a` ensures that the references `x` and `y` and the return value all live at least as long as the scope of the lifetime `'a`.

Additionally, prefer using the `Copy` trait for types that are small and simple in structure, such as numeric types and tuples thereof. Types implementing the `Copy` trait can seamlessly allow multiple ownerships by copying the data rather than transferring ownership.

Leverage Rust's documentation and built-in tools, such as the Rust Compiler's feedback, `rustfmt` for consistent formatting, and `clippy` for linting, to highlight potential ownership and borrowing pitfalls in your code.

Lastly, continually practice writing Rust code and peruse community resources such as forums, existing projects, and the official Rust documentation. This helps in gaining a deeper understanding of idiomatic patterns and best practices, striving towards writing more efficient and safe Rust programs.

Chapter 4

Working with Data: Variables and Data Types

This chapter examines the use and management of data in Rust, focusing on variables and data types. It covers variable declaration, shadowing, and the distinction between scalar and compound data types, including integers, floating-point numbers, booleans, tuples, and arrays. The chapter also explores string handling, including ownership with strings, and the use of the Option and Result types for managing null values and error handling. Additional topics include type aliases, type inference, constants, static variables, and pattern matching with variables.

4.1 Introduction to Variables in Rust

Variables in Rust are fundamental entities that represent memory locations where values can be stored. Unlike many other languages, Rust emphasizes safety and efficiency, and its variable management system is designed to uphold these principles. To declare a variable in Rust, the let keyword is used. Here is a basic example of a variable declaration:

```
let x = 5;
```

In this example, the variable x is assigned the value 5. One key feature is that variables are immutable by default in Rust. This means that once a value is assigned to a variable, it cannot be changed. Attempting to modify an immutable variable will result in a compilation error. For instance:

```
let y = 10;
y = 20; // This will fail
```

To allow a variable to be mutable, the mut keyword must be used. Here is how you can declare a mutable variable:

```
let mut z = 15;
z = 30; // This is allowed
```

This declaration enables the programmer to change the value of z after its initialization.

Another feature of variable declaration in Rust is the ability to define the variable's type explicitly. Although Rust often infers types automatically, specifying types can make the code more readable and help avoid potential errors. Here is an example of explicit type annotation:

```
let a: i32 = 25;
```

In this case, the variable a is explicitly declared as an i32 type, which is a 32-bit signed integer.

Rust also supports constant variables which remain immutable for the entire duration of their scope. Constants are declared using the const keyword, and their types must always be annotated. Unlike regular variables, constants can be declared in any scope, including global scope. An example of a constant declaration is as follows:

```
const MAX_POINTS: u32 = 100_000;
```

Notice the use of snake case for naming constants, which is a Rust convention. The underscore in the number is used for readability and has no effect on the value.

Shadowing is another important concept related to variables in Rust. Shadowing allows a new variable to override a previous variable of the same name within a certain scope. This can be useful for transforming a variable's value while keeping it immutable. Here is how shadowing works:

```
let b = 5;
let b = b + 1; // b is now 6
let b = b * 2; // b is now 12
```

Each occurrence of b is treated as a new variable, which means that shadowed variables can have different types. For example:

```
let c = "initial";
let c = c.len(); // c is now a usize type
```

Variables have different lifetimes, depending on where they are declared. For example, a variable declared within a function is scoped to that function and cannot be accessed outside of it. Here is an example illustrating variable scope:

```
fn main() {
    let d = 5;
    {
        let e = 10;
        println!("e is {}", e); // This works
    }
    println!("d is {}", d); // This also works
    // println!("e is {}", e); // This will fail: e is out of scope
}
```

In this example, e is only accessible within the inner block where it is declared, while d is accessible throughout the main function.

Variable ownership and scope rules are critical for memory safety in Rust. When a variable goes out of scope, Rust automatically deallocates the memory associated with it, preventing memory leaks.

Type inference in Rust allows for streamlined and concise code, by letting the compiler determine the type from the context. However, there are times where specifying type is necessary, particularly for complex types, ensuring clarity and reducing ambiguity in the code's logic.

Rust's approach to variables encompasses immutability, explicit typing, type inference, constants, and variable scopes, ensuring efficient and safe management of memory and data throughout the program's lifecycle.

4.2 Variable Shadowing

Variable shadowing is a key concept in Rust that allows the redeclaration of a variable in the same scope, which effectively hides the previous declaration of that variable. This feature offers flexibility by enabling the transformation of variable values within a particular scope without mutating the original variable. This contrasts with other languages where modification of a variable requires mutable signatures or results in syntax errors due to multiple declarations.

Consider the following example:

```
fn main() {
    let x = 5;
    let x = x + 1;
    let x = x * 2;
    println!("The value of x is: {}", x);
}
```

In this code, the variable x is declared three times. Each subsequent declaration shadows the previous one. Initially, x is assigned the value 5. The second declaration adds 1 to x, resulting in 6. The final declaration multiplies x by 2, resulting in 12. This final value of x is then printed, outputting:

```
The value of x is: 12
```

This ability to shadow variables signifies that let does not merely bind a name to a value but can re-bind the name to a new value within the same scope. Importantly, shadowing is distinct from mutable variables, although both can change the value associated with a variable name. To understand this further, compare shadowing to using mutable variables:

```
fn main() {
    let mut y = 5;
    y = y + 1;
    y = y * 2;
    println!("The value of y is: {}", y);
}
```

Here, the variable y is declared mutable with mut, allowing its value to change. The output of this code is:

```
The value of y is: 12
```

While both techniques achieve similar results in this simple case, shadowing allows the developer to redefine the variable's type:

```
fn main() {
```

```
    let spaces = " ";
    let spaces = spaces.len();
    println!("The number of spaces is: {}", spaces);
}
```

In this example, the variable spaces is first declared as a string slice holding several spaces. The second declaration rebinds spaces to the integer value representing the length of the string, effectively changing its type from &str to usize. This type-changing capability is a distinctive advantage of shadowing over mutable bindings, as mutable bindings require the variable to maintain the same type.

Scope boundaries play a crucial role in variable shadowing. When the scope ends, previous bindings are no longer shadowed and become accessible again. Examine the following program:

```
fn main() {
    let a = 10;

    {
        let a = 20;
        println!("The value of a in the inner scope: {}", a);
    }

    println!("The value of a in the outer scope: {}", a);
}
```

Inside the inner scope delineated by the curly braces, a is shadowed and takes the value 20. Outside this scope, the original value of a, which is 10, persists. The output is:

```
The value of a in the inner scope: 20
The value of a in the outer scope: 10
```

Shadowing variables therefore provides controlled scope-specific redefinitions without permanently altering the original bindings. This feature is especially useful in iterative processes or temporary value transformations.

Consider a situation involving iterations over frequently transforming values in functional pipelines:

```
fn main() {
    let mut sum = 0;

    for i in 0..5 {
        let value = i * 2;
        sum += value;
    }

    println!("Sum of the values: {}", sum);
}
```

In each loop iteration, value is declared and shadowed with a new computed value (i * 2). The sequential shadowing ensures the correct computation of sum. The final output will be:

```
Sum of the values: 20
```

The versatility of variable shadowing allows for efficient and straightforward handling of temporary or new values within a scope, enhancing the expressiveness and functionality of Rust programs.

4.3 Scalar Data Types: Integers, Floating-Point Numbers, and Booleans

In Rust, scalar data types represent single values as opposed to compound types which group multiple values together. Scalar types include integers, floating-point numbers, and booleans. Understanding these types and their properties is crucial for effective memory management and performance optimization in Rust programs.

Integers in Rust can be classified into signed and unsigned integers. Signed integers allow for negative values, while unsigned integers only represent non-negative values. The specific type determines the range of values an integer can store. For instance, an i8 can store values from -128 to 127, whereas a u8 stores values from 0 to 255.

Below is an example of integer declaration and usage in Rust:

```
fn main() {
    let signed_integer: i32 = -42;
    let unsigned_integer: u32 = 42;
    println!("Signed integer: {}", signed_integer);
    println!("Unsigned integer: {}", unsigned_integer);
}
```

When executing the above code, the output would be:

```
Signed integer: -42
Unsigned integer: 42
```

Rust allows for specifying different sizes for integers: 8, 16, 32, 64, and 128 bits (e.g., i8, u16, i32, etc.). Additionally, Rust provides isize and usize types, which are either 32 or 64 bits depending on the architecture.

Floating-point numbers are used when fractional values are needed. Rust conforms to the IEEE-754 standard with single-precision (32-bit f32) and double-precision (64-bit f64) representations. By default, Rust infers floating-point literals as f64 due to its greater precision and range.

General usage of floating-point numbers in Rust can be demonstrated as follows:

```
fn main() {
    let float_number: f32 = 3.14;
    let double_number = 2.71828; // inferred as f64
    println!("Float number: {}", float_number);
    println!("Double number: {}", double_number);
}
```

Executing the above will produce:

```
Float number: 3.14
Double number: 2.71828
```

Rust provides a range of operations for integers and floating-point numbers, including addition, subtraction, multiplication, division, and remainder. The std::ops module encompasses these operations, ensuring type-safety.

Booleans in Rust are simple data types representing true or false. They are denoted by the bool keyword and can be utilized in control flow mechanisms such as if expressions or loops.

An example of boolean declaration and control flow:

```
fn main() {
    let is_active: bool = true;
    let is_complete = false; // inferred as bool
    if is_active {
        println!("The process is active.");
    } else {
        println!("The process is not active.");
    }
    println!("Is the process complete? {}", is_complete);
}
```

This produces:

```
The process is active.
Is the process complete? false
```

Booleans are integral to logical operations, which are essential for conditional statements and decision-making processes. Rust supports the standard logical operations such as AND (&&), OR (||), and NOT (!).

For instance:

```
fn main() {
    let a = true;
    let b = false;
    println!("a AND b: {}", a && b);
```

```
    println!("a OR b: {}", a || b);
    println!("NOT a: {}", !a);
}
```

The corresponding output will be:

```
a AND b: false
a OR b: true
NOT a: false
```

Knowledge of scalar data types in Rust, including their properties and operations, facilitates the effective design of robust, efficient programs. Proper utilization of integers, floating-point numbers, and booleans is fundamental to achieving optimal performance and reliable behavior in computational tasks.

4.4 Compound Data Types: Tuples and Arrays

In Rust, compound data types allow the grouping of multiple values into a single type. Among the most fundamental compound types are tuples and arrays. These types offer varying mechanisms for grouping and accessing multiple values and demonstrate Rust's emphasis on safety and performance.

Tuples are a general way of grouping together a number of values of different types. When you need to combine mixed types, tuples are an optimal choice.

```
fn main() {
    let tuple1: (i32, f64, u8) = (500, 6.4, 1);
    println!("Tuple contains: {:?}", tuple1);
    let (x, y, z) = tuple1;
    println!("Values extracted: x = {}, y = {}, z = {}", x, y, z);
}
```

Using the code above, the expression let tuple1: (i32, f64, u8) = (500, 6.4, 1); declares a tuple variable tuple1 that contains three distinct types: i32, f64, and u8. You can output tuple values using the println! macro; {:\} is used for debugging output.

Pattern matching enables extracting individual values from tuples: let (x, y, z) = tuple1; destructures tuple1 into its component values. Following this, you can access each element individually through x, y, and z.

Accessing tuple elements directly via indexing is another salient feature in Rust. let value = tuple1.0; accesses the first element. The subsequent elements can be accessed similarly using tuple1.1 and tuple1.2.

Arrays are collections of elements of the same type. They are particularly useful for fixed-size, sequential data organization. Arrays utilize stack allocation, which ensures fast and predictable access times.

```
fn main() {
    let array1: [i32; 4] = [1, 2, 3, 4];
    println!("Array contains: {:?}", array1);
    let first = array1[0];
    let second = array1[1];
    println!("First two elements: {}, {}", first, second);
}
```

In the code above: let array1: [i32; 4] = [1, 2, 3, 4]; declares an array of i32 with a length of 4. The array elements are accessed via indexing.

The array's length is accessed using the len() method: array1.len() returns the length of the array, providing a method to ensure operations remain within bounds.

It is essential to acknowledge that array bounds are checked at runtime. If an attempt to access an out-of-bounds index occurs, Rust will terminate the program, helping maintain memory safety.

Another feature of Rust arrays is their inclusion in a slice, a view into a contiguous sequence of elements within a collection, which provides a way to reference a segment of an array.

```
fn main() {
    let array1: [i32; 4] = [1, 2, 3, 4];
    let slice: &[i32] = &array1[1..3];
    println!("Slice contains: {:?}", slice);
}
```

The code highlights how to create a slice from an array: let slice: &[i32] = &array1[1..3]; creates a slice that references elements from index 1 to index 3 of array1. This feature of Rust allows for flexible data manipulation without copying the array elements.

Examining both tuples and arrays showcases the diversity and flexibility of Rust's compound data types, enabling developers to efficiently organize and manipulate data collections while ensuring type safety and performance.

4.5 Strings and String Slices

Rust offers robust support for string handling, a critical requirement for many applications. Its string management paradigm ensures memory safety while providing operational efficiency. Rust's core string types are String and &str. Understanding their characteristics and how to use them efficiently is essential.

String is a growable, heap-allocated data structure provided by Rust's std::collections module. It is the most versatile string type, supporting various operations such as concatenation, modification, and dynamic resizing.

```
fn main() {
    let mut s = String::from("Hello, "); // Create a mutable String
    s.push_str("world!"); // Append a string slice to String
    println!("{}", s); // Output: Hello, world!
}
```

In the example above, the String::from method initializes a String with the contents "Hello, ". The push_str method appends a string slice to the string, demonstrating String's mutable nature.

&str, or string slice, is an immutable reference to a sequence of UTF-8 encoded bytes within a string. It can point either to a part of a String or a string literal, ensuring efficient memory usage. Slices are often leveraged for borrowing strings without requiring additional allocations.

```
fn main() {
    let s = "Hello, world!"; // String literal (type: &str)
    let part = &s[0..5]; // Slice of the string literal
    println!("{}", part); // Output: Hello
}
```

String slices are denoted using the syntax &s[start..end], where start and end are the byte positions within the string.

A deep understanding of String and &str involves their memory management and ownership rules. When a String is created, it owns the allocated memory, and when it goes out of scope, the memory is deallocated. Conversely, a &str is usually a reference to an existing string, meaning it does not own the data; hence, it adheres to Rust's borrowing rules to ensure memory safety.

Characteristics and Operations

* String:

- Heap-allocated, growable.
- Mutable, can be modified.
- Has methods like push_str, push, and insert for mutability.

* &str:

- Immutable, fixed-size view of a string.
- Can reference a part of a String or string literal.
- Borrowing is applicable, ensuring efficient memory usage without duplication.

To convert between String and &str, Rust provides methods that facilitate these operations conveniently.

```
fn main() {
    let s = String::from("hello");

    // Obtaining a string slice from a String
    let slice = &s[0..2];
    println!("{}", slice); // Output: he

    // Converting &str to String for ownership
    let slice_literal: &str = "world";
    let owned_string: String = slice_literal.to_string();
    println!("{}", owned_string); // Output: world
}
```

String Methods and Manipulation

The String type offers numerous useful methods for string manipulation. Below are a few commonly used methods:

```
fn main() {
    let mut s = String::from("hello ");

    // Append a character
    s.push('w');

    // Append a string slice
    s.push_str("orld");

    // Replace substrings
    let new_s = s.replace("world", "Rust");

    println!("{}", new_s); // Output: hello Rust

    // Check string length
    println!("{}", s.len()); // Output: 11
}
```

Comparing Strings and Slices

Comparing String and &str is common in many applications. This comparison is straightforward using Rust's PartialEq trait.

```
fn main() {
    let s1 = String::from("hello");
    let s2 = "hello";

    assert_eq!(s1, s2); // Compare String with &str, evaluates true
    println!("s1 and s2 are equal"); // This line will be printed
}
```

String Slicing and Iteration

Rust provides tools for slicing and iterating over strings while maintaining safety and efficiency.

```
fn main() {
    let s = String::from("hello");

    // Iterate over characters
    for c in s.chars() {
        print!("{} ", c);
    }
    // Output: h e l l o

    println!();

    // Iterate over bytes
    for b in s.bytes() {
        print!("{} ", b);
    }
    // Output: 104 101 108 108 111
}
```

The chars() method iterates over Unicode scalar values, whereas bytes() iterates over raw bytes. Both approaches are beneficial depending on the operations performed—whether manipulating textual data or examining byte patterns.

4.6 Understanding Ownership with Strings

Ownership is a core concept in Rust, ensuring memory safety without a garbage collector. Understanding ownership is particularly crucial when working with strings, as strings involve more complex memory management compared to scalar types.

In Rust, strings come in two main types: String and &str (string slices). Each type has different ownership and usage characteristics, and grasping these differences is essential for efficient and safe string handling.

String is a heap-allocated, growable string type. Because String is heap-allocated, it provides the flexibility to store dynamic text content that can be modified at runtime. On the other hand, &str is an immutable reference to a string slice, often used for static strings or substrings.

Consider the following example of creating and modifying a String:

```
let mut s1 = String::from("Hello");
s1.push_str(", world!");
println!("{}", s1); // Output: Hello, world!
```

In this example, s1 initially holds the string "Hello". The method push_str appends ", world!" to s1, resulting in "Hello, world!". This shows the mutable nature of String, allowing for dynamic modifications.

Conversely, &str is an immutable reference. Attempting to mutate a &str will result in a compile-time error:

```
let s2 = "Hello, world!";
s2.push_str(" This will cause error."); // This line will not compile
```

Rust enforces rules to ensure memory safety through ownership semantics. The ownership rule states that each value in Rust has a single owner, and the owner handles the cleanup of the value when it goes out of scope. When dealing with strings, this rule has significant implications for performance and memory safety.

Ownership Transfers with Strings

Ownership can be transferred, or moved, from one variable to another. This transfer invalidates the original owner, ensuring no dangling pointers exist. For instance:

```
let s1 = String::from("Hello");
let s2 = s1; // Ownership of s1 is moved to s2
println!("{}", s1); // This line will cause compile-time error
```

Since s1's ownership is moved to s2, attempting to use s1 after the move results in a compile-time error, preventing access to invalid memory.

Alternatively, cloning a String can be performed to generate a deep copy:

```
let s1 = String::from("Hello");
let s2 = s1.clone();
println!("{}", s1); // s1 can still be used
println!("{}", s2); // s2 is an independent copy
```

In this case, both s1 and s2 are independent strings, and each can be used safely without affecting the other.

String Slices and Borrowing

String slices (&str) borrow from strings and do not own the underlying data. Borrowing allows functions and code to access the data without transferring ownership. Borrowing can be either mutable or immutable, but only one mutable reference can exist at a time.

Consider the example below:

```
fn take_borrowed_str(s: &str) {
    println!("{}", s);
}

let s1 = String::from("Hello");
take_borrowed_str(&s1);
println!("{}", s1); // s1 can still be used as it is not moved
```

Here, the function take_borrowed_str borrows s1 as an immutable reference (&s1). After the function call, s1 remains valid and can be used subsequently because ownership was not transferred.

String Slices and Lifetime Annotations

Lifetime annotations are necessary to ensure references are valid as long as they are used. Lifetime describes how long a reference is valid. When dealing with string slices that borrow data, Rust's compiler uses lifetimes to guarantee memory safety.

Consider the following function returning a string slice:

```
fn first_word(s: &str) -> &str {
    let bytes = s.as_bytes();
    for (i, &item) in bytes.iter().enumerate() {
        if item == b' ' {
            return &s[0..i];
        }
    }
    &s[..]
}
```

The function first_word returns a slice of the given string s up to the first space. Since the returned slice is a part of the input string s, the lifetime of the output slice must match the lifetime of the input reference &str.

Lifetimes are inferred by the compiler in simple cases, but explicit lifetime annotations might be necessary for more complex functions:

```
fn longest<'a>(x: &'a str, y: &'a str) -> &'a str {
    if x.len() > y.len() {
```

```
        x
    } else {
        y
    }
}
```

In this function, longest takes two string slices with the same lifetime 'a and returns a string slice with that lifetime. This ensures that the returned reference is valid for as long as both input references are valid.

Understanding and correctly applying ownership, borrowing, and lifetimes with strings in Rust ensures that programs are memory safe and efficient. This foundational knowledge is critical for working effectively with more complex data structures and concurrent programming in Rust.

4.7 Option Type for Handling Null Values

The Option type in Rust provides a robust way to handle potential absence of a value. In many programming languages, null values are used to signify the absence of a value. However, using null can often lead to null pointer exceptions and only surfaces at runtime, making error detection challenging. Rust's Option type offers a safer alternative by encoding the possibility of absence within the type system itself.

The Option type is an enum, declared as follows:

```
enum Option<T> {
    Some(T),
    None,
}
```

Here, T is a generic type. The Option enum can have one of two variants: * Some(T), representing the presence of a value, wrapping a value of type T. * None, representing the absence of a value.

Consider a function that may or may not return a string based on some conditions.

```
fn get_name(input: bool) -> Option<String> {
    if input {
        Some(String::from("Alice"))
    } else {
        None
    }
}
```

This function returns an Option<String>, which can either be

Some(String) if input is true, or None if input is false.

Handling the Option type requires explicit pattern matching or methods to address both variants. The use of the match expression ensures that all possible cases (variants) are covered, preventing runtime errors due to unhandled cases:

```
fn print_name(input: bool) {
    let name = get_name(input);

    match name {
        Some(n) => println!("The name is: {}", n),
        None => println!("No name provided"),
    }
}
```

Alternatively, using methods provided by the Option type often results in more concise code. Common methods include unwrap, unwrap_or, map, and and_then:

* unwrap: Extracts the value inside Some variant, panicking if it is None.

```
let name = get_name(true).unwrap();
println!("The name is: {}", name);
```

* unwrap_or: Provides a default value if the Option is None.

```
let name = get_name(false).unwrap_or(String::from("Default Name"));
println!("The name is: {}", name);
```

* map: Applies a function to the value inside Some if it exists, otherwise does nothing.

```
let name = get_name(true).map(|n| format!("Hello, {}", n));
match name {
    Some(greeting) => println!("{}", greeting),
    None => println!("No name to create a greeting"),
}
```

* and_then: Chains multiple computations that return an Option, flattening the result.

```
fn get_greeting(name: Option<String>) -> Option<String> {
    name.and_then(|n| Some(format!("Hello, {}", n)))
}

let greeting = get_greeting(get_name(true));
match greeting {
    Some(g) => println!("{}", g),
    None => println!("No name to greet"),
}
```

The Option type exemplifies Rust's emphasis on safety and correctness by eliminating null references, making it obligatory for developers to consider the presence and absence of values explicitly. This design choice not only mitigates common runtime errors but also ensures that code is self-documenting regarding whether a value might be optional.

Understanding and effectively utilizing the Option type is critical for writing robust Rust programs, especially when dealing with potentially absent data. This proficiency enhances error handling practices and aligns with Rust's goals of safety and zero-cost abstractions.

4.8 Result Type for Error Handling

Error handling in Rust is distinctive due to its emphasis on safety and its prevention of many common bugs associated with error states in programming. A pivotal construct in this context is the Result type, which is used for returning and propagating errors. The Result type is an enumeration (enum) that includes two variants: Ok and Err. The Ok variant is used when a value is returned successfully, while the Err variant is employed when an error occurs.

The definition of the Result enum is as follows:

```
enum Result<T, E> {
    Ok(T),
    Err(E),
}
```

Here, T represents the type of the value that is returned in a successful case, and E signifies the type of the error that occurs.

To demonstrate the practical utility of the Result type, consider a function that attempts to divide two numbers, returning an error if the divisor is zero:

```
fn divide(dividend: f64, divisor: f64) -> Result<f64, String> {
    if divisor == 0.0 {
        return Err(String::from("Cannot divide by zero"));
    }
    Ok(dividend / divisor)
}
```

In the above function, divide takes two f64 arguments and returns a Result<f64, String>. If the divisor is zero, the function returns an Err with an appropriate error message; otherwise, it returns the quotient wrapped in Ok.

To call this function and handle the result, we might use pattern matching:

```
fn main() {
    match divide(4.0, 2.0) {
        Ok(result) => println!("Quotient: {}", result),
        Err(e) => println!("Error: {}", e),
    }

    match divide(4.0, 0.0) {
        Ok(result) => println!("Quotient: {}", result),
        Err(e) => println!("Error: {}", e),
    }
}
```

The output of this program will be:

```
Quotient: 2
Error: Cannot divide by zero
```

Pattern matching on the Result type allows for explicit handling of both success and error cases, making the control flow clear and robust against various failure modes. Rust's Result offers several methods to augment flexibility and convenience, which are frequently leveraged in error handling.

unwrap is a method that extracts the value in an Ok or panics if the value is an Err. Although unwrap can be convenient, its use is cautioned against in scenarios where a failure scenario is likely or unpredictable:

```
fn example_unwrap() {
    let result = divide(4.0, 2.0).unwrap(); // Safe usage
    println!("Quotient: {}", result);

    let result = divide(4.0, 0.0).unwrap(); // This will panic
    println!("Quotient: {}", result);
}
```

To avoid panic and handle errors more gracefully, expect can be utilized. It behaves similarly to unwrap but lets you specify an error message:

```
fn example_expect() {
    let result = divide(4.0, 2.0).expect("Division failed");
    println!("Quotient: {}", result);

    let result = divide(4.0, 0.0).expect("Division failed"); // This will panic with a
         custom message
    println!("Quotient: {}", result);
}
```

Beyond unwrap and expect, Rust provides combinator methods such as map, and_then, and or_else, which enable chaining operations on Result values more effectively.

For instance, map allows the transformation of an Ok value while leaving an Err untouched:

```
fn example_map() {
    let result = divide(4.0, 2.0).map(|value| value * 2.0);
    match result {
        Ok(result) => println!("Double the quotient: {}", result),
        Err(e) => println!("Error: {}", e),
    }

    let result = divide(4.0, 0.0).map(|value| value * 2.0);
    match result {
        Ok(result) => println!("Double the quotient: {}", result),
        Err(e) => println!("Error: {}", e),
    }
}
```

Sometimes, error handling benefits from encapsulating additional context about an error. For more complex operations requiring rich error information, and_then can transform a successful result or propagate errors seamlessly:

```
fn example_and_then() {
    let result = divide(4.0, 2.0).and_then(|value| divide(value, 2.0));
    match result {
        Ok(result) => println!("Final quotient: {}", result),
        Err(e) => println!("Error: {}", e),
    }

    let result = divide(4.0, 0.0).and_then(|value| divide(value, 2.0));
    match result {
        Ok(result) => println!("Final quotient: {}", result),
        Err(e) => println!("Error: {}", e),
    }
}
```

Rust's Result type fosters robust error management by encouraging developers to handle both potential success and failure paths conscientiously. Its design allows for the development of safe and predictable systems, adhering to Rust's broader philosophy of performance, reliability, and concurrency.

```
Double the quotient: 4.0
Error: Cannot divide by zero

Final quotient: 1.0
Error: Cannot divide by zero
```

4.9 Type Aliases and Type Inference

Rust provides powerful abstractions to improve code readability and maintainability, including type aliases and type inference. These features allow for cleaner code and reduce redundancy, leading to more efficient and error-resistant programming practices.

Type aliases are mechanisms that enable programmers to create new names for existing types. This can be particularly useful when dealing with complex types. By defining a type alias, a programmer can simplify type annotations and improve code readability without introducing new types.

To define a type alias in Rust, the type keyword is used followed by the new type name and the original type. For example:

```
type Kilometers = i32;
type ComplexNumber = (f64, f64);
```

In this example, Kilometers is an alias for i32, and ComplexNumber is an alias for a tuple containing two f64 values. Type aliases do not create new types, but they can make existing types easier to use and understand. Consider the following function:

```
fn add_distance(dist1: Kilometers, dist2: Kilometers) -> Kilometers {
    dist1 + dist2
}

fn display_complex(c: ComplexNumber) {
    println!("Real part: {}, Imaginary part: {}", c.0, c.1);
}
```

Here, Kilometers and ComplexNumber enhance code readability by providing meaningful names for the types. This can be especially beneficial when types are more complex, such as nested tuples or long generic chains.

Type inference is another powerful feature of Rust that allows the compiler to deduce the type of variables based on available information. This makes code shorter and less verbose, while still maintaining type safety. Rust's type inference is robust enough to determine types in most cases without explicit annotations.

For example, when declaring a variable, if the type can be inferred from the assigned value, there is no need to specify the type explicitly:

```
let x = 42; // Type is inferred as i32
let y = 3.14; // Type is inferred as f64
let name = "Alice"; // Type is inferred as &str
```

This inference works in more complex contexts as well. When using functions, the return type can often be inferred:

```
fn square(x: i32) -> i32 {
    x * x
}
```

```
let result = square(10); // Type of result is inferred as i32
```

Rust's type inference simplifies code by eliminating unnecessary type annotations. This is particularly useful when dealing with collections and iterators. Take the following example, which demonstrates type inference with vectors:

```
let numbers = vec![1, 2, 3, 4, 5]; // Type is inferred as Vec<i32>
```

In this case, the compiler infers that numbers is a vector of i32 because the elements are all integers. When combining type inference with method chaining, Rust remains expressive and concise:

```
let doubled_numbers: Vec<i32> = numbers.iter().map(|x| x * 2).collect();
```

Here, the compiler can infer the type of the closure |x| x * 2, the iterator method return types, and the final collection type. This level of inference drastically reduces the amount of boilerplate code.

However, there are limits to type inference. The compiler might not always deduce the type, especially in more complex scenarios where the type could be ambiguous. In such situations, explicit type annotations are necessary:

```
let value: i32 = "42".parse().expect("Not a number");
```

In this instance, the result of "42".parse() could be any type that implements the FromStr trait. Therefore, an explicit type annotation is required for the variable value to specify that the expected type is i32.

Type aliases and type inference in Rust foster an efficient development process by simplifying type management and making code cleaner and more manageable. Well-defined type aliases can make complicated type signatures more understandable, while effective use of type inference minimizes verbosity without sacrificing type safety. These features are instrumental in both small-scale and enterprise-level Rust applications.

4.10 Working with Constants and Static Variables

In Rust, constants and static variables serve roles distinct from regular variables, providing a means to define data that remains unchanging throughout a program's execution. Grasping their proper use is pivotal for writing efficient and clear code, particularly when dealing with values that need global access or immutability enforced by the compiler.

Constants in Rust are immutable values that must be assigned at compile time. These are annotated with the const keyword and are required to have explicit types. Constants can be set only to expressions that can be evaluated at compile time, such as literals, constant functions, and expressions composed of other constants.

For example, you can define a constant as follows:

```
// Defining a constant
const MAX_POINTS: u32 = 100_000;
```

In this case, MAX_POINTS is a constant of type u32, and its value is set to 100000. The use of underscores in the numeric value enhances readability.

Key attributes of constants in Rust include:

- Constants live for the entire lifetime of a program.
- They are immutably assigned with values determinable at compile time.
- There can be no runtime derived assignment.

Static variables, in contrast, hold a singular instance of data for the program's run and are defined with the static keyword. Like constants, they require explicit type definitions. Static variables primarily differ from constants in their ability to hold mutable data, albeit this mutability comes with the caveat of ensuring thread-safety, typically involving usage of synchronization primitives like Mutex or RwLock.

An example of a static variable is:

```
// Defining a static variable
static LANGUAGE: &str = "Rust";
```

LANGUAGE is a static string slice that persists for the program's duration, ensuring it's accessible globally within the code.

Mutable static variables can also be defined but should be used with caution:

```
// Defining a mutable static variable
static mut COUNTER: u32 = 0;
```

Here, COUNTER is defined as a mutable static variable. Accessing or modifying COUNTER is unsafe and must be enclosed within an unsafe block:

```
// Modifying a mutable static variable within an unsafe block
unsafe {
    COUNTER += 1;
}
```

Given their global scope and extended lifetime, mutable static variables should be carefully managed to avoid data races or inconsistent state. Best practices include restricting their usage and preferring other concurrency constructs like channels or atomic types.

The choice between constants and static variables hinges on the specific requirements:

- Use const for values that never change during program execution and are known at compile time.

- Use static for data that might require mutability or for safely sharing data across threads.

In practical terms, leveraging constants and static variables involves understanding their memory management, scope, and synchronization when used concurrently. Mastery of these constructs facilitates robust and efficient Rust code, contributing to the language's goals of safety and performance.

4.11 Pattern Matching with Variables

Pattern matching is a powerful feature in Rust that allows for the checking and unpacking of data structures based on their shape and content. This mechanism is particularly useful when dealing with complex data types and can be used to simplify the control flow of a program. Understanding pattern matching in the context of variables is essential for writing idiomatic and efficient Rust code.

In Rust, patterns are used primarily in match expressions and if let constructs. A pattern can be as simple as a literal value or as complex as a nested data structure. Let's first consider the basic usage of pattern matching with a match expression.

The match expression is used to compare a value against a series of patterns and execute code based on which pattern matches. Here's an example of a basic match expression:

```
let number = 3;

match number {
    1 => println!("One!"),
    2 => println!("Two!"),
    3 => println!("Three!"),
    _ => println!("Something else"),
}
```

In this example, the value of number is compared against the patterns '1', '2', and '3'. When a match is found, the corresponding code block is executed. The underscore (_) is a wildcard pattern that matches any value and acts as a catch-all, ensuring that all possible values are accounted for.

Pattern matching can also be used to destructure compound data types such as tuples, arrays, and structs. Consider the following tuple example:

```
let tuple = (1, "hello", 3.5);

match tuple {
    (1, "hello", x) => println!("The third value is {}", x),
    _ => println!("No match found"),
}
```

In this case, the pattern (1, "hello", x) is used to destructure the tuple (1, "hello", 3.5). If the first two elements of the tuple match the specified values, the third element is bound to the variable x.

Similarly, when working with arrays, you can use patterns to match and destructure elements:

```
let array = [1, 2, 3, 4, 5];

match array {
    [1, 2, ..] => println!("Starts with 1, 2"),
    [.., 4, 5] => println!("Ends with 4, 5"),
    _ => println!("No match found"),
}
```

Here, the two patterns [1, 2, ..] and [.., 4, 5] use the .. syntax to indicate any number of elements in between, allowing for flexible matching of array contents.

Pattern matching in Rust also extends to the Option and Result types, which are commonly used for error handling and dealing with optional values. The following example demonstrates matching on an Option<i32>:

```
let optional_value: Option<i32> = Some(10);

match optional_value {
    Some(value) => println!("Got a value: {}", value),
    None => println!("No value"),
}
```

In this case, the match expression handles the Some and None variants of the Option<i32> type. If the variant is Some, the contained value is extracted and used in the code block.

For more complex error handling scenarios, pattern matching can be applied to the Result type. Consider the following example:

```
enum Error {
    NotFound,
    PermissionDenied,
}

fn process_result(result: Result<i32, Error>) {
    match result {
        Ok(value) => println!("Success with value: {}", value),
        Err(Error::NotFound) => println!("Error: Not Found"),
        Err(Error::PermissionDenied) => println!("Error: Permission Denied"),
    }
}
```

In the process_result function, the match expression deconstructs the Result<i32, Error> type into its Ok and Err variants. Each variant is then handled appropriately within its corresponding code block.

Pattern matching can also be integrated with the control flow using the if let construct, which provides a concise way to match and simultaneously bind variables:

```
if let Some(value) = optional_value {
    println!("Got a value via if let: {}", value);
} else {
    println!("No value via if let");
}
```

The if let construct is particularly useful when you care about handling only one specific pattern and want to avoid the verbosity of a full match expression for simple scenarios.

Lastly, patterns can incorporate guards, which are additional if conditions specified after a pattern in a match expression:

```
match number {
    x if x % 2 == 0 => println!("Even number"),
    x if x % 2 != 0 => println!("Odd number"),
    _ => println!("Not a valid number"),
}
```

In this example, the guards if x % 2 == 0 and if x % 2 != 0 refine the patterns to match even and odd numbers, respectively. Using guards adds another level of precision to pattern matching, enabling complex conditions to be elegantly expressed and managed in Rust programs.

Understanding and leveraging pattern matching with variables enhances code readability and robustness, making it an indispensable tool for Rust developers. By mastering this feature, you can write more concise and expressive code, analogous to leveraging advanced control structures found in other mature programming languages.

Chapter 5

Control Flow in Rust

This chapter addresses how Rust manages control flow, beginning with conditional statements like if and else, and continuing with match for pattern matching. It explores various looping constructs, including loop, while, and for, and discusses control flow modifiers such as break and continue. The chapter examines error handling using match and Result, as well as the utilization of logical operators, the ? operator for early returns, and pattern matching with if let. Finally, it covers idiomatic control flow patterns and the use of guard clauses.

5.1 Introduction to Control Flow

In Rust, as with most programming languages, control flow constructs dictate the order in which statements and instructions are executed. These constructs allow you to introduce decision-making, looping, and branching into your programs, making them more dynamic and responsive to varying conditions. Understanding Rust's control flow mechanisms is pivotal to writing effective and efficient Rust code.

At the core of Rust's control flow capabilities are constructs such as if, else, match, loop, while, and for. Each of these serves a specific purpose and provides a unique way to manage the execution path of a program.

The if statement is used for simple conditional branching. It evaluates a boolean expression and, based on its value, decides which block of code to execute. For example:

```
let x = 5;

if x > 0 {
    println!("x is positive");
} else {
    println!("x is not positive");
}
```

In the above snippet, the condition $x > 0$ is evaluated. If true, the code inside the first block is executed, otherwise, the code inside the else block is executed.

For more complex branching based on multiple criteria, Rust provides the match statement. It allows you to compare a value against a series of patterns and execute the associated block of code based on the first matching pattern. Here is an example demonstrating the use of match:

```
let number = 7;

match number {
    1 => println!("One"),
    2 => println!("Two"),
    3 => println!("Three"),
    _ => println!("Something else"),
}
```

The match statement compares number to the specified patterns (1, 2, 3). If number does not match any of these patterns, the wildcard pattern _ is used, which acts as a catch-all.

Looping constructs in Rust include loop, while, and for. These loops help in executing a block of code repeatedly based on a defined condition or for a specific range.

A loop construct sets up an infinite loop that will run until explicitly terminated with the break statement. For example:

```
let mut counter = 0;

loop {
    counter += 1;
    if counter == 5 {
        break;
    }
}
println!("Counter stopped at: {}", counter);
```

In the above code, the loop construct will continually increment counter until it equals 5, whereupon the break statement will exit the loop.

The while loop continues execution as long as its condition remains true. Here is an example:

```
let mut number = 3;

while number != 0 {
    println!("{}!", number);

    number -= 1;
}
println!("Liftoff!");
```

In this example, the loop will print each number before decreasing it, continuing until number reaches zero.

The for loop in Rust is most commonly used to iterate over elements in a collection, such as arrays, vectors, or ranges. Consider the following example:

```
let array = [10, 20, 30, 40, 50];

for elem in array.iter() {
    println!("The value is: {}", elem);
}
```

The for loop iterates over each element in the array and prints it out.

Rust also provides mechanisms to control loop execution using the break and continue statements. break is used to exit a loop early, while continue skips to the next iteration of the loop. Here is an example demonstrating both:

```
for i in 1..10 {
    if i == 5 {
        continue; // Skip the rest of the current iteration when i is 5
    }
    if i == 8 {
        break; // Exit the loop when i is 8
    }
    println!("i: {}", i);
}
```

Understanding the nuances of Rust's control flow constructs allows developers to write clear, efficient, and idiomatic code. These constructs, combined with Rust's strict ownership, and concurrency paradigms, enable the creation of reliable and performant software.

By leveraging the power of Rust's control flow mechanisms, programmers can efficiently direct the execution of their code, effectively handle errors, and manage complex conditions and patterns.

5.2 Conditional Statements: if and else

Conditional statements are fundamental for directing the flow of a program based on certain conditions. In Rust, the most commonly used conditional statement is the if statement, often coupled with else to handle alternative branches.

An if statement evaluates an expression and executes a block of code if the expression evaluates to true. The syntax is straightforward:

```
if expression {
    // block of code to execute if the expression is true
}
```

Here's a concrete example:

```
let number = 5;

if number > 3 {
    println!("The number is greater than 3.");
}
```

In this example, the condition is number > 3, which evaluates to true. Consequently, the block inside the if statement gets executed, printing "The number is greater than 3." to the console.

To handle an alternative case when the condition is false, we use the else keyword:

```
if expression {
    // block of code to execute if the expression is true
} else {
    // block of code to execute if the expression is false
}
```

Consider this example:

```
let number = 2;

if number > 3 {
    println!("The number is greater than 3.");
} else {
    println!("The number is not greater than 3.");
}
```

In this case, number > 3 evaluates to false, so the block inside the else statement is executed, resulting in the output:

```
The number is not greater than 3.
```

Rust allows chaining multiple conditions with else if. This is particularly useful when you need to check several conditions in sequence:

```
if condition1 {
    // block of code to execute if condition1 is true
} else if condition2 {
    // block of code to execute if condition2 is true
} else {
    // block of code to execute if none of the above conditions are true
}
```

Here's a practical example:

```
let number = 5;

if number > 6 {
    println!("The number is greater than 6.");
} else if number == 5 {
    println!("The number is exactly 5.");
} else {
    println!("The number is less than 5.");
}
```

The condition number > 6 is false, but the condition number == 5 is true, so the corresponding block is executed, producing:

```
The number is exactly 5.
```

It's important to note that in Rust, the condition after if must be a boolean. Using non-boolean conditions will result in a compile-time error:

```
let number = 5;

// This will cause a compile-time error
if number {
    println!("The number is non-zero.");
}
```

Attempting to compile this will yield:

```
/tmp/rust_isrsn/src/main.rs:3:8: error: mismatched types:
 expected `bool`,
    found `{integer}`
(expected bool, found integer)
if number {
   ^~~~~
```

To correct this, you need to ensure the condition evaluates to a boolean:

```
let number = 5;

if number != 0 {
    println!("The number is non-zero.");
}
```

Rust's if and else constructs can also be used to assign values based on conditions. This is achieved by leveraging the expression-based nature of Rust:

```
let number = 5;
let message = if number > 6 {
    "The number is greater than 6."
} else {
    "The number is not greater than 6."
};
println!("{}", message);
```

This will result in:

```
The number is not greater than 6.
```

The variable message is assigned the value from the block that executes, demonstrating the expressive power of Rust's conditional constructs.

Understanding how to effectively use if and else statements is crucial for controlling the flow of Rust programs. These constructs enable handling multiple paths based on varying conditions efficiently and effectively, ensuring robust and maintainable code.

5.3 Using match for Pattern Matching

Pattern matching in Rust is an expressive control flow construct that allows you to branch based on the structure and contents of values. The match statement is particularly powerful and flexible, enabling you to destructure complex data types and execute code based on their composition.

The general syntax of the match statement is as follows:

```
match value {
    pattern1 => expression1,
    pattern2 => expression2,
    pattern3 => expression3,
    _ => default_expression,
}
```

Here, value is the item being matched, and pattern1, pattern2, and pattern3 are patterns we are trying to match against the value. If a pattern matches, the corresponding expression is executed. The underscore (_) is a special pattern that matches any value and is often used as a catch-all default case.

To illustrate, consider a simple example where we match against an integer:

```
let number = 3;
```

```
match number {
    1 => println!("One"),
    2 => println!("Two"),
    3 => println!("Three"),
    _ => println!("Other number"),
}
```

This code will output:

```
Three
```

The integer 3 matches the third pattern, so the corresponding block println!("Three") is executed.

Matching Multiple Patterns

Rust's match allows multiple patterns to run the same code by using the pipe (|) symbol to combine them.

```
let number = 2;

match number {
    1 | 2 | 3 => println!("One, Two, or Three"),
    _ => println!("Other number"),
}
```

In this case, number is 2, which matches one of the patterns in 1 | 2 | 3 and results in the output:

```
One, Two, or Three
```

Destructuring with match

match is not limited to simple integer values; it can destructure complex data types such as tuples, structs, and enums.

Matching Tuples

Tuples can be destructured within a match statement:

```
let pair = (2, -2);

match pair {
    (x, y) if x == y => println!("The numbers are equal"),
    (x, y) if x + y == 0 => println!("{} and {} are opposites", x, y),
    (x, _) => println!("First element is {}", x),
}
```

For the tuple (2, -2), the second arm (x, y) if x + y == 0 matches and produces:

```
2 and -2 are opposites
```

Matching Enums

Enums are particularly well-suited to match statements. Consider an enum representing a binary tree:

```
enum BinaryTree {
    Leaf(i32),
    Node(Box<BinaryTree>, i32, Box<BinaryTree>),
}

let tree = BinaryTree::Node(
    Box::new(BinaryTree::Leaf(1)),
    2,
    Box::new(BinaryTree::Leaf(3)),
);

match tree {
    BinaryTree::Leaf(value) => println!("Leaf with value {}", value),
    BinaryTree::Node(left, value, right) => {
        println!("Node with value {}", value);
        // further processing can be done on left and right
    },
}
```

For this tree, the match statement will match the BinaryTree::Node pattern and execute the code within the corresponding block.

Patterns and Refutability

Patterns in match can be irrefutable or refutable. Irrefutable patterns, such as those used in let statements, always succeed. Refutable patterns, used in match arms, may fail. Rust ensures that all possible values are covered either by explicit patterns or by a catch-all pattern (_).

match provides a compile-time guarantee of exhaustive pattern matching, ensuring that all possible cases are handled. For enums, this means all variants must have corresponding match arms or be covered by the catch-all pattern. This feature helps eliminate many classes of bugs associated with incomplete handling of possible cases.

Using Guards in match

Guards provide an additional layer of control within a match statement. They add a condition that must be fulfilled for the associated pattern to match. Consider modifying the earlier tuple example to use guards:

```
let pair = (5, 5);

match pair {
    (x, y) if x == y => println!("The numbers are equal"),
    (x, y) if x + y == 10 => println!("{} and {} sum to ten", x, y),
    (x, _) => println!("First element is {}", x),
}
```

Here, the guard if x + y == 10 adds additional control logic. For the given pair, it will match (x, y) if x == y and produce the output:

```
The numbers are equal
```

Exploring Advanced Pattern Matching

Rust's match statement supports an extensive range of patterns, including ranges, references, and even ignoring specific fields in larger patterns.

Matching Ranges

You can match ranges of values using ..=:

```
let number = 7;

match number {
    1..=5 => println!("One through Five"),
    6..=10 => println!("Six through Ten"),
    _ => println!("Other number"),
}
```

In this case, number is 7, which matches the range 6..=10, producing:

```
Six through Ten
```

Ignoring Values

You can ignore specific values within a pattern using an underscore (_):

```
let origin = (0, 0);

match origin {
    (0, y) => println!("On the y-axis at {}", y),
    (x, 0) => println!("On the x-axis at {}", x),
    _ => println!("Somewhere else"),
}
```

For the point (0, 0), the pattern (0, y) will match, resulting in the output:

```
On the y-axis at 0
```

Through the comprehensive capabilities of match, Rust provides powerful tools for making code both readable and expressive, all while maintaining strict type safety and exhaustive checking. This effectively eliminates many bugs associated with incomplete patterns and unhandled cases.

5.4 Loops in Rust: loop, while, and for

In Rust, loops allow for repetitive execution of code blocks. Rust provides three primary looping constructs: loop, while, and for. Each of these constructs serves particular use cases, and understanding their functionality and appropriate application is critical for writing efficient and idiomatic Rust programs.

The loop keyword provides the simplest form of infinite looping. An infinite loop continues execution until explicitly terminated by a break statement. This can be useful for cases where the loop's exit condition may not be known initially or depends on asynchronous events.

```
fn main() {
    let mut counter = 0;
    loop {
        counter += 1;
        println!("Counter: {}", counter);
        if counter == 10 {
            break;
        }
    }
}
```

The above example demonstrates a basic use of the loop construct to incrementally count to ten. The break statement terminates the loop when the counter reaches ten, preventing an infinite loop.

The while keyword facilitates execution of a code block as long as a specified condition evaluates to true. This form of looping is particularly useful when the number of iterations is not predetermined but depends on dynamic conditions during runtime.

```
fn main() {
    let mut number = 1;
    while number <= 5 {
        println!("Number: {}", number);
        number += 1;
    }
}
```

Here, the while loop continues execution as long as number <= 5. Once the variable number exceeds five, the loop terminates.

The for loop allows iterating over a collection, such as arrays or ranges, and is often more ergonomic and safe compared to other loop constructs. Rust's for loop leverages the IntoIterator trait, facilitating iteration over any datatype that implements this trait.

```
fn main() {
```

```
    let numbers = [1, 2, 3, 4, 5];
    for number in numbers.iter() {
        println!("Number: {}", number);
    }
}
```

In the above for loop, the number variable iteratively takes on each value from the numbers array. The .iter() method returns an iterator over the array, enabling element access within the loop body.

Rust also supports looping through ranges, which is particularly effective for numeric sequences.

```
fn main() {
    for number in 1..6 {
        println!("Number: {}", number);
    }
}
```

The range 1..6 generates numbers from 1 to 5, excluding the upper bound, making the for loop run five iterations. To include the upper bound, Rust provides the ..= syntax.

```
fn main() {
    for number in 1..=6 {
        println!("Number: {}", number);
    }
}
```

Now, number iterates from 1 through 6 inclusively, illustrating the flexibility and expressiveness of Rust's range syntax.

Understanding and effectively utilizing these looping constructs is essential for implementing repetitive tasks in Rust. The loop, while, and for loops each provide a unique set of functionalities suited for different scenarios. Choosing the appropriate looping construct based on the problem requirements contributes to writing clear, efficient, and idiomatic Rust code.

5.5 Controlling Loop Execution with break and continue

The constructs break and continue play a crucial role in controlling the flow of loops in Rust. These keywords allow for more nuanced and flexible loop control, enabling developers to exit loops or skip iterations based on specific conditions. Understanding and utilizing these control flow modifiers can significantly enhance your ability to write efficient and clear code.

The break statement is used to terminate a loop immediately. When break is encountered within a loop, the loop stops executing, and control is transferred to the code following the loop. This is particularly useful in situations where the loop no longer needs to run once a certain condition is met. Here is an example illustrating the use of break:

```
fn main() {
    let mut counter = 0;

    loop {
        counter += 1;

        if counter == 10 {
            break;
        }
    }

    println!("The loop has been broken after {} iterations.", counter);
}
```

In this example, a loop increments a counter variable until it reaches 10. When the counter equals 10, break is executed, stopping the loop. The program then prints the number of iterations performed.

The continue statement, on the other hand, causes the current iteration of the loop to end immediately, skipping to the next iteration without executing the remaining code in the block for the current iteration. This is useful when certain conditions are met that signal the current loop iteration should be skipped. Below is an example of using continue:

```
fn main() {
    for number in 0..10 {
        if number % 2 == 0 {
            continue;
        }

        println!("Odd number: {}", number);
    }
}
```

This example iterates over the range from 0 to 9, but only prints odd numbers. When the loop encounters an even number (determined by the condition number % 2 == 0), continue is executed, skipping the println! statement for that iteration, i.e., even numbers are not printed.

Understanding the interplay between break and continue is crucial for writing well-structured loops. Consider a scenario where both break and continue are used together within a loop:

```
fn main() {
    let numbers = [1, 2, 3, 0, 4, 5];

    for &number in numbers.iter() {
        if number == 0 {
            println!("Zero found, stopping loop.");
            break;
        } else if number % 2 == 0 {
            println!("Even number found: {}, skipping.", number);
            continue;
        }

        println!("Processing number: {}", number);
    }
}
```

In this example, the loop iterates through an array of integers. If a zero is encountered, the loop is terminated with break. If an even number (other than zero) is found, continue is executed, and the iteration for that number is skipped. Otherwise, the number is processed (printed in this case). The printed output will reflect this behavior:

```
Processing number: 1
Even number found: 2, skipping.
Processing number: 3
Zero found, stopping loop.
```

Employing break and continue statements enhances loop control, facilitating the writing of more readable and efficient code. It's crucial to use them judiciously to avoid creating complex and hard-to-follow code flow. When used appropriately, they can simplify logic by clearly defining conditions under which certain code paths should be exited or skipped. ‘‘‘

5.6 Error Handling with match and Result

Rust emphasizes safety and provides robust error handling mechanisms to prevent runtime failures. One of the most powerful features in Rust is the Result type, which is used for returning and propagating errors. The Result type is an enum with two variants: Ok and Err. The Ok variant indicates that an operation was successful and contains the resultant value, while the Err variant signifies that an error occurred and holds an error value.

The match statement is extensively used to handle these Result values explicitly. By matching on the Result type, programmers can ensure that errors are handled in a controlled manner, preventing unexpected crashes. Let us delve into the mechanics of match and Result to appreciate how they contribute to error handling.

Consider the following Rust code, which attempts to open a file and read its contents:

```
use std::fs::File;
use std::io::{self, Read};

fn read_file(file_path: &str) -> Result<String, io::Error> {
    let mut file = File::open(file_path)?;
    let mut contents = String::new();
    file.read_to_string(&mut contents)?;
    Ok(contents)
}
```

In this example, the function read_file returns a Result<String, io::Error>. The ? operator is syntactic sugar for propagating errors; however, to fully comprehend the underlying mechanisms, it is important to explore error handling using match.

When an operation returns a Result, it can be matched to handle the success and error cases accordingly. The following code illustrates how to achieve this:

```
use std::fs::File;
use std::io::{self, Read};

fn read_file(file_path: &str) -> Result<String, io::Error> {
    let file_result = File::open(file_path);

    let mut file = match file_result {
        Ok(file) => file,
        Err(e) => return Err(e),
    };

    let mut contents = String::new();
    match file.read_to_string(&mut contents) {
        Ok(_) => Ok(contents),
        Err(e) => Err(e),
    }
}
```

In this version, the file_result is explicitly matched to handle both the Ok and Err cases. If File::open is successful, the opened file is returned; otherwise, the error is propagated using return Err(e).

Similarly, the result of file.read_to_string is matched to handle potential errors during the read operation. If successful, the file contents are returned wrapped in Ok; if an error occurs, it is returned as Err.

The match statement ensures that every possible outcome is considered and addressed, making the code resilient to runtime failures. By leveraging Rust's exhaustive pattern matching, programmers can design error handling pathways that are both explicit and robust.

To further illustrate, consider a slightly more complex scenario where multiple file operations are performed, each of which could fail:

```
use std::fs;
use std::io::{self, Read};

fn process_file(file_path: &str) -> Result<String, io::Error> {
    // Attempt to open the file
    let mut file = match File::open(file_path) {
        Ok(file) => file,
        Err(e) => return Err(e),
    };

    // Read the file contents
    let mut contents = String::new();
    if let Err(e) = file.read_to_string(&mut contents) {
        return Err(e);
    }

    // Additional processing can be added here

    Ok(contents)
}
```

In this example, the use of if let provides a concise alternative to match, which is particularly useful when handling simple cases. However, the principle remains the same: every function that can fail is handled explicitly, ensuring that errors are propagated or managed as necessary.

When dealing with multiple potential failure points, it is essential to maintain clarity and comprehensibility. This can be achieved by using well-structured match statements and clearly indicating the pathways for both success and failure.

To summarize, the match statement and Result type lie at the heart of Rust's error handling strategy. By embracing these constructs, developers can write programs that are both safe and predictable, effectively mitigating the risk of unexpected runtime errors.

5.7 Combining Conditions with Logical Operators

In Rust, control flow within conditional statements can be significantly enhanced and fine-tuned using logical operators. These operators allow the combination of multiple conditions into a single if or match expression, thus enabling the creation of more intricate and expressive branching logic.

Rust supports the common logical operators && (logical AND), || (logical OR), and ! (logical NOT). Each of these operators plays a crucial role in evaluating and combining boolean expressions.

The && operator returns true if both operands are true; otherwise, it returns false. This behavior is especially useful for scenarios where multiple conditions must be met. For instance, consider the case where a value must fall within a specific range:

```
let x = 20;
if x > 10 && x < 30 {
    println!("x is between 10 and 30");
}
```

In this example, the if statement checks whether x is both greater than 10 and less than 30. Only if both conditions are satisfied does the block execute, printing the message.

The || operator, on the other hand, evaluates to true if at least one of its operands is true. This operator is typically used when any of multiple conditions may trigger the execution of a block. For example:

```
let y = 8;
if y < 5 || y > 15 {
    println!("y is either less than 5 or greater than 15");
}
```

Here, the if statement verifies whether y is less than 5 or greater than 15. If either condition holds true, the block's statements get executed.

The ! operator negates a boolean expression. When used in combination with && or ||, it can invert the truth value of a condition, which is useful for scenarios that require exclusion conditions:

```
let z = false;
if !z {
    println!("z is false");
}
```

As a fundamental construct, logical operators support the creation of complex expressions by combining multiple conditions. This is often seen in scenarios requiring nested checks or compound conditions:

```
let a = 5;
let b = 12;
let c = 18;

if (a < 10 && b > 10) || c == 18 {
    println!("Complex condition met");
}
```

In this snippet, the if statement evaluates the combined condition where either $a < 10$ and $b > 10$ must both be true, or $c == 18$ must be true. The expression makes use of parentheses to clearly define the precedence of evaluation.

Rust's logical operators support short-circuit evaluation, meaning that they do not evaluate the right-hand operand if the left-hand operand determines the result. For example, in an && operation, if the left-hand operand is false, the right-hand operand is not evaluated because the final result will necessarily be false. This characteristic can be harnessed to avoid unnecessary computations or potential runtime errors:

```
let d = 4;

if d != 0 && (10 / d) > 1 {
    println!("d is not zero, and 10 divided by d is greater than 1");
}
```

In this example, the division operation 10 / d only occurs if d != 0, hence preventing a possible division by zero error.

Employing logical operators effectively can lead to more readable and maintainable code. It allows combining multiple checks into a single line, thus reducing the verbosity of nested conditional statements. An understanding and correct application of these operators are essential for error-free, efficient, and clear control flow in Rust programs. By mastering the use of these operators, developers can enhance the precision and functionality of conditional logic within their Rust applications.

5.8 Early Return with the ? Operator

Rust provides an idiomatic approach to handle early returns when working with functions that may result in errors. This approach is facilitated by the ? operator, which offers a concise way to propagate errors in a function. The ? operator simplifies code that deals with functions returning a Result or Option by eliminating the need for explicit match statements to handle the different outcomes.

When appending the ? operator to a Result or Option, it checks the value. If the value is Ok or Some, it unwraps and returns the contained value. If the value is Err or None, it causes the function to return immediately with that Err or None.

To utilize the ? operator, ensure that the function's return type is compatible with the potential Err or None being returned. The common practice in Rust is to define functions with a return type of Result<T,

E> or Option<T>.

Consider the following illustrative example:

```
fn read_file_content(filepath: &str) -> std::io::Result<String> {
    let mut file = std::fs::File::open(filepath)?;
    let mut contents = String::new();
    file.read_to_string(&mut contents)?;
    Ok(contents)
}
```

In this function, read_file_content, the ? operator is used after attempting to open a file and read its contents. If either of these operations fails, the function will immediately return the corresponding Err.

Expanding the Example

For a deeper understanding, let's dissect what happens step by step:

1. std::fs::File::open(filepath): This attempts to open the file at the given path. 2. ?: If opening the file fails, Err is returned from the function immediately. 3. let mut contents = String::new();: An empty String is created to store the file contents. 4. file.read_to_string(&mut contents): This reads the file contents into the String. 5. ?: If reading the file fails, Err is returned from the function immediately. 6. Ok(contents): If both operations succeed, the file contents are returned encapsulated in Ok.

Example with Option

The ? operator works similarly with Option. The following example demonstrates this behavior:

```
fn get_second_element(vec: &Vec<i32>) -> Option<i32> {
    let second = vec.get(1)?;
    Some(*second)
}
```

In this example, get_second_element, the ? operator is used to handle the Option returned by vec.get(1). If the vector has a second element, it is returned wrapped in Some. If not, the function returns None immediately.

Error Conversion

Often, functions may require converting one error type to another before propagating it with ?. This can be achieved using the From trait implemented for error conversion:

```
use std::num::ParseIntError;

fn string_to_number(input: &str) -> Result<i32, ParseIntError> {
```

```
    let number: i32 = input.parse()?;
    Ok(number)
}
```

In this function, string_to_number, the ? operator propagates the parsing error if the input string does not contain a valid number. The error type ParseIntError is returned, demonstrating how error types can be managed and propagated concisely.

The ? operator also works seamlessly within more complex function combinations, particularly when nested within other high-level operations. Efficient use of ? encourages writing clean, maintainable code and reduces verbosity, aiding developers in focusing on core logic rather than error handling boilerplate.

The ? operator is integral in making Rust code more readable and expressive, streamlining the process of error propagation and contributing to the overall robustness and resiliency of Rust applications.

5.9 Pattern Matching with match and if let

Pattern matching in Rust is a powerful feature that enables developers to destructure and examine complex data structures succinctly and safely. Pattern matching is primarily facilitated by the match expression and the if let construct. Understanding how to leverage these tools is essential for writing idiomatic and efficient Rust code.

The match expression compares a value against a series of patterns and executes the code associated with the first matching pattern. This functionality expands beyond simple equality checks and enables rich, complex conditions to be expressed more declaratively.

match statements resemble switch statements in other programming languages but with enhanced power and flexibility. A match expression begins with the match keyword, followed by the value being matched, and a series of arms. Each arm consists of a pattern and an associated block of code.

```
// Define an enumeration
enum Coin {
    Penny,
    Nickel,
    Dime,
    Quarter,
}

fn value_in_cents(coin: Coin) -> u8 {
```

```
    match coin {
        Coin::Penny => 1,
        Coin::Nickel => 5,
        Coin::Dime => 10,
        Coin::Quarter => 25,
    }
}

fn main() {
    let coin = Coin::Dime;
    println!("Value in cents: {}", value_in_cents(coin));
}
```

Upon executing the main function, the output will be:

```
Value in cents: 10
```

This example illustrates how match can be used to map the variants of an enum to specific values. Each pattern within the match corresponds to one of the enum's variants.

In addition to matching enum variants, match can deconstruct structs and tuples, allowing for seamless manipulations of their contents.

```
// Define a struct
struct Point {
    x: i32,
    y: i32,
}

fn main() {
    let point = Point { x: 0, y: 7 };

    match point {
        Point { x, y: 0 } => println!("Point lies on the x-axis at {}", x),
        Point { x: 0, y } => println!("Point lies on the y-axis at {}", y),
        Point { x, y } => println!("Point at ({}, {})", x, y),
    }
}
```

The output from this particular snippet will be:

```
Point lies on the y-axis at 7
```

This demonstrates pattern matching on a struct where specific fields are matched and notated using similar syntax to struct definitions. The Point struct is deconstructed, and depending on the values of x and y, different messages are printed.

The if let construct is a more concise way to match a single pattern while ignoring others. It can be thought of as syntactic sugar for a match that runs code only for one of its cases.

```
fn main() {
    let config_max = Some(3u8);
```

```
    match config_max {
        Some(max) => println!("The maximum is configured to be {}", max),
        _ => (),
    }

    // Using if let
    if let Some(max) = config_max {
        println!("The maximum is configured to be {}", max);
    }
}
```

In both cases, if config_max contains Some(3), the message will be printed. While the match statement requires an exhaustive set of patterns, including the wildcard pattern (_), if let provides a more compact, readable alternative when only one pattern matters.

if let is particularly useful when working with Option or Result types. It avoids the need to handle the None or Err case explicitly, thus making the code clearer.

```
fn main() {
    let some_value: Option<i32> = Some(5);
    if let Some(value) = some_value {
        println!("There is a value: {}", value);
    }

    let another_value: Result<i32, &str> = Ok(10);
    if let Ok(value) = another_value {
        println!("The operation was successful: {}", value);
    }
}
```

In these examples, if let is used to execute code only when Some or Ok variants are present, respectively. This avoids the need for verbose match statements to achieve the same effect.

Pattern matching with match and if let equips developers with tools to write expressive and maintainable code. These constructs enable clear handling of complex data and flow control, facilitating robust and error-prone software development.

5.10 Using Guard Clauses in Pattern Matching

Guard clauses in Rust add a powerful layer of expressiveness and control within pattern matching, particularly when utilizing the match construct. A guard clause introduces an additional condition that must be satisfied for a particular pattern to be selected. This mechanism permits more granular control over which pattern a value should match, thereby enhancing code readability and precision.

In Rust, guard clauses are specified using the if keyword following a pattern. Here is a fundamental example to illustrate the syntax and usage of guard clauses:

```
fn main() {
    let number = 21;

    match number {
        n if n % 2 == 0 => println!("{} is even", n),
        n if n % 2 != 0 => println!("{} is odd", n),
        _ => println!("Invalid number"),
    }
}
```

The provided example evaluates whether a number is even or odd using guard clauses. The pattern, n if n % 2 == 0, only matches when the number is divisible by 2 (even), and the pattern, n if n % 2 != 0, matches when the number is not divisible by 2 (odd). The underscore _ serves as a catch-all pattern but remains unexecuted due to preceding exhaustive patterns.

Consider another scenario where multiple guards are necessary to refine pattern matching. Each guard evaluates a different aspect, further narrowing down valid cases:

```
fn classify_number(x: i32) -> &'static str {
    match x {
        n if n > 0 && n % 2 == 0 => "Positive even",
        n if n > 0 && n % 2 != 0 => "Positive odd",
        n if n < 0 && n % 2 == 0 => "Negative even",
        n if n < 0 && n % 2 != 0 => "Negative odd",
        _ => "Zero",
    }
}

fn main() {
    let numbers = vec![10, -3, 0, 14, -17];
    for num in numbers {
        println!("{} is {}", num, classify_number(num));
    }
}
```

Each match clause features a guard, weaving together conditions on the positivity or negativity of the number as well as its evenness or oddness. The function, classify_number, thus categorizes an integer into precise categories.

It is crucial to recognize that guards offer more than pattern guards in a purely boolean context. Combining multiple conditions and various data types within guard expressions creates more sophisticated pattern matching schemes:

```
fn main() {
    let data: Vec<(i32, &str)> = vec![(10, "A"), (-20, "B"), (15, "C")];

    for (value, label) in data {
        match (value, label) {
            (x, "A") if x > 0 => println!("{} is positive and labeled A", x),
            (x, "B") if x < 0 => println!("{} is negative and labeled B", x),
            (x, _) if x % 5 == 0 => println!("{} is multiple of 5", x),
            _ => println!("{} with label {} does not match any condition", value, label)
                ,
        }
    }
}
```

In this instance, the pattern match considers both elements in the tuple and utilizes guards to selectively match combinations, such as positive numbers labeled "A" or negative numbers labeled "B". The third clause captures any number that is a multiple of 5, irrespective of its label.

Implementing guards yields code that is more robust and easier to understand, particularly when conditions are intricately connected. However, ineffectual or overly complex guards can lead to challenging-to-read and maintain code. Thus, it is essential to strike a balance between match pattern clarity and guard complexity.

Rust enforces comprehensive pattern matching, ensuring all possible cases are handled. If none of the patterns and their guards in a match expression apply, a compile-time error ensures no runtime case is neglected. Thus, incorporating guard clauses demands cautiously designed patterns and conditions to cover all potential cases adequately.

5.11 Idiomatic Control Flow Patterns in Rust

The concept of idiomatic control flow patterns in Rust revolves around utilizing language features to write code that is both safe and expressive. Rust promotes several idioms that enhance readability, efficiency, and reliability. This section delves into common strategies and idioms in Rust's control flow mechanisms, illustrating their usage with examples. Each idiom leverages Rust's powerful type system, pattern matching capabilities, and control flow constructs to manage execution paths effectively.

Early Returns with the ? Operator: The ? operator is extensively used for error handling in Rust. It enables concise propagation of errors without the need for explicit match statements. When a function returns a Result<T, E> or Option<T>, the ? operator can be appended to a method call, yielding a value on success or returning an error immediately. This idiom is valuable for simplifying functions that perform a sequence of operations that each might fail.

```
// Function demonstrating the '?' operator for early returns
fn read_username_from_file() -> Result<String, io::Error> {
    let mut f = File::open("username.txt")?;
    let mut s = String::new();
    f.read_to_string(&mut s)?;
    Ok(s)
}
```

In the example above, File::open may fail, in which case it returns an Err. The ? operator ensures the function exits early, returning the error encountered.

Pattern Matching with match: The match expression in Rust is a powerful construct for pattern matching. It allows branching based on the structure and contents of values. With match, different patterns can be specified, making code more robust and error-resistant.

```
// Example of pattern matching with match
fn get_color_code(color: &str) -> &str {
    match color {
        "red" => "FF0000",
        "green" => "00FF00",
        "blue" => "0000FF",
    _ => "unknown color",
    }
}
```

In this function, match evaluates the color string and returns corresponding color codes. The wildcard pattern _ catches any unmatched values, providing a default response.

Using if let for Concise Conditional Assignments: The if let construct simplifies handling Option and Result types when only specific branches are of interest. It combines pattern matching and conditional logic, reducing verbosity.

```
// Example using if let for conditional assignment
if let Some(name) = user_name {
    println!("User name is: {}", name);
}
```

Instead of using a complete match statement, if let checks if user_name is Some and binds the inner value to name, executing the body of the if statement if the pattern matches.

Guard Clauses in match Expressions: A guard is an additional if condition in a match arm, used to refine matching criteria. Guards are effective for adding constraints to patterns, ensuring more granular control flow.

```
// Example of guard clauses in match expressions
fn classify_number(num: i32) -> &'static str {
    match num {
        x if x > 0 => "positive",
        x if x < 0 => "negative",
        _ => "zero",
    }
}
```

Here, guards refine the matching process by adding conditions to the patterns, distinguishing between positive, negative, and zero values.

Error Handling with combinator methods: Rust's standard library offers methods like map, and_then, or_else, which are combinators used with Result and Option types. These methods provide concise ways to handle errors and chain operations without elaborate control flow constructs.

```
// Using combinator methods for error handling
fn process_input(input: &str) -> Result<i32, ParseIntError> {
    input.parse::<i32>().map(|num| num * 2)
}
```

In this example, map transforms the successful Result value by doubling it, propagating errors automatically if parsing fails.

Loop Labels for Nested Loops: Nested loops can lead to complex control flow. Loop labels clarify which loop is affected by break and continue statements. Labels improve readability and ensure the correct loop exits or continues.

```
// Example of loop labels for nested loops
'outer: for i in 0..5 {
    for j in 0..5 {
        if i + j == 3 {
            break 'outer;
        }
        println!("{} {}", i, j);
    }
}
```

The label 'outer: prefixes the outer loop, and break 'outer; exits the outer loop when the condition is met.

These idiomatic patterns contribute to writing robust, efficient, and clear Rust code by leveraging the language's features effectively. Understanding and applying these idioms will facilitate managing complex control flows in various contexts.

Chapter 6

Functions and Error Handling

This chapter explores the definition, scope, and usage of functions in Rust, including function parameters, return values, and lifetime considerations. It introduces closures and higher-order functions, then delves into Rust's robust error handling mechanisms. Readers will learn about the Result and Option types, the ? operator for simplifying error propagation, and the creation of custom error types. The distinction between recoverable and unrecoverable errors is highlighted, along with best practices in error handling to ensure code reliability and clarity.

6.1 Defining and Calling Functions

In Rust, defining a function is pivotal for code organization, reusability, and modularity. A function in Rust begins with the fn keyword followed by the function name and a set of parentheses which may contain parameters. After the parentheses, the function's return type is optionally specified using the -> symbol. The body of the function is encapsulated within curly braces {}.

Consider the following example of a simple function definition and call:

```
fn main() {
    // Call the function
    greet("Alice");
```

```
}

// Define a function
fn greet(name: &str) {
    println!("Hello, {}!", name);
}
```

In this example, the greet function takes one parameter, name, which is a string slice of type &str. The function body uses the println! macro to format and print a greeting. The main function serves as the entry point and calls the greet function with the argument “Alice”.

Function Parameters

Parameters to a function are declared within the parentheses following the function name. Parameters must have explicit types, as Rust does not perform type inference for function parameters. The syntax for declaring parameters is name: type. Multiple parameters are separated by commas.

```
fn add(a: i32, b: i32) -> i32 {
    a + b
}

fn main() {
    let sum = add(5, 3);
    println!("The sum is: {}", sum);
}
```

In this snippet, the add function takes two parameters of type i32 and returns an i32. The function body computes the sum of a and b. Note that the return type is specified after the -> symbol.

Return Values

Functions in Rust can return values. If a return type is specified, the function body must conclude with an expression that matches this type. If the function does not explicitly return a value, it implicitly returns the unit type ().

```
fn square(x: i32) -> i32 {
    x * x
}

fn main() {
    let result = square(4);
    println!("The square is: {}", result);
}
```

The function square takes an i32 parameter and returns its square. The result is used in main and printed.

Implicit Returns

Rust allows functions to return values without an explicit return statement. The last line of a function without a semicolon is treated as the return value.

```
fn subtract(a: i32, b: i32) -> i32 {
    a - b
}
```

In the subtract function, a - b is returned implicitly because it is the last line and lacks a semicolon.

Function Signatures

Function signatures consist of the function name, parameters, and return type. They provide the function's interface without its implementation. Signatures are crucial for understanding how a function can be used.

```
fn divide(numerator: f64, denominator: f64) -> f64 {
    numerator / denominator
}
```

The divide function signature states that it takes two f64 arguments and returns an f64 result.

Main Function

The main function in Rust serves as the program's entry point. It has a unique signature with no parameters and a return type of ().

```
fn main() {
    println!("Program started!");
}
```

The main function in this example prints a message indicating that the program has started.

Function Overloading

Rust does not support function overloading. Each function must have a unique name. However, it is possible to achieve similar functionality using traits and generics, which will be explored in subsequent sections.

Best Practices for Function Definitions

When defining functions, it's important to follow best practices for clarity and maintainability:

- Use descriptive names for functions and parameters that indicate their purpose.

- Keep functions small and focused on a single task or concept.
- Document functions using Rust's documentation comments, ///, to provide context and usage examples.
- Avoid global state, favoring parameter passing to enhance reusability and testability.

The choice of function definition and calling conventions greatly influences code clarity and reusability. A disciplined approach to function design is essential for writing maintainable and efficient Rust code.

6.2 Function Parameters and Return Values

In Rust, functions are a primary means of implementing code modularity and reusability. Function parameters and return values are essential aspects of function definition and utility. Understanding how to define, pass, and manipulate these elements will equip us with a solid foundation for more complex programming constructs.

Function parameters allow us to pass values or references into functions, enabling functions to act on varying inputs. Parameters in Rust are explicitly typed, and their types must be specified in the function signature. Here is a basic example:

```
fn add(a: i32, b: i32) -> i32 {
    a + b
}
```

In this example, a and b are parameters of type i32, and the function returns an i32 value that is the sum of a and b. Note the use of the -> symbol to indicate the return type of the function.

Parameters can also be passed by reference, which is useful for functions that need to read, but not modify, the argument values. This prevents unnecessary copying of data. For instance:

```
fn print_sum(a: &i32, b: &i32) {
    println!("Sum is: {}", a + b);
}
```

In this function, a and b are references to i32 values. The ampersand (&) denotes that the parameters are references.

Rust also supports mutable references, enabling functions to modify the inputs. Here's an example:

```
fn increment(value: &mut i32) {
    *value += 1;
}
```

In this case, the increment function takes a mutable reference to an i32 value and increments it. The * operator is used to dereference the mutable reference, allowing us to modify the original value.

Return values in Rust are specified using the -> symbol in the function signature, followed by the return type. Functions can return any type, including primitive types, tuples, structs, and enums. Here is a function that returns a tuple:

```
fn swap(a: i32, b: i32) -> (i32, i32) {
    (b, a)
}
```

The swap function takes two i32 parameters and returns a tuple containing the values in reverse order.

Rust functions can also return references. When returning references, it's crucial to specify lifetimes to ensure the returned reference lives as long as the function caller expects. Here's an example:

```
fn get_first_char(s: &str) -> &str {
    &s[..1]
}
```

In this function, the return type &str uses the same lifetime as the input reference s. This ensures that the returned slice does not outlive the input string slice.

It's important to handle the potential for functions to return no meaningful value. Rust provides the Option type for such situations. Here's an example where a function returns an Option<i32>:

```
fn divide(numerator: i32, denominator: i32) -> Option<i32> {
    if denominator == 0 {
        None
    } else {
        Some(numerator / denominator)
    }
}
```

The divide function returns None if the denominator is zero, indicating an invalid division, otherwise it returns the result wrapped in Some.

Understanding these concepts will significantly enhance our ability to write robust and flexible functions in Rust, enabling more precise control over how functions interact with their inputs and outputs.

6.3 Understanding Function Scope and Lifetime

In Rust, managing function scope and lifetime is crucial for writing safe and efficient code. Rust enforces strict rules to ensure that memory is managed correctly, preventing common issues such as null pointer dereferencing and use-after-free errors. In this section, we shall explore these concepts in detail, focusing on how they relate to functions.

At a high level, scope refers to the region of a program where a particular variable is valid. Lifetime, on the other hand, indicates how long a variable's data is valid and can be used safely. Understanding the interplay between scope and lifetime is essential for mastering Rust's ownership system.

Consider the following function that demonstrates variable scope:

```
// Function demonstrating variable scope
fn scope_example() {
    let x = 5; // x is valid from this point forward
    {
        let y = 10; // y is valid from this point forward
        println!("Inside inner scope: x = {}, y = {}", x, y);
    } // y goes out of scope here
    println!("Outside inner scope: x = {}", x);
} // x goes out of scope here
```

In the example above, the variable x is defined in the outer scope of the function scope_example, meaning it is accessible throughout the function's execution until the function's closure. The variable y, however, is defined within an inner block, making it accessible only within that block. Once the block ends, y goes out of scope, and any attempt to access it beyond that point will result in a compilation error.

Lifetimes are essential for ensuring that references do not outlive the data they point to. Rust uses lifetime annotations to keep track of how long references are valid. These annotations are usually inferred by the compiler, but in complex scenarios, explicit annotations are required.

Consider a function that returns a reference to a value:

```
// Function that returns a reference
fn longest<'a>(s1: &'a str, s2: &'a str) -> &'a str {
    if s1.len() > s2.len() {
```

```
        s1
    } else {
        s2
    }
}

// Example usage
fn main() {
    let string1 = String::from("long string");
    let string2 = String::from("short");
    let result = longest(&string1, &string2);
    println!("The longest string is {}", result);
}
```

In the function longest, the lifetime annotation 'a specifies that the references s1 and s2 must live at least as long as the reference returned by the function. This ensures that the returned reference remains valid, preventing dangling references.

The Rust compiler employs a sophisticated borrow checker to enforce these lifetime rules. This ensures that all references are valid for as long as they are used, preventing issues like use-after-free. Lifetime annotations can be more complex in functions that involve multiple references or more intricate data structures.

Consider a more advanced example with multiple lifetimes:

```
// Struct with a reference field
struct ImportantExcerpt<'a> {
    part: &'a str,
}

// Function that uses the struct
impl<'a> ImportantExcerpt<'a> {
    fn announce_and_return_part(&self, announcement: &str) -> &str {
        println!("Attention please: {}", announcement);
        self.part
    }
}

// Example usage
fn main() {
    let novel = String::from("Call me Ishmael. Some years ago...");
    let first_sentence = novel.split('.').next().expect("Could not find a '.'");
    let excerpt = ImportantExcerpt { part: first_sentence };

    let result = excerpt.announce_and_return_part("Here is an important excerpt:");
    println!("Excerpt: {}", result);
}
```

In this example, the struct ImportantExcerpt holds a reference to a string slice with a lifetime of 'a. The method announce_and_return_part has the same lifetime annotation for its self reference and the return value. This ensures that the struct's reference and the return value maintain the necessary scope and lifetime constraints, preventing invalid references.

Understanding and correctly applying function scope and lifetime annotations is fundamental to leveraging Rust's safety guarantees. By effectively managing these aspects, developers can write robust, efficient code that adheres to Rust's strict memory safety rules without unnecessary complexity.

6.4 Closures: Anonymous Functions

Closures in Rust are anonymous functions you can save in a variable or pass as arguments to other functions. Unlike regular functions defined with the fn keyword, closures are more flexible and can capture variables from their enclosing scope. This capability is significant because it allows for certain programming patterns that regular functions cannot accommodate.

To begin, examine a simple closure. The syntax for defining a closure in Rust is as follows:

```
// A simple closure that takes two arguments and returns their sum.
let add = |x, y| x + y;
```

Here, add is a closure taking two parameters, x and y, and returning their sum. Notice that unlike the fn keyword used for regular functions, closures use pipes | | to delimit their parameters.

Closures can infer the types of their parameters and return values, which simplifies their syntax. However, you can optionally annotate the types for clarity:

```
// A closure with explicit parameter types
let add: |i32, i32| -> i32 = |x: i32, y: i32| -> i32 { x + y };
```

In this example, the types for parameters x and y are explicitly defined as i32.

One of the primary strengths of closures is their ability to capture variables from their environment. Rust allows closures to capture values in three different ways, corresponding to the three types of borrows in Rust: by reference, by mutable reference, and by value.

- Fn: the closure captures variables by reference.
- FnMut: the closure captures variables by mutable reference.

- FnOnce: the closure captures variables by value.

Consider the following example that captures an external variable by reference:

```
let y = 5;
let add_y = |x| x + y;
println!("Result: {}", add_y(10)); // Output: 15
```

In this snippet, add_y captures y from the surrounding environment and uses it within the closure.

Mutable closures can modify captured variables. Here's an example:

```
let mut z = 0;
let mut update_z = |x| z += x;
update_z(5);
println!("z: {}", z); // Output: z: 5
```

The closure update_z modifies the value of z, reflecting the capability to mutate its environment.

For situations where the closure needs to take ownership of captured variables, you can use the move keyword:

```
let p = vec![1, 2, 3];
let owns_p = move |q| q == p;
println!("Is p owned? {}", owns_p(vec![1, 2, 3])); // Output: true
// println!("Cannot use p here: {:?}", p); // This line would cause an error
```

By employing the move keyword, the closure owns_p takes ownership of p, making it inaccessible after the closure captures it.

Closures are not only succinct but also powerful within iterators and higher-order functions. They are commonly used with iterator methods such as map, filter, and for_each to perform transformations and computations on data collections.

Consider this example using map:

```
let numbers = vec![1, 2, 3];
let squared_numbers: Vec<_> = numbers.iter().map(|&x| x * x).collect();
println!("{:?}", squared_numbers); // Output: [1, 4, 9]
```

Here, a closure within the map method squares each element of the numbers vector. The collect method then transforms the iterator into a Vec of squared values.

Rust's idiomatic use of closures in functional programming patterns allows for more expressive and concise code. This paradigm is further complemented by Rust's strong type system and borrowing rules, ensuring safety and performance. Understanding these intricacies is crucial for leveraging Rust's full potential in writing robust, efficient, and expressive code.

6.5 Using Higher-Order Functions

Higher-order functions are functions that can take other functions as arguments and/or return them as results. In Rust, this powerful feature enables more abstract and flexible code design. Understanding higher-order functions is essential for mastering functional programming principles within Rust.

A function can be passed as an argument to another function using either function pointers or closures. Function pointers have the type fn, and closures have types derived from their implementation, such as Fn, FnMut, and FnOnce.

To illustrate higher-order functions, consider a simple example where a function is passed to another function.

```
fn apply<F>(f: F, x: i32) -> i32
where
    F: Fn(i32) -> i32
{
    f(x)
}

fn square(x: i32) -> i32 {
    x * x
}

fn main() {
    let result = apply(square, 5);
    println!("The result is: {}", result);
}
```

In this example, apply is a higher-order function that accepts a function f and an integer x. The function f is applied to x within apply. The square function is simply a function that returns the square of its input. When apply is called in main with square and 5, it prints:

```
The result is: 25
```

Closures, which are anonymous functions, offer a more flexible approach by capturing their environment. The following example demonstrates how a closure can be used with a higher-order function:

```
fn apply_to_10<F>(f: F) -> i32
```

```
where
    F: Fn(i32) -> i32
{
    f(10)
}

fn main() {
    let add_three = |x| x + 3;
    let result = apply_to_10(add_three);
    println!("The result is: {}", result);
}
```

This code captures the closure add_three which adds 3 to any integer passed to it, and applies it to 10 using the higher-order function apply_to_10, resulting in:

```
The result is: 13
```

Rust also allows passing mutable closures. These closures can modify values from their environment. To use mutable closures, we need to define them using the FnMut trait. Consider the following example:

```
fn apply_mut<F>(mut f: F, x: i32) -> i32
where
    F: FnMut(i32) -> i32
{
    f(x)
}

fn main() {
    let mut multiplier = 2;
    let mut multiply = |x| {
        multiplier *= x;
        multiplier
    };
    let result = apply_mut(multiply, 3);
    println!("The result is: {}", result);
}
```

The closure multiply modifies its environment by changing the value of multiplier. The output of the program is:

```
The result is: 6
```

This demonstrates how Rust closures can capture and modify their environment, allowing for more powerful functional programming constructs.

Additionally, higher-order functions can return closures. The returned closures can capture and utilize their environment, leading to complex and dynamic functionality. Here is an example:

```
fn create_multiplier(factor: i32) -> impl Fn(i32) -> i32 {
    move |x| x * factor
}

fn main() {
    let multiplier = create_multiplier(4);
    let result = multiplier(3);
    println!("The result is: {}", result);
}
```

In this case, the function create_multiplier returns a closure that multiplies its input by a given factor. The move keyword ensures that the factor is captured by value, not borrowed. This provides:

```
The result is: 12
```

Higher-order functions improve code reuse and abstraction, serve critical roles in iterator chains, and facilitate functional approaches to problem-solving. By appropriately using function pointers, closures, and traits like Fn, FnMut, and FnOnce, programmers can unlock the full potential of higher-order functions, leading to more expressive and concise Rust code.

6.6 Error Handling: The Basics

Error handling in Rust is a critical aspect of ensuring program reliability and robustness. Unlike many other programming languages that make use of exceptions for error management, Rust opts for a more explicit and structured approach that encourages handling errors directly. This section aims to introduce the fundamental concepts and constructs used in Rust for basic error handling.

In Rust, the primary mechanism for managing errors is through the use of the Result and Option types, rather than exceptions. Let us delve into Result, which is a more commonly used type for error handling.

Result is an enum that looks like this:

```
enum Result<T, E> {
    Ok(T),
    Err(E)
}
```

The Result type is parameterized over two types: T and E. T represents the type of the value returned in the success case, while E represents the type of the error. The Result type has two variants:

- Ok(T): Indicates a successful operation containing a value of type T.
- Err(E): Indicates an operation that resulted in an error, containing an error value of type E.

Consider a function that performs division and returns a Result type to handle the possibility of division by zero.

```
fn divide(a: f64, b: f64) -> Result<f64, String> {
    if b == 0.0 {
        Err(String::from("Division by zero"))
    } else {
        Ok(a / b)
    }
}
```

Calling this divide function can yield either an Ok result or an Err:

```
let result = divide(4.0, 2.0);
match result {
    Ok(value) => println!("Result: {}", value),
    Err(e) => println!("Error: {}", e),
}
```

The match expression is instrumental in unpacking the Result type. Depending on whether the Result is Ok or Err, the corresponding block of code is executed.

For ease of use, Rust provides several methods for working with Result types, including unwrap, expect, and is_ok/is_err.

- unwrap(): Extracts the value for Ok, panicking if the variant is Err.

```
let result = divide(4.0, 0.0);
let value = result.unwrap(); // This will cause a panic
```

- expect(msg): Similar to unwrap, but allows specifying a custom panic message.

```
let result = divide(4.0, 0.0);
let value = result.expect("Custom error message: Division by zero detected");
```

- is_ok()/is_err(): Test the Result value without unpacking.

```
let result = divide(4.0, 0.0);
if result.is_err() {
    println!("Encountered an error during division.");
}
```

Another fundamental error handling component in Rust is the Option type, which indicates the presence or absence of a value and can be used to handle cases where a value may or may not exist.

The Option enum is defined as follows:

```
enum Option<T> {
    Some(T),
    None
}
```

The Option type has two variants:

- Some(T): Contains a value of type T.
- None: Represents the absence of a value.

An example function using Option could be one that searches for an element in a vector and returns None if the element is not found:

```
fn find_index(vec: &Vec<i32>, val: i32) -> Option<usize> {
    for (index, &element) in vec.iter().enumerate() {
        if element == val {
            return Some(index);
        }
    }
    None
}
```

Using this function might look like this:

```
let numbers = vec![1, 2, 3, 4, 5];
match find_index(&numbers, 3) {
    Some(index) => println!("Found at index: {}", index),
    None => println!("Value not found"),
}
```

Similar to Result, Option has methods like unwrap, expect, and is_-some/is_none.

If a pattern where the error propagates through several layers of function calls, Rust provides the ? operator to simplify and streamline error propagation.

6.7 Working with Result and Option Types

Understanding Result and Option types in Rust is crucial for effective error handling and ensuring code reliability. Both types are enums that encapsulate a value or the absence of a value, providing a robust system to handle optional or error-prone computations.

The Option type is used when a value can be present or absent. It is defined as:

```
enum Option<T> {
    Some(T),
    None,
}
```

Here, T represents a generic type. Option<T> can either be Some(T), indicating the presence of a value of type T, or None, representing the absence of a value.

Consider the following example where an optional value might be returned from a function:

```
fn find_user(username: &str) -> Option<&str> {
    let users = vec!["alice", "bob", "carol"];
    for user in users {
        if user == username {
            return Some(user);
        }
    }
    None
}
```

In the above function, find_user returns an Option<&str>, which can be Some(&str) if the user is found in the list, or None if the user is not found.

To handle the Option type, pattern matching is often used:

```
let username = "alice";
match find_user(username) {
    Some(user) => println!("Found user: {}", user),
    None => println!("User not found"),
}
```

The Result type is essential for error handling in Rust, representing either a success or an error. It is defined as:

```
enum Result<T, E> {
    Ok(T),
    Err(E),
}
```

T represents the type of the value in the success case, and E represents the type of the error.

Consider a function that performs a division operation and returns a Result type to indicate both success and failure:

```
fn divide(dividend: f64, divisor: f64) -> Result<f64, String> {
    if divisor == 0.0 {
        return Err(String::from("Cannot divide by zero"));
    }
    Ok(dividend / divisor)
}
```

In the divide function, if the divisor is zero, it returns Err with an error message. Otherwise, it returns Ok with the result of the division.

Handling the Result type can also be achieved through pattern matching:

```
match divide(4.0, 2.0) {
    Ok(result) => println!("Result: {}", result),
    Err(e) => println!("Error: {}", e),
}
```

Rust also provides convenient methods to work with Option and Result types. For instance, unwrap can be used to extract the contained value while panicking if the value is None or Err:

```
let some_number: Option<i32> = Some(10);
let number = some_number.unwrap();
println!("Number: {}", number); // prints "Number: 10"
```

```
let result = divide(4.0, 2.0).unwrap();
println!("Division result: {}", result); // prints "Division result: 2"
```

However, using unwrap carries the risk of panicking and should be avoided in robust applications. Instead, methods like unwrap_or, unwrap_or_else, and unwrap_or_default can provide safer ways to handle these cases by returning a default value or executing a closure:

```
let number = some_number.unwrap_or(0);
println!("Number: {}", number); // prints "Number: 10"
```

```
let default_division = divide(4.0, 0.0).unwrap_or_else(|err| {
    println!("Error: {}", err);
    0.0
});
println!("Default division: {}", default_division); // prints "Error: Cannot divide by
    zero" and then "Default division: 0"
```

Additionally, Result types can be used with the ? operator to simplify the propagation of errors. The ? operator can be placed after a Result value, returning the contained value if it is Ok, or returning from the function if it is Err:

```
fn calculate(dividend: f64, divisor: f64) -> Result<f64, String> {
    let result = divide(dividend, divisor)?;
```

```
    Ok(result * 2.0)
}
```

In this calculate function, if divide returns an Err, the calculate function will return immediately with that Err. If Ok is returned, the result is doubled and returned.

By mastering the use of Option and Result types, Rust programmers can write safe, reliable, and easily maintainable code, effectively handling scenarios where values might be absent or operations might fail.

6.8 The ? Operator for Simplifying Error Handling

The ? operator in Rust is a syntactic sugar that simplifies error handling by reducing boilerplate code. It automatically propagates errors in functions that return the Result or Option types. This operator can be used in functions that return Result<T, E> or Option<T>, streamlining the error propagation process and enhancing code readability.

To understand how the ? operator functions, let's start with a basic example that does not use the ? operator. Consider the following function that reads a file and parses its content into an integer.

```
use std::fs::File;
use std::io::{self, Read};
use std::num::ParseIntError;

fn read_file_to_integer(filename: &str) -> Result<i32, Box<dyn std::error::Error>> {
    let mut file = File::open(filename)?;
    let mut contents = String::new();
    file.read_to_string(&mut contents)?;
    let number: i32 = contents.trim().parse()?;
    Ok(number)
}
```

In the above example, the ? operator is used to propagate errors from the File::open, file.read_to_string, and contents.parse calls. Each of these methods returns a Result type, and if any of them return an Err, the function will cease execution and return the Err to the caller. This replaces the need for explicit match statements or other error-checking mechanics, thus making the code cleaner.

When the ? operator is used, it effectively performs the following actions:

- It calls the Into trait that converts the error type into the required error type for the function.
- It checks if the result is Ok. If it is, the Ok value is extracted and the computation continues.
- If the result is Err, the function returns early with this Err value.

Here is a more detailed decomposition of how the ? operator works internally. Suppose we rewrite the previous example without using the ? operator:

```
fn read_file_to_integer(filename: &str) -> Result<i32, Box<dyn std::error::Error>> {
    let mut file = match File::open(filename) {
        Ok(file) => file,
        Err(e) => return Err(Box::new(e)),
    };
    let mut contents = String::new();
    match file.read_to_string(&mut contents) {
        Ok(_) => {},
        Err(e) => return Err(Box::new(e)),
    }
    let number: i32 = match contents.trim().parse() {
        Ok(num) => num,
        Err(e) => return Err(Box::new(e)),
    };
    Ok(number)
}
```

Comparing the two implementations, it is evident that the use of the ? operator leads to more concise and readable code.

The ? operator also works with the Option type. If the value is None, it will return None; otherwise, it will unwrap the value and proceed. Consider the following example:

```
fn square_root(value: Option<f64>) -> Option<f64> {
    let val = value?;
    Some(val.sqrt())
}
```

In the square_root function, the ? operator checks the given Option<f64>. If value is None, the function returns None. If it is Some(val), it proceeds to compute the square root.

When working with functions that return an Option or Result, the ? operator thus introduces an efficient way to handle error propagation without cluttering the code with numerous match blocks or unwrap calls. It ensures that the function exit conditions are managed more gracefully and with less boilerplate.

An important aspect to remember is that the ? operator can only be used in functions that return Result or Option. If used in a context where the return type is not Result or Option, the compiler will produce an error.

In practice, the ? operator improves both the quality and readability of Rust code by promoting more functional error handling patterns, making code bases easier to maintain and understand.

6.9 Creating Custom Error Types

Creating custom error types is a fundamental aspect of error handling in Rust, allowing developers to define and manage specific error scenarios uniquely pertinent to their application context. This process not only enhances the clarity and reliability of the code but also provides a structured way to convey error information.

To define a custom error type, it is standard practice to create an enum that represents various error conditions that might occur within the application. Enums in Rust are a versatile tool for defining types that can be one of several variants, each optionally carrying associated data. Here is a basic example of a custom error type using an enum:

```
enum MyCustomError {
    IoError(std::io::Error),
    ParseError(std::num::ParseIntError),
    NotFound,
}
```

In this example, MyCustomError is an enum that categorizes three different kinds of errors: 'IoError' for I/O related errors, 'ParseError' for errors related to parsing integers, and 'NotFound' for a generic error representing a missing item.

To make the custom error type more idiomatic and integrate well with Rust's error handling ecosystem, it is advisable to implement the std::fmt::Display and std::error::Error traits for it. The Display trait allows us to control how the error is formatted into a human-readable string, while the Error trait integrates with Rust's other error handling functionalities.

Here is an example of implementing these traits for our custom error type:

```
use std::fmt;

impl fmt::Display for MyCustomError {
```

```
    fn fmt(&self, f: &mut fmt::Formatter<'_>) -> fmt::Result {
        match *self {
            MyCustomError::IoError(ref err) => write!(f, "I/O Error: {}", err),
            MyCustomError::ParseError(ref err) => write!(f, "Parse Error: {}", err),
            MyCustomError::NotFound => write!(f, "Item not found"),
        }
    }
}

impl std::error::Error for MyCustomError {
    fn source(&self) -> Option<&(dyn std::error::Error + 'static)> {
        match *self {
            MyCustomError::IoError(ref err) => Some(err),
            MyCustomError::ParseError(ref err) => Some(err),
            MyCustomError::NotFound => None,
        }
    }
}
```

In this implementation, fmt::Display::fmt method is used to define human-readable messages for each variant of our custom error. The std::error::Error::source method specifies the underlying cause of the error, if available. For wrapped errors like 'IoError' and 'ParseError', the source is provided, but for a generic error like 'NotFound', it returns 'None'.

To provide more utility, custom error types often implement the From trait, allowing seamless conversion from common error types into the custom error type. This facilitates the use of the ? operator for error propagation, enhancing ergonomics in function implementations.

```
impl From<std::io::Error> for MyCustomError {
    fn from(err: std::io::Error) -> MyCustomError {
        MyCustomError::IoError(err)
    }
}

impl From<std::num::ParseIntError> for MyCustomError {
    fn from(err: std::num::ParseIntError) -> MyCustomError {
        MyCustomError::ParseError(err)
    }
}
```

These implementations of the From trait allow for automatic conversion of I/O errors and parse errors into MyCustomError without extra boilerplate code. This feature is particularly useful when functions return a Result<T, E> type, and you want to propagate errors using the ? operator.

Here is an example function utilizing the custom error type:

```
fn open_and_parse_file(filename: &str) -> Result<i32, MyCustomError> {
    use std::fs::File;
    use std::io::{self, Read};
```

```
    use std::num::ParseIntError;

    let mut file = File::open(filename)?;
    let mut contents = String::new();
    file.read_to_string(&mut contents)?;

    let number: i32 = contents.trim().parse()?;
    Ok(number)
}
```

In this function, 'File::open' returns a 'Result<File, std::io::Error>', and the 'parse' method returns a 'Result<i32, std::num::ParseIntError>'. Since both of these error types implement From conversions to MyCustomError, the ? operator can be used to automatically convert and propagate errors.

It's important to further adapt custom error types to the specific requirements of the application domain. Custom error types can include additional context or metadata that might be necessary for debugging or conveying more detailed error information. Here is an example of enhancing MyCustomError with custom messages:

```
enum MyCustomError {
    IoError(std::io::Error),
    ParseError(std::num::ParseIntError),
    NotFound(String),
}

impl fmt::Display for MyCustomError {
    fn fmt(&self, f: &mut fmt::Formatter<'_>) -> fmt::Result {
        match *self {
            MyCustomError::IoError(ref err) => write!(f, "I/O Error: {}", err),
            MyCustomError::ParseError(ref err) => write!(f, "Parse Error: {}", err),
            MyCustomError::NotFound(ref message) => write!(f, "Not Found: {}",
                message),
        }
    }
}

impl std::error::Error for MyCustomError {
    fn source(&self) -> Option<&(dyn std::error::Error + 'static)> {
        match *self {
            MyCustomError::IoError(ref err) => Some(err),
            MyCustomError::ParseError(ref err) => Some(err),
            MyCustomError::NotFound(_) => None,
        }
    }
}
```

By including a String with the NotFound variant, we enable more descriptive error messages, specifying what exactly was not found.

Adopting these practices, custom error types can significantly streamline and clarify error handling in Rust applications, promoting both robustness and ease of maintenance.

6.10 Recoverable vs. Unrecoverable Errors

In Rust, distinguishing between recoverable and unrecoverable errors is crucial for writing robust and reliable code. This section will delve into the characteristics of these errors, how to identify them, and the appropriate strategies for handling each type.

Recoverable errors are those from which the program can gracefully recover, allowing it to continue running. They are expected as part of the program's normal operation, such as a failed file read due to a non-existent file. In Rust, recoverable errors are handled using the Result type, which encapsulates the possibility of success (Ok) and failure (Err).

```
use std::fs::File;
use std::io::ErrorKind;

fn open_file() -> Result<File, std::io::Error> {
    let f = File::open("hello.txt");
    match f {
        Ok(file) => Ok(file),
        Err(ref error) if error.kind() == ErrorKind::NotFound => {
            match File::create("hello.txt") {
                Ok(fc) => Ok(fc),
                Err(e) => Err(e),
            }
        },
        Err(error) => Err(error),
    }
}
```

In the example above, the open_file function attempts to open a file. If the file does not exist, it handles the ErrorKind::NotFound error by attempting to create the file. This is a typical case of handling a recoverable error. The function returns a Result<File, std::io::Error> type, which indicates that it may either succeed with a File or fail with an std::io::Error.

On the other hand, unrecoverable errors are those from which the program cannot logically recover. These errors signify bugs in the code, such as out-of-bounds array access or attempt to divide by zero. Rust handles unrecoverable errors using the panic! macro, which terminates the program and provides a backtrace of the error.

```
fn main() {
    let v = vec![1, 2, 3];
    println!("{}", v[99]);
}
```

This code will produce an unrecoverable error because it attempts to access an index that does not exist in the vector. When the program encounters this, it will panic:

```
thread 'main' panicked at 'index out of bounds: the len is 3 but the index is 99', src/main.rs:2:20
note: run with `RUST_BACKTRACE=1` environment variable to display a backtrace
```

Using panic! is reserved for situations where further execution of the program is impossible or could lead to more severe bugs. However, it is often recommended to avoid panic! in library code, as it directly terminates the program. Instead, library code should return Result or Option types, allowing the calling code to decide how to handle the error.

Another common scenario is transforming a potentially unrecoverable error into a recoverable one. This approach allows the programmer to handle errors gracefully even if they might not typically expect them.

```
fn checked_division(dividend: i32, divisor: i32) -> Result<i32, String> {
    if divisor == 0 {
        Err(String::from("Division by zero"))
    } else {
        Ok(dividend / divisor)
    }
}
```

Here, the checked_division function returns a Result<i32, String>, making the division operation, which could potentially panic, into a recoverable error that the caller can handle appropriately.

Another important aspect is the distinction between unwrap and expect methods on Result and Option types. While unwrap will cause the program to panic on an Err or None, expect allows the programmer to provide a custom panic message, giving more context about the error.

```
use std::env;

fn main() {
    let home = env::var("HOME").expect("HOME environment variable is not set.");
    println!("Home directory: {}", home);
}
```

In this example, if the HOME environment variable is not set, the program will panic with a custom message, helping to quickly identify and address the issue.

Finally, it is essential to follow best practices when deciding between recoverable and unrecoverable errors. Only panic when absolutely necessary, prefer returning Result or Option in functions, and use custom error types to make error handling more descriptive and meaningful. This ensures that your Rust programs are both safe and clear in conveying error states.

Recognizing when to treat an error as recoverable or unrecoverable, and handling it appropriately, is a foundational aspect of writing robust Rust programs.

6.11 Best Practices in Error Handling

Effective error handling mechanisms are essential for maintaining robust and reliable software systems. This section will discuss best practices in error handling within the Rust programming language, aligning with its paradigms of memory safety and concurrency without compromising performance.

- **Use the Result and Option Types:** Rust provides the Result and Option types for handling errors and optional values, respectively. These types enforce explicit error handling at compile-time, preventing many runtime issues.

Result is used for error handling and is defined as follows:

```
enum Result<T, E> {
    Ok(T),
    Err(E),
}
```

The Option type is used when a value could be absent:

```
enum Option<T> {
    Some(T),
    None,
}
```

- **Avoid Silent Failures:** Avoid using patterns that could silently ignore errors. For example, do not just unwrap Result and Option indiscriminately with unwrap() or expect(). Instead, leverage pattern matching or appropriate combinators to handle the failure cases.

Consider a function read_file which attempts to read file contents:

```
use std::fs::File;
use std::io::{self, Read};

fn read_file(file_path: &str) -> Result<String, io::Error> {
    let mut file = File::open(file_path)?;
    let mut contents = String::new();
```

```
    file.read_to_string(&mut contents)?;
    Ok(contents)
}
```

This function uses the ? operator to propagate errors, making the code more concise.

- **Propagate Errors Using the ? Operator:** The ? operator simplifies error propagation in functions that return Result. This operator will automatically return an Err if the expression it is applied to results in an error.

Example of using the ? operator:

```
fn parse_config(filename: &str) -> Result<Config, Box<dyn Error>> {
    let contents = read_file(filename)?;
    let parsed = toml::from_str(&contents)?;
    Ok(parsed)
}
```

- **Define Custom Error Types:** For complex applications, define custom error types to provide more context about failures. This can be achieved using enum to enumerate different error kinds.

Example of a custom error type:

```
#[derive(Debug)]
enum MyError {
    IoError(io::Error),
    ParseError(toml::de::Error),
}

impl From<io::Error> for MyError {
    fn from(error: io::Error) -> Self {
        MyError::IoError(error)
    }
}

impl From<toml::de::Error> for MyError {
    fn from(error: toml::de::Error) -> Self {
        MyError::ParseError(error)
    }
}
```

- **Document Error Handling Behavior:** Clearly document the error handling behavior of your functions. Indicate which errors might be returned and under what conditions, helping users of your API handle errors appropriately.

Example of a documented function signature:

```
/**
 * Opens the specified file and reads its contents.
 *
 * # Errors
 *
 * Will return 'Err' if the file cannot be opened or read.
 */
fn read_file(file_path: &str) -> Result<String, io::Error>;
```

- **Differentiate Between Recoverable and Unrecoverable Errors:** Rust distinguishes between recoverable errors (e.g., file not found) and unrecoverable errors (e.g., out of memory). Use Result for recoverable errors and panic! for unrecoverable ones.

Example of using panic! for unrecoverable errors:

```
fn allocate_memory(size: usize) -> *mut u8 {
    let ptr = unsafe { libc::malloc(size) };
    if ptr.is_null() {
        panic!("Out of memory: failed to allocate {} bytes", size);
    }
    ptr
}
```

- **Use Logging for Debugging:** Employ logging to provide additional insights into the application's state and failures. The log crate can be used for this purpose, along with various logging levels (Error, Warn, Info, Debug, Trace).

Example of using the log crate:

```
use log::{info, warn, error};

fn process_data() {
    info!("Processing data...");
    if let Err(e) = perform_step_1() {
        warn!("Step 1 failed: {:?}", e);
        return;
    }
    if let Err(e) = perform_step_2() {
        error!("Step 2 failed: {:?}", e);
    }
}
```

- **Graceful Degradation Under Failure:** Design your application to gracefully degrade under failure scenarios. This might involve providing fallback options, retrying operations, or presenting user-friendly error messages.

Example of graceful degradation:

```
fn fetch_data(api_endpoint: &str) -> Result<Data, FetchError> {
    match send_request(api_endpoint) {
        Ok(data) => Ok(data),
        Err(e) => {
            log::warn!("Primary API endpoint failed: {:?}", e);
            log::info!("Attempting backup API endpoint...");
            send_request("backup.api.endpoint")
        },
    }
}
```

Integrating these best practices assures that error handling in Rust not only aligns with the language's philosophies of safety and performance but also enhances the overall robustness and reliability of the software system. Employ these patterns and practices to develop resilient applications capable of gracefully handling unexpected situations.

Chapter 7

Structs and Enums

This chapter introduces Rust's powerful type constructs, structs and enums. It covers defining and instantiating various types of structs, including tuple and unit-like structs, and the use of methods and associated functions with structs. The chapter then details enums, their definition, and usage, including enums with data and pattern matching. The integration of structs and enums is explored to illustrate complex data modeling, followed by best practices for using these constructs effectively in Rust programs.

7.1 Introduction to Structs

In Rust, a *struct*, short for structure, is a custom data type that allows the grouping of related data under a single name. This construct is akin to structs in the C programming language but with additional functionalities and safety guarantees. Structs in Rust are primarily utilized to create types that represent real-world entities by bundling related variables, called fields, into a cohesive unit. Each field in a struct is defined by a name and a type, providing a clear structure and organization to the data.

To define a struct in Rust, use the struct keyword, followed by the name of the struct and a pair of curly braces containing the fields. The syntax is straightforward and consists of specifying each field's name, followed by a colon, and then the field's type. Consider the following example, which defines a struct named Rectangle:

```
struct Rectangle {
    width: u32,
    height: u32,
}
```

In this example, the Rectangle struct has two fields, width and height, both of which are of type u32. Once the struct is defined, instances of the struct can be created by specifying the values for each field. Here's how you can create an instance of Rectangle:

```
let rect1 = Rectangle {
    width: 30,
    height: 50,
};
```

The instance rect1 represents a rectangle with a width of 30 units and a height of 50 units. Accessing the fields of a struct instance is done using dot notation, which provides a means to read or modify the values of the fields. For example, to access the width of rect1, you would use the following syntax:

```
println!("The width of the rectangle is: {}", rect1.width);
```

This line prints the width of the rectangle, utilizing Rust's robust macro system for formatted output.

Structs are essential for creating complex data types that encapsulate multiple values, making them more manageable and easier to understand. Rust's ownership, borrowing, and lifetime rules apply to structs just as they do to other types, ensuring memory safety without a garbage collector. As the complexity and length of your programs increase, organizing data with structs becomes crucial for maintaining clarity and reducing errors.

When defining a struct, it is possible to provide field names that are the same as local variables within the function, utilizing Rust's shorthand syntax for struct instantiation. This feature is especially useful for reducing redundancy and improving code readability. Consider the following example, where local variables width and height are used to create an instance of Rectangle:

```
fn main() {
    let width = 30;
    let height = 50;

    let rect1 = Rectangle {
        width,
        height,
    };
```

```
    println!("The width of the rectangle is: {}", rect1.width);
}
```

In this case, the compiler automatically maps the local variable names to the struct field names, resulting in cleaner code.

Structs can also be used in conjunction with traits to define common behaviors or functionalities. Traits are collections of methods that can be implemented for different types, similar to interfaces in other programming languages. By implementing traits for your structs, you can define shared behavior across multiple types, ensuring consistency and reusability.

Consider the following example where the Rectangle struct implements the Debug trait to enable formatted printing:

```
use std::fmt;

#[derive(Debug)]
struct Rectangle {
    width: u32,
    height: u32,
}

fn main() {
    let rect1 = Rectangle {
        width: 30,
        height: 50,
    };

    println!("{:?}", rect1);
}
```

The #[derive(Debug)] attribute automatically provides an implementation of the Debug trait for the Rectangle struct, allowing instances of Rectangle to be printed in a programmer-friendly format. The output of the program would be:

```
Rectangle { width: 30, height: 50 }
```

The ability to customize and extend the functionality of structs through traits is a powerful feature of Rust, promoting code reuse and modular design.

Understanding and utilizing structs effectively is foundational for writing robust and maintainable Rust programs. Structs provide a means to represent complex data in a clear and concise manner, ensuring that your code remains organized and easy to understand.

7.2 Defining and Instantiating Structs

Rust provides a flexible and powerful way to define custom data types through structs. A struct, short for structure, is a composite data type that groups together variables under a single name. The variables within a struct are called fields, and they can have different types. This is useful for modeling more complex data that fits logically together.

To define a struct in Rust, you use the struct keyword followed by the name of the struct and a pair of curly braces containing the fields. Each field has a name and a type, separated by a colon.

```
struct User {
    username: String,
    email: String,
    sign_in_count: u64,
    active: bool,
}
```

In this example, we define a struct named User with four fields: username, email, sign_in_count, and active. The data types for these fields are String, String, u64, and bool, respectively.

Once a struct is defined, you can create instances of that struct. Creating an instance of the User struct involves specifying concrete values for each of the fields, enclosed in curly braces.

```
let user1 = User {
    username: String::from("user1"),
    email: String::from("user1@example.com"),
    sign_in_count: 1,
    active: true,
};
```

Here, user1 is an instance of the User struct. Each field is assigned a value: username and email fields are assigned string values created using String::from, while sign_in_count and active are assigned a u64 and a bool value, respectively.

Rust provides a shorthand syntax for initializing a struct where some fields have the same name as local variables in the current scope. This can help to reduce redundancy and make the code cleaner.

```
let username = String::from("user2");
let email = String::from("user2@example.com");
let user2 = User {
    username,
    email,
    sign_in_count: 2,
    active: false,
};
```

In this case, username and email are variables in the local scope, and we use shorthand initialization for these fields when creating user2. The values of the local variables are moved to the struct fields having the same name.

Updating struct instances can be streamlined using the struct update syntax. This syntax allows you to create a new instance of a struct, using most of the values from another instance, while updating some of the fields.

```
let user3 = User {
    email: String::from("user3@example.com"),
    ..user2
};
```

The user3 instance is created by copying the values of the fields username, sign_in_count, and active from user2, while updating the email field to a new value. The ..user2 syntax indicates that the remaining fields should be the same as in user2.

It is crucial to note that the struct update syntax moves the fields from the original instance, making it unusable after the update if any of the fields implement the Drop trait. Additionally, Rust employs ownership rules to prevent data races and ensure memory safety. If a field in the original instance has ownership traits, it will be moved rather than borrowed.

Structs in Rust can also be defined with references as fields, though special considerations are required due to Rust's ownership and borrowing system. When a struct has reference fields, you must specify lifetimes, ensuring that the references remain valid as long as the struct is in use.

```
struct UserRef<'a> {
    username: &'a str,
    email: &'a str,
    sign_in_count: u64,
    active: bool,
}

let username = "user4";
let email = "user4@example.com";
let user4 = UserRef {
    username,
    email,
    sign_in_count: 4,
    active: true,
};
```

In this example, UserRef is a struct with lifetimes 'a specified for the reference fields username and email. The lifetimes ensure that the referenced data lives at least as long as the struct instance.

By leveraging these techniques for defining and instantiating structs, Rust allows for precise and efficient data modeling, accommodating a wide array of use cases while upholding safety and performance guarantees.

7.3 Struct Update Syntax

In Rust, the struct update syntax provides an efficient way to create a new instance of a struct based on an existing instance. This technique is particularly useful when you want to duplicate most of the field values from one struct into another while modifying a few specific fields. The syntax makes the code more concise and readable, eliminating the need to manually copy each field.

Consider the following example where we define a simple struct:

```
struct Point {
    x: i32,
    y: i32,
}
```

We can create an instance of Point as follows:

```
let point1 = Point { x: 5, y: 10 };
```

Suppose we want to create a new point, point2, with the same x value as point1 but a different y value. The struct update syntax allows us to achieve this without repeating the x field. The right-hand side of the update syntax is the original instance from which fields are copied:

```
let point2 = Point { y: 20, ..point1 };
```

In this statement, the fields of point1 are used to populate the new point2 instance, except for y, which is explicitly set to 20. This results in point2 having x equal to 5 and y equal to 20.

The struct update syntax is concise, but it is essential to understand its behavior in terms of ownership and borrowing. When we use the struct update syntax, Rust applies its usual borrowing rules. If we attempt to use point1 after the update, we might encounter an error, as the fields of point1 may have been moved into point2.

```
println!("point1.x: {} and point1.y: {}", point1.x, point1.y); // Error
```

The code above will result in a compile-time error because point1 is partially moved. To address this, we must use a clone of point1 if we still need to access point1 afterward:

```
let point2 = Point { y: 20, ..point1.clone() };
```

For the clone() method to work, the Point struct must derive the Clone trait, as follows:

```
#[derive(Clone)]
struct Point {
    x: i32,
    y: i32,
}
```

Once the Point struct implements Clone, the cloned fields are now available for future use. Using the struct update syntax, one should also be cautious when working with non-Copy types, such as those that implement the Clone trait but are not implicitly copyable due to ownership semantics.

Additionally, struct update syntax can be combined with other Rust features to build more complex data structures. Consider another struct, Rectangle, which contains two Point instances as its fields.

```
struct Rectangle {
    top_left: Point,
    bottom_right: Point,
}
```

We can create a rectangle instance and later create another rectangle with some updated fields using the struct update syntax:

```
let rect1 = Rectangle {
    top_left: Point { x: 0, y: 10 },
    bottom_right: Point { x: 10, y: 0 },
};

let rect2 = Rectangle {
    top_left: Point { x: 5, y: 15 },
    ..rect1 // All fields from rect1 except top_left
};
```

In this example, rect2 is created by copying the bottom_right field from rect1, while the top_left field is explicitly set to a new value.

Understanding the struct update syntax's functionality and nuances is essential for writing efficient and idiomatic Rust code that takes full advantage of Rust's ownership and borrowing rules.

7.4 Tuple Structs

In Rust, tuple structs provide a useful means of combining multiple values into a single compound structure, similar to classic tuples but with distinct types. They differ from traditional structs by not requiring named fields, which can simplify their declaration and instantiation, especially when labels are unnecessary or would otherwise obfuscate the meaning. Here, we will investigate the definition, construction, and utilization of tuple structs comprehensively.

To define a tuple struct, we use the struct keyword followed by the struct name and a tuple-like list of types enclosed in parentheses. Below is a Rust code snippet demonstrating the declaration of a tuple struct named Color:

```
struct Color(i32, i32, i32);
```

This definition establishes Color as a tuple struct with three i32 components, representing the red, green, and blue channels of an RGB color.

To instantiate a tuple struct, we provide the values corresponding to its fields in parentheses, similar to how we work with tuples. For example:

```
let black = Color(0, 0, 0);
let white = Color(255, 255, 255);
let custom_color = Color(128, 64, 32);
```

Here, black, white, and custom_color are instances of the Color tuple struct. Accessing the individual fields of a tuple struct follows the index-based syntax familiar from tuples:

```
println!("Red: {}, Green: {}, Blue: {}", custom_color.0, custom_color.1, custom_color
    .2);
```

The above code accesses and prints each component of the custom_-color.

Tuple structs are beneficial in various contexts. Here we illustrate a tuple struct Point, representing a point in a 2D space:

```
struct Point(f64, f64);

let origin = Point(0.0, 0.0);
let point = Point(3.5, -2.1);

println!("Origin is at ({}, {})", origin.0, origin.1);
println!("Point is at ({}, {})", point.0, point.1);
```

Tuple structs can also be employed to create newtypes, which are single-element tuple structs used to introduce a distinct type even when the underlying type is the same. This is especially advantageous for type safety and avoiding type mismatch errors.

```
struct Meters(f64);
struct Seconds(f64);

let distance = Meters(700.0);
let time = Seconds(300.0);
```

In the above example, despite both Meters and Seconds being based on f64, they are distinct types, preventing accidental mixing of values that represent different concepts.

Methods can be implemented for tuple structs similarly to regular structs. Here is an implementation of a method for the Point struct:

```
impl Point {
    fn distance_from_origin(&self) -> f64 {
        (self.0.powi(2) + self.1.powi(2)).sqrt()
    }
}

let p = Point(3.0, 4.0);
println!("Distance from origin: {}", p.distance_from_origin());
```

The method distance_from_origin calculates the Euclidean distance of the point from the origin. The implementation of methods and the use of impl blocks for tuple structs maintain uniformity with named fields structs, making tuple structs versatile and easy to integrate where field names are redundant.

Tuple structs exhibit the typical behaviors and patterns observed in structures, being a lightweight and efficient option for grouping data with a strict type system encapsulation. They enhance the type safety and expressiveness of Rust code while maintaining simplicity when named fields are not essential.

7.5 Unit-Like Structs

In Rust, unit-like structs are a special type of struct that do not contain any fields. They are defined using the same struct keyword as other structs, but their definition does not include a field list. Unit-like structs can be useful in scenarios where you need to create types for specific purposes such as marker types, singleton patterns, or as flags in APIs to convey additional type information.

A unit-like struct is defined as follows:

```
struct UnitLike;
```

In this example, UnitLike is a unit-like struct. Notice that there are no braces or field definitions following the struct name. This differentiates it from other types of structs that contain fields or data.

One of the primary usages of unit-like structs is to implement traits when you need to enforce specific behaviors or constraints in your code. Consider the following example where a unit-like struct is used to implement a trait for authentication purposes:

```
struct Authenticated;

trait AuthCheck {
    fn check_auth(&self) -> bool;
}

impl AuthCheck for Authenticated {
    fn check_auth(&self) -> bool {
        // Authentication logic could go here.
        true
    }
}
```

In the code above, Authenticated is a unit-like struct used to implement the AuthCheck trait. The check_auth method is defined to return true, indicating successful authentication. This unit-like struct acts as a marker type, and the trait implementation provides the specific behavior for types carrying this marker.

Unit-like structs can also be utilized in context-dependent designs where specific types need differentiation without carrying additional data. For instance, they can be employed in a type-safe API with finite possible states:

```
struct Started;
struct Stopped;

struct Engine<State> {
    state: State,
}

impl Engine<Started> {
    fn new() -> Self {
        Engine { state: Started }
    }
}

impl Engine<Stopped> {
    fn new() -> Self {
        Engine { state: Stopped }
    }
}
```

```
impl Engine<Started> {
    fn stop(self) -> Engine<Stopped> {
        Engine { state: Stopped }
    }
}

impl Engine<Stopped> {
    fn start(self) -> Engine<Started> {
        Engine { state: Started }
    }
}

// Usage example
let stopped_engine = Engine::<Stopped>::new();
let started_engine = stopped_engine.start();
```

In the above example, Started and Stopped are unit-like structs representing the states of an Engine. The Engine struct is parameterized by a generic State type. This design ensures that the methods stop and start are only called when the Engine is in the correct state, providing a type-safe way to handle state transitions.

Unit-like structs can also be used as fieldless types in enums. Consider the following example where unit-like structs are embedded within an enum to represent different states without additional data:

```
enum ConnectionState {
    Connected,
    Disconnected,
    InProgress,
}

impl ConnectionState {
    fn is_connected(&self) -> bool {
        match self {
            ConnectionState::Connected => true,
            _ => false,
        }
    }
}

let connection_status = ConnectionState::Connected;

if connection_status.is_connected() {
    println!("The connection is active.");
}
```

In this example, the ConnectionState enum has three variants: Connected, Disconnected, and InProgress, all of which are represented as unit-like structs without fields. The is_connected method uses pattern matching to determine if the current state of the connection is Connected.

Employing unit-like structs provides several benefits:

- **Type Safety**: They help create distinct types for specific states or markers, enforcing compile-time checks.
- **Code Clarity**: By using unit-like structs, it becomes evident to the reader that these types do not carry data but are used to define specific behaviors or states.
- **Efficient Representation**: Since unit-like structs do not contain data, they have a minimal memory footprint.

To further solidify understanding, consider constructing more complex examples where unit-like structs coordinate with other Rust constructs. For example, when integrating unit-like structs with other Rust features like concurrency primitives or advanced trait implementations. Through practical applications and use cases like the ones presented, the utility and clarity brought by unit-like structs become apparent.

7.6 Methods and Associated Functions

In Rust, impl blocks facilitate the addition of methods and associated functions to structs and enums. This section elucidates how to define and use these methods and functions, enhancing the functionality of your data types.

A method is a function that is defined within the context of a struct (or enum) and operates on an instance of that struct (or enum). Methods are defined using the impl keyword, and they require a reference to self, meaning they have access to the instance's data.

Consider a simple struct:

```
struct Rectangle {
    width: u32,
    height: u32,
}
```

To define methods for the Rectangle struct, we use an impl block in which we define functions that take self as a parameter. Here is how you can implement a method that computes the area of a Rectangle:

```
impl Rectangle {
    fn area(&self) -> u32 {
        self.width * self.height
    }
}
```

In this example, the method area borrows self immutably (&self), which allows it to read the data in the Rectangle instance without changing it. The method returns the product of width and height.

To call this method, you must have an instance of the struct:

```
fn main() {
    let rect = Rectangle {
        width: 30,
        height: 50,
    };

    println!("The area of the rectangle is {} square pixels.", rect.area());
}
```

The output from running this example would be:

```
The area of the rectangle is 1500 square pixels.
```

Methods can also take ownership of self or borrow it mutably if they need to mutate the instance's data. Here is an additional method that describes the rectangle by taking ownership of self:

```
impl Rectangle {
    fn describe(self) {
        println!("This rectangle is {} pixels wide and {} pixels tall.", self.width, self.
            height);
    }
}
```

When you call describe, ownership of rect is moved to this method, and rect can no longer be used after this call.

```
fn main() {
    let rect = Rectangle {
        width: 30,
        height: 50,
    };

    rect.describe();
}
```

The output:

```
This rectangle is 30 pixels wide and 50 pixels tall.
```

If a method needs to mutate the instance's state, it should take &mut self:

```
impl Rectangle {
    fn enlarge(&mut self, scale: u32) {
        self.width *= scale;
        self.height *= scale;
    }
}
```

Calling this method requires a mutable instance of Rectangle:

```
fn main() {
    let mut rect = Rectangle {
        width: 30,
        height: 50,
    };

    rect.enlarge(2);
    println!("The enlarged rectangle is {} pixels wide and {} pixels tall.", rect.width,
        rect.height);
}
```

The output:

```
The enlarged rectangle is 60 pixels wide and 100 pixels tall.
```

Associated functions, on the other hand, don't take self as a parameter and are typically used for constructors or utility functions that are related to the type but don't operate on an instance.

Here is an example of an associated function that acts as a constructor for the Rectangle struct:

```
impl Rectangle {
    fn new(width: u32, height: u32) -> Rectangle {
        Rectangle { width, height }
    }
}
```

You can call this function without creating an instance first:

```
fn main() {
    let rect = Rectangle::new(30, 50);

    println!("The area of the rectangle is {} square pixels.", rect.area());
}
```

The associated function new provides a function signature starting with the struct name and is invoked using the :: operator. This pattern is a common convention in Rust.

Finally, it's important to note that Rust allows multiple impl blocks to be defined for a given struct. This feature allows logically grouping related methods, even if they operate on the same struct:

```
impl Rectangle {
    fn can_hold(&self, other: &Rectangle) -> bool {
        self.width > other.width && self.height > other.height
    }
}
```

This method checks if one rectangle can completely contain another:

```
fn main() {
```

```
    let rect1 = Rectangle::new(30, 50);
    let rect2 = Rectangle::new(10, 40);

    println!("Can rect1 hold rect2? {}", rect1.can_hold(&rect2));
}
```

Output:

```
Can rect1 hold rect2? true
```

Understanding how to define and use methods and associated functions harnesses the full potential of Rust's type systems, providing flexible and effective ways to manage and manipulate data within your programs. The careful encapsulation of functionality within impl blocks aligns with Rust's focus on safety and clarity.

7.7 Introduction to Enums

Enums in Rust, short for "enumerations," represent a type that can hold different values, each potentially with different types and amounts of associated data. Enumerations are a fundamental part of the Rust language, offering capabilities beyond those found in many other programming languages. Here, we explore what enums are, how they are defined, and how they are used within the context of Rust programming.

To define an enum, the enum keyword is used, followed by a name and a set of variants enclosed in curly braces. Each variant can be a standalone value or can include associated data, making enums versatile in their ability to model different kinds of data.

Consider the following example that defines a simple enum named IpAddrKind to represent IPv4 and IPv6 addresses:

```
enum IpAddrKind {
    V4,
    V6,
}
```

In this case, IpAddrKind has two variants: V4 and V6. These variants do not hold any data, and thus are simply markers indicating which type of IP address we are dealing with.

To create instances of 'IpAddrKind', we can do the following:

```
let four = IpAddrKind::V4;
let six = IpAddrKind::V6;
```

Here, four is an instance of IpAddrKind::V4 and six is an instance of IpAddrKind::V6. These instances are called variants of the IpAddrKind enum. Though this example does not contain associated data, enums in Rust can also store data alongside each variant.

Suppose we want each variant of IpAddrKind to store an actual IP address. We can modify our enum to do so:

```
enum IpAddr {
    V4(String),
    V6(String),
}
```

With this definition, both variants carry a String to store the IP address. Now we can create instances of IpAddr with actual addresses:

```
let home = IpAddr::V4(String::from("127.0.0.1"));
let loopback = IpAddr::V6(String::from("::1"));
```

This design allows enum variants to hold and encapsulate different data types, a feature that is quite powerful. Enums can also include more complex data structures as needed. Consider a more detailed example where enum variants hold different types of data:

```
enum Message {
    Quit,
    Move { x: i32, y: i32 },
    Write(String),
    ChangeColor(i32, i32, i32),
}
```

Here, Message is an enum with four variants:

- Quit: No associated data.
- Move: Includes an anonymous struct with x and y coordinates.
- Write: Contains a String.
- ChangeColor: Has three i32 values.

To instantiate these variants, we use the following constructs:

```
let quit = Message::Quit;
let move_to = Message::Move { x: 10, y: 20 };
let write_text = Message::Write(String::from("Hello"));
let change_color = Message::ChangeColor(255, 0, 0);
```

Each instance of Message can hold different types of data, allowing for a unified way to handle multiple kinds of information. This polymorphic behavior is a powerful feature of Rust enums.

Understanding and using enums effectively often involves pattern matching. Rust provides a powerful match control flow operator that can be used to inspect and handle different variants of an enum:

```
fn print_message(msg: Message) {
    match msg {
        Message::Quit => println!("Quit variant does not contain any data."),
        Message::Move { x, y } => println!("Move to coordinates: x = {}, y = {}", x, y
            ),
        Message::Write(text) => println!("Write this message: {}", text),
        Message::ChangeColor(r, g, b) => println!("Change color to red: {}, green: {},
            blue: {}", r, g, b),
    }
}
```

The match statement works by comparing the value of msg against each enum variant, executing the corresponding code for the first matching variant. Each arm of the match statement can destructure the values held by the enum, accessing the data stored within.

Enums are also utilized in the context of error handling in Rust through the Option and Result types. These provide a robust method for dealing with potential absence of values or errors, ensuring that Rust code can be written in a way that is both safe and expressive.

The Option enum is defined by the standard library as follows:

```
enum Option<T> {
    Some(T),
    None,
}
```

Here, Option<T> can be either Some holding a value of type T, or None indicating the absence of a value. Similarly, the Result enum is defined to handle success or error states:

```
enum Result<T, E> {
    Ok(T),
    Err(E),
}
```

Variants of Result are Ok containing a success value of type T and Err containing an error value of type E. Utilizing Option and Result facilitates error handling and null safety in Rust, promoting the development of reliable software.

Understanding enums and their usage in pattern matching is crucial for mastering Rust's type system and ensuring code safety and architectural clarity. Enums provide a flexible and powerful method for representing state and data, significantly enhancing the expressiveness and robustness of Rust programs.

7.8 Defining and Using Enums

In Rust, an enum is a type that can represent one of several possible variants. Each variant in an enum can optionally hold associated data, sometimes in different types, making enums exceptionally versatile for defining custom data types. The ability to define complex state machines, represent values that could be one of many different types, and handle errors and cases effectively is a significant feature of Rust.

Here is a basic example to introduce the syntax and usage of enums:

```
enum Direction {
    North,
    South,
    East,
    West,
}
```

In this example, the Direction enum can have one of four possible values: North, South, East, or West. To use this enum in a function or variable, you can follow this example:

```
fn navigate(direction: Direction) {
    match direction {
        Direction::North => println!("Going North!"),
        Direction::South => println!("Going South!"),
        Direction::East => println!("Going East!"),
        Direction::West => println!("Going West!"),
    }
}
```

Calling this function with an enum value would look like the following:

```
let my_direction = Direction::North;
navigate(my_direction);
```

Output: Going North!

Enums can also hold data. Each variant can contain a different type and amount of data. Here is how you can define and use such enums:

```
enum Message {
    Quit,
    Move { x: i32, y: i32 },
    Write(String),
    ChangeColor(i32, i32, i32),
}
```

In this example, the Message enum contains four variants. Here are details about the different variants: - Quit: No data associated. - Move: Contains named fields x and y (both i32). - Write: Contains a single

String. - ChangeColor: Contains three i32 values representing RGB color values.

To handle such enums, you'd use the match expression to cover all variants:

```
fn process_message(msg: Message) {
    match msg {
        Message::Quit => println!("Quit message received"),
        Message::Move { x, y } => println!("Move to coordinates: ({}, {})", x, y),
        Message::Write(text) => println!("Text message: {}", text),
        Message::ChangeColor(r, g, b) => println!("Change color to RGB: ({}, {}, {})",
            r, g, b),
    }
}
```

Here is an example on how you might call this function:

```
let msg1 = Message::Quit;
let msg2 = Message::Move { x: 10, y: 20 };
let msg3 = Message::Write(String::from("Hello, world!"));
let msg4 = Message::ChangeColor(255, 0, 0);

process_message(msg1);
process_message(msg2);
process_message(msg3);
process_message(msg4);
```

```
Output:
Quit message received
Move to coordinates: (10, 20)
Text message: Hello, world!
Change color to RGB: (255, 0, 0)
```

Beyond these fundamental uses, enums are instrumental in error handling, especially with the Result type which is defined as follows:

```
enum Result<T, E> {
    Ok(T),
    Err(E),
}
```

The Result enum is a standard way to return an outcome from an operation that can succeed or fail. The Ok variant holds a success value (of type T), and the Err variant holds an error value (of type E). Using Result in function return types assists in error propagation and handling, illustrated as follows:

```
fn divide(a: i32, b: i32) -> Result<i32, String> {
    if b == 0 {
        Err(String::from("Division by zero"))
    } else {
        Ok(a / b)
    }
}
```

```
fn handle_division_result() {
    match divide(10, 2) {
        Ok(result) => println!("Result: {}", result),
        Err(e) => println!("Error: {}", e),
    }
}
```

Output: Result: 5

Output for divide(10, 0):
Error: Division by zero

Enums in Rust also support the feature of implementing methods using impl blocks. This allows encapsulation of behavior directly related to the enum. Here's an example:

```
impl Message {
    fn call(&self) {
        match self {
            Message::Quit => println!("Quit message received"),
            Message::Move { x, y } => println!("Move to coordinates: ({}, {})", x, y),
            Message::Write(text) => println!("Text message: {}", text),
            Message::ChangeColor(r, g, b) => println!("Change color to RGB: ({}, {},
                {})", r, g, b),
        }
    }
}

fn main() {
    let msg = Message::Move { x: 10, y: 20 };
    msg.call();
}
```

Output:
Move to coordinates: (10, 20)

Enums provide a powerful mechanism for handling diverse data types and states within a single, cohesive type. Their integration with pattern matching, variant data, and method implementations makes them an indispensable feature of Rust.

7.9 Enums with Data

Enums in Rust allow for the definition of a type that can represent multiple distinct variants. Each variant can be associated with data, thereby enabling the representation of a variety of complex types and states concisely. This section delves into defining and using enums with data, emphasizing their utility in safe and efficient programming.

To declare an enum with data in Rust, use the enum keyword. The data associated with each variant can vary in type and quantity. Here is a simple example to illustrate this:

```
enum IpAddr {
    V4(u8, u8, u8, u8),
    V6(String),
}
```

In this example, the IpAddr enum can either be a V4 variant which contains four u8 values, or a V6 variant which contains a String. Each variant has a different type and amount of associated data.

To create instances of these enum variants, specify the variant name followed by its associated data in parentheses:

```
let home = IpAddr::V4(127, 0, 0, 1);
let loopback = IpAddr::V6(String::from("::1"));
```

Accessing the data in an enum typically involves pattern matching. Pattern matching allows for the exhaustive handling of different enum variants in a concise manner. The following example shows how this is done using the match expression:

```
fn route(ip: IpAddr) {
    match ip {
        IpAddr::V4(a, b, c, d) => println!("IPv4: {}.{}.{}.{}", a, b, c, d),
        IpAddr::V6(addr) => println!("IPv6: {}", addr),
    }
}
```

To invoke this function:

```
route(home); // Output: IPv4: 127.0.0.1
route(loopback); // Output: IPv6: ::1
```

Enums offer significant flexibility, allowing variants to hold any type of data, including custom structs. Consider the following example, where each variant holds a distinct type:

```
struct Point {
    x: f64,
    y: f64,
}

enum Shape {
    Circle { radius: f64 },
    Rectangle { width: f64, height: f64 },
    PointShape(Point),
}
```

Constructing instances of this enum involves specifying the variant and providing the associated data:

```
let circle = Shape::Circle { radius: 5.0 };
```

```
let rectangle = Shape::Rectangle { width: 10.0, height: 20.0 };
let point = Shape::PointShape(Point { x: 3.0, y: 4.0 });

fn describe(shape: Shape) {
    match shape {
        Shape::Circle { radius } => println!("Circle with radius {}", radius),
        Shape::Rectangle { width, height } => println!("Rectangle with width {} and
            height {}", width, height),
        Shape::PointShape(Point { x, y }) => println!("Point at ({}, {})", x, y),
    }
}
```

When invoked, the describe function elucidates the variant and its data:

```
describe(circle); // Output: Circle with radius 5
describe(rectangle); // Output: Rectangle with width 10 and height 20
describe(point); // Output: Point at (3, 4)
```

Furthermore, enum variants can encapsulate complex data, such as references, boxes, and even other enums, making them highly versatile for modeling nuanced, real-world data structures and state.

Box type can be used with enums to handle recursive structures gracefully. The following enum represents a linked list:

```
enum List {
    Cons(i32, Box<List>),
    Nil,
}
```

This enum can be instantiated to create a linked list by boxing recursive references:

```
let list = List::Cons(1, Box::new(List::Cons(2, Box::new(List::Nil))));
```

Enums with associated data enable the representation of multiple states with embedded data, ensuring that each variant is handled safely and efficiently during execution. Whether modeling network protocols, graphic shapes, or recursive structures, enums provide a powerful mechanism to encompass a wide variety of data in Rust programs.

7.10 Pattern Matching with Enums

In Rust, pattern matching is a powerful feature that allows you to destructure and examine enums succinctly and expressively. This systematic approach involves writing patterns to compare values against, and executing code based on the structure of these values. Pattern matching is most commonly achieved using the match expression, which provides a way to handle multiple cases through pattern matching. Let's delve into the mechanics and use cases of pattern matching with enums in Rust.

To illustrate pattern matching with enums, we will consider the following enum definition:

```
enum Message {
    Quit,
    ChangeColor(i32, i32, i32),
    Move { x: i32, y: i32 },
    Write(String),
}
```

Here we define an enum Message with four variants: Quit, ChangeColor with tuple data, Move with named fields, and Write with a single String data.

A match expression against a Message value works as follows:

```
fn process_message(msg: Message) {
    match msg {
        Message::Quit => {
            println!("The Quit variant has no data to process.");
        },
        Message::ChangeColor(r, g, b) => {
            println!("Change the color to red: {}, green: {}, blue: {}", r, g, b);
        },
        Message::Move { x, y } => {
            println!("Move by x: {}, y: {}", x, y);
        },
        Message::Write(text) => {
            println!("Text message: {}", text);
        },
    }
}
```

The function process_message takes a Message enum instance and processes it based on its variant. Each arm of the match expression:

- Handles the Message::Quit variant by printing a message indicating no additional data.
- Destructures the Message::ChangeColor variant and extracts the r, g, and b values from the tuple data, subsequently printing the RGB values.
- Destructures the Message::Move variant using named fields x and y, printing the coordinates.
- Extracts the text from the Message::Write variant, then prints the text.

Each pattern in the match arms must be exhaustive, covering all possible variants of the enum. If not, we must include a wild card arm (_) to account for any remaining cases.

Using an exhaustive match:

```
fn process_message_v2(msg: Message) {
    match msg {
        Message::Quit => println!("Quit has no data."),
        Message::ChangeColor(r, g, b) => println!("RGB({}, {}, {})", r, g, b),
        Message::Move { x, y } => println!("Move by ({}, {})", x, y),
        Message::Write(text) => println!("Text: {}", text),
        _ => println!("Other message type encountered."),
    }
}
```

Advantages of pattern matching in Rust include type safety and clear, concise code. Pattern matching ensures all variants are handled correctly; any missing variant generates a compile-time error.

Advanced usage of pattern matching includes combining match guards to add conditional checks. Match guards are additional if conditions within a pattern.

For example, extending ChangeColor pattern:

```
fn process_message_v3(msg: Message) {
    match msg {
        Message::ChangeColor(r, g, b) if r == 0 => println!("Zero red component"),
        Message::ChangeColor(r, g, b) => println!("Color: {}, {}, {}", r, g, b),
        _ => println!("Unmatched message"),
    }
}
```

Here, we handle ChangeColor differently if the red component is zero, showcasing the addition of match guards for more granular control.

Similarly, nested pattern matching can destructure complex enums within other enums or nested structures:

```
enum ComplexMessage {
    Success(Message),
    Error(String),
}

fn process_complex_message(cmsg: ComplexMessage) {
    match cmsg {
        ComplexMessage::Success(msg) => process_message_v2(msg),
        ComplexMessage::Error(err) => println!("Error: {}", err),
    }
}
```

We define an enum ComplexMessage that nests Message enums within the Success variant. The match expression decomposes the nested

Message and processes it accordingly.

Pattern matching in Rust ensures safe, expressive, and maintainable code. By leveraging the power of match, handling complex data structures becomes both intuitive and efficient.

7.11 Combining Structs and Enums

In complex Rust programs, combining structs and enums provides greater flexibility and expressiveness in data modeling. This combination allows for the creation of intricate data structures that can represent a wide variety of states and behaviors. The interoperability of structs and enums enables more readable, maintainable, and scalable code.

To elucidate the concept, consider a scenario where we are modeling a geometric shape. Each shape can either be a circle, rectangle, or triangle, with associated data such as radius for circles and width and height for rectangles.

We start by defining the enum to represent the different shape types, each variant of the enum can hold different data that describes the shape.

```
enum Shape {
    Circle { radius: f64 },
    Rectangle { width: f64, height: f64 },
    Triangle { base: f64, height: f64 },
}
```

Here, Shape is an enum with three variants: Circle, Rectangle, and Triangle. Each variant stores different fields relevant to the shape it represents. The Circle variant holds a radius, the Rectangle variant holds a width and height, and the Triangle variant holds a base and height.

Next, let's define a struct that will hold additional common data pertinent to any shape, such as a unique identifier and a color.

```
struct GeometricShape {
    id: u32,
    color: String,
    shape: Shape,
}
```

The GeometricShape struct contains an id to uniquely identify each shape, a color, and an instance of the Shape enum. This allows each GeometricShape to have properties common to all shapes while also possessing shape-specific details.

Let's instantiate a few geometric shapes using these definitions.

```
fn main() {
    // Create a circle
    let circle = GeometricShape {
        id: 1,
        color: String::from("Red"),
        shape: Shape::Circle { radius: 10.0 },
    };

    // Create a rectangle
    let rectangle = GeometricShape {
        id: 2,
        color: String::from("Blue"),
        shape: Shape::Rectangle {
            width: 20.0,
            height: 10.0,
        },
    };

    // Create a triangle
    let triangle = GeometricShape {
        id: 3,
        color: String::from("Green"),
        shape: Shape::Triangle {
      base: 15.0,
      height: 7.0
      },
    };
}
```

In these examples, we instantiated geometric shapes with varying attributes. Each shape contains a unique identifier and a color, in addition to their specific geometric properties.

To interact with these shapes, we can implement methods that operate on the GeometricShape struct, as well as methods specific to the Shape enum. For instance, we can calculate the area for each shape variant.

Let's define a method to calculate the area of a shape. We'll start by implementing a method for the Shape enum.

```
impl Shape {
    fn area(&self) -> f64 {
        match *self {
            Shape::Circle { radius } => std::f64::consts::PI * radius * radius,
            Shape::Rectangle { width, height } => width * height,
            Shape::Triangle { base, height } => 0.5 * base * height,
        }
    }
}
```

This method uses pattern matching to implement the correct area calculation formula for each shape variant. Now, we can also implement a method for the GeometricShape struct that utilizes the shape's area method.

```
impl GeometricShape {
    fn describe(&self) {
        println!("ID: {}, Color: {}, Area: {}",
            self.id, self.color, self.shape.area());
    }
}
```

The describe method prints out the shape's identifier, color, and area. We can now utilize these methods in our main function to interact with our geometric shapes:

```
fn main() {
    // Create a circle
    let circle = GeometricShape {
        id: 1,
        color: String::from("Red"),
        shape: Shape::Circle { radius: 10.0 },
    };

    // Create a rectangle
    let rectangle = GeometricShape {
        id: 2,
        color: String::from("Blue"),
        shape: Shape::Rectangle {
            width: 20.0,
            height: 10.0,
        },
    };

    // Create a triangle
    let triangle = GeometricShape {
        id: 3,
        color: String::from("Green"),
        shape: Shape::Triangle {
            base: 15.0,
            height: 7.0
        },
    };

    // Describe each shape
    circle.describe();
    rectangle.describe();
    triangle.describe();
}
```

Executing the main function would produce the following output:

```
ID: 1, Color: Red, Area: 314.1592653589793
ID: 2, Color: Blue, Area: 200.0
ID: 3, Color: Green, Area: 52.5
```

This example demonstrates the power and versatility of combining structs and enums. We encapsulated shared information inside the GeometricShape struct while allowing for the complexity and variability inherent in different shapes via the Shape enum. This approach is widely applicable in various domains requiring sophisticated data representation, including but not limited to geometric modeling, user interface components, and state management in complex systems.

7.12 Best Practices for Structs and Enums

In this section, we focus on best practices for utilizing structs and enums efficiently in Rust programming. These practices aim to enhance code readability, maintainability, and performance. By adhering to these guidelines, developers can write robust and efficient Rust programs that leverage the language's safety and concurrency features.

Firstly, it is crucial to design structs with clear and specific responsibilities. Each struct should represent a single concept or a tightly related set of data. Avoid creating structs that do too much as it complicates maintenance and diminishes readability. Structs should encapsulate all relevant data and expose methods that operate on that data, thus adhering to the principle of encapsulation.

Consider the use of trait implementations to define behavior:

```
struct Rectangle {
    width: u32,
    height: u32,
}

impl Rectangle {
    fn area(&self) -> u32 {
        self.width * self.height
    }

    fn can_hold(&self, other: &Rectangle) -> bool {
        self.width > other.width && self.height > other.height
    }
}
```

Here, Rectangle is a well-defined struct encapsulating properties and behaviors related to rectangles. The methods area and can_hold logically belong to Rectangle and enhance the usability and readability of the code.

Secondly, favor immutability by default. In Rust, variables and fields are immutable by default. This is a beneficial feature as it aids in avoiding unintended side effects. Use mutability only when necessary:

```
let rect1 = Rectangle { width: 30, height: 50 };
let rect2 = Rectangle { width: 10, height: 40 };

println!("Can rect1 hold rect2? {}", rect1.can_hold(&rect2));
```

In the above example, rect1 and rect2 are immutable. This immutability guarantees that their dimensions will not change, preventing bugs caused by unintended modifications.

For enums, it is recommended to define variants that comprehensively cover the domain of the type. Each variant should clearly represent a distinct case. Enums are most powerful when used with pattern matching, enabling exhaustive and safe handling of different cases:

```
enum TrafficLight {
    Red,
    Yellow,
    Green,
}

impl TrafficLight {
    fn duration(&self) -> u32 {
        match *self {
            TrafficLight::Red => 60,
            TrafficLight::Yellow => 3,
            TrafficLight::Green => 45,
        }
    }
}
```

This pattern matching ensures that every possible variant of TrafficLight is addressed, promoting safety and clarity.

When combining structs and enums, consider their complementary roles. Enums can be used to represent state or variant types, while structs encapsulate data and behavior. For instance:

```
struct Engine {
    horsepower: u32,
}

enum CarType {
    Sedan,
    Coupe,
    Hatchback,
}

struct Car {
    make: String,
    model: String,
    engine: Engine,
    car_type: CarType,
}
```

This example demonstrates a clear separation of concerns: Engine encapsulates the properties of the engine, CarType enumerates the types of cars, and Car integrates both alongside other relevant data.

Appropriately leveraging Rust's advanced features such as generics and traits with structs and enums can significantly enhance flexibility. Define traits to specify shared behavior among different structs and use generics to allow for type flexibility:

```
trait Shape {
    fn area(&self) -> f64;
}

struct Circle {
    radius: f64,
}

impl Shape for Circle {
    fn area(&self) -> f64 {
        std::f64::consts::PI * self.radius * self.radius
    }
}

struct Square {
    side: f64,
}

impl Shape for Square {
    fn area(&self) -> f64 {
        self.side * self.side
    }
}

fn print_area<T: Shape>(shape: T) {
    println!("The area is {}", shape.area());
}
```

In this code, Shape is a trait that defines a shared behavior, and Circle and Square implement this trait, enabling them to be used interchangeable where Shape is expected.

Lastly, while using complex data structures, ensure proper documentation. Document each struct, enum, and method to describe its purpose, inputs, outputs, and any important considerations. This practice improves maintainability and serves as a valuable reference for other developers.

By following these practices, developers can utilize Rust's structs and enums optimally, leading to code that is both performant and easy to understand.

Chapter 8

Collections and Iterators

This chapter covers Rust's standard collections and iterators, starting with vectors, strings, hash maps, and hash sets. It explains how to efficiently manage and manipulate data using these collections. The chapter also delves into iterating over collections, utilizing built-in iterators, and creating custom iterators. Advanced iterator techniques, such as consuming adaptors and chaining operations, are explored to demonstrate their robustness and flexibility. Performance considerations with collections and iterators are provided to ensure optimal usage in practical applications.

8.1 Introduction to Collections

In Rust, collections are data structures used to store multiple values. These collections provide powerful capabilities to manage and manipulate data efficiently. The primary collections available in the Rust standard library include Vec, String, HashMap, and HashSet. Each collection type serves different purposes and exhibits unique properties, making them suitable for various scenarios.

Vec, or vectors, are dynamic arrays allowing storage of values of the same type. They can grow and shrink in size as needed, making them highly flexible for handling sequences where the size is not known at compile time. String is a collection that specifically holds UTF-8 encoded text. Although String can be seen as a specialized Vec of bytes, it guarantees that the stored data is valid UTF-8, providing robust text manipulation capabilities.

HashMap is a key-value storage collection that allows for efficient retrieval of values based on their associated keys. This is particularly useful when you need to associate data with unique identifiers. HashSet, on the other hand, stores unique values without any associated data, making it ideal for collections where the uniqueness of elements is required.

The flexibility and power of these collections come from their implementation using traits in Rust. The Collection trait, although not a literal trait in Rust, conceptually represents common functionalities shared by these collection types. Each actual collection type implements specific traits that define their behavior. For example, the Vec type implements the Deref and DerefMut traits for dereferencing operations, Index and IndexMut for indexing, and Extend to extend with items.

Here is an example of creating and using a vector in Rust:

```
fn main() {
    let mut vec = Vec::new();
    vec.push(1);
    vec.push(2);
    vec.push(3);

    for elem in &vec {
        println!("{}", elem);
    }
}
```

The output of this program will be:

```
1
2
3
```

In the above example, we initialize a mutable vector, add three integers to it using the push method, and then iterate over the elements, printing each one.

Collections in Rust provide numerous methods for manipulation. For instance, vectors offer methods like push, pop, insert, and remove. Strings offer methods such as push_str, replace, and split. HashMaps provide insert, get, and remove, while HashSets include insert, contains, and remove.

A key consideration when working with collections is ownership and borrowing, which ensures memory safety and concurrency without data races. When you pass a collection to a function, you can either move it, borrow it immutably, or borrow it mutably.

```
fn borrow_vector(v: &Vec<i32>) {
    println!("The vector contains: {:?}", v);
}

fn main() {
    let vec = vec![1, 2, 3];
    borrow_vector(&vec);

    println!("Original vector retains ownership: {:?}", vec);
}
```

Output:

```
The vector contains: [1, 2, 3]
Original vector retains ownership: [1, 2, 3]
```

This example demonstrates borrowing a vector immutably for printing, allowing the original vector to retain ownership and remain unmutated.

Understanding the semantics of borrowing and ownership is critical when manipulating collections to prevent common pitfalls like use-after-free errors or data races in concurrent settings.

Next, consider an example that utilizes a HashMap for key-value storage:

```
use std::collections::HashMap;

fn main() {
    let mut scores = HashMap::new();
    scores.insert("Alice", 50);
    scores.insert("Bob", 30);

    match scores.get("Alice") {
        Some(score) => println!("Alice's score: {}", score),
        None => println!("No score found for Alice"),
    }
}
```

Output:

```
Alice's score: 50
```

In this example, a HashMap is used to store scores for players identified by their names. This demonstrates efficient retrieval using the get method.

Collections also interplay with iterators, allowing for transformations and evaluations on data sequences. Iterators provide a way to traverse elements in a collection without exposing the underlying representation. This allows for concise and expressive code through iterator adaptors. Methods such as map, filter, and fold can be used to perform complex transformations in a functional programming style.

The comprehensive usage of collections in Rust exemplifies the language's emphasis on safety, performance, and concurrency, making it a robust choice for developing both critical systems and general applications.

8.2 Vectors: Growing Arrays

Vectors in Rust are implemented as the structure Vec<T>, where T represents the type of the elements held within the vector. The primary characteristic of vectors is their ability to dynamically grow and shrink in size while maintaining contiguous memory allocation. This feature makes vectors a powerful tool for managing and manipulating sequences of elements.

To define and initialize a vector, the vec! macro is typically employed. This macro can generate a new vector containing specified elements:

```
// Create an empty vector of i32 type
let mut v: Vec<i32> = Vec::new();

// Create a vector with initial elements
let v = vec![1, 2, 3, 4, 5];
```

Vectors in Rust ensure that all elements are stored contiguously, which facilitates fast indexing and iteration. Elements within a vector can be accessed using indexing, typically yielding an Option type to handle potential out-of-bounds access safely.

```
// Accessing elements of a vector
let v = vec![10, 20, 30];
let first = v[0];
let second = v[1];
```

One essential feature of vectors is their ability to dynamically grow. This is achieved through the push method, which appends an element to the end of the vector. If the vector's current capacity is insufficient, it will automatically allocate additional memory to accommodate the new elements.

```
// Growing a vector by adding elements
let mut v = vec![1, 2];
v.push(3);
v.push(4);

// Vector after push operations: [1, 2, 3, 4]
```

Similarly, vectors can shrink in size using the pop method, which removes the last element from the vector and returns an Option of the element. This method is particularly useful when dealing with stack-like structures.

```
// Shrinking a vector by removing the last element
let mut v = vec![1, 2, 3, 4];
let last = v.pop(); // last contains Some(4)

// Vector after pop operation: [1, 2, 3]
```

It's crucial to highlight the distinction between borrowing immutably and mutably when working with vectors. Rust's ownership rules necessitate careful management of references to ensure memory safety.

```
// Immutable and mutable borrowing
let mut v = vec![1, 2, 3];

// Immutable borrow
let first = &v[0];

// Mutable borrow
let last = &mut v[2];
*last = 5;

// Vector after mutation: [1, 2, 5]
```

Vectors in Rust have numerous utility methods that enhance their functionality. Some notable methods include len to determine the number of elements in the vector, is_empty to check if the vector contains no elements, and clear to remove all elements.

```
// Utility methods for vectors
let v = vec![1, 2, 3];

// Get the length of the vector
let length = v.len();

// Check if the vector is empty
let empty = v.is_empty(); // returns false

// Clear the vector
let mut v = vec![1, 2, 3];
v.clear(); // Vector is now empty
```

Vectors also allow slicing operations, which enable the creation of references to sub-sequences of the vector. Slicing a vector yields a slice, which is a view into the vector and does not own the data.

```
// Slicing a vector
let v = vec![1, 2, 3, 4, 5];
let slice = &v[1..4]; // slice contains [2, 3, 4]
```

Slices are vital for efficient data manipulation as they provide a way to work with parts of a vector without the overhead of copying elements.

For more advanced operations, vectors can interact with iterators. Converting a vector into an iterator allows for functional programming paradigms such as map, filter, and collect.

```
// Using iterators with vectors
let v = vec![1, 2, 3, 4, 5];

// Apply a square function to all elements
let squared: Vec<i32> = v.iter().map(|&x| x * x).collect(); // squared contains [1, 4, 9,
     16, 25]
```

Iterators provide a powerful and expressive way to manipulate vectors, enabling concise and readable code.

Furthermore, vectors can be manipulated using the insert and remove methods, which offer precise control over the position of elements within the vector. The insert method allows for adding an element at a specified index, while the remove method deletes an element from a specific index.

```
// Inserting and removing elements
let mut v = vec![1, 2, 3];

// Insert 4 at index 1
v.insert(1, 4); // Vector is now [1, 4, 2, 3]

// Remove element at index 2
v.remove(2); // Vector is now [1, 4, 3]
```

Managing the capacity and allocation of vectors is another crucial aspect of their use. The with_capacity method is favored when the size of the vector is known in advance, as it pre-allocates memory, reducing the overhead of multiple allocations.

```
// Pre-allocating memory with capacity
let mut v = Vec::with_capacity(10);
// Vector with an initial capacity for 10 elements
```

Understanding vectors is fundamental to leveraging Rust's collection capabilities effectively. Mastery of vector operations paves the way for efficient data management and optimization, quintessential for robust and high-performance Rust applications.

8.3 String Collections

String manipulation is a fundamental part of many applications, and Rust provides several types of string collections to handle various use cases effectively. Let's explore the primary types of string collections in Rust: String and &str, and how to use them efficiently.

Rust's String type is an owned, growable, and mutable UTF-8 encoded string. It's a dynamic array of bytes that ensures UTF-8 compliance, making it suitable for general-purpose string manipulation. In contrast, &str is a reference to a string slice which is immutable and usually borrowed from a String or a string literal.

```
fn main() {
    let mut s = String::from("Hello, ");
    s.push_str("world!");
    println!("{}", s); // Outputs: Hello, world!
}
```

In the code snippet above, String::from creates a new String from a string literal. The push_str method appends a string slice to an existing String. This operation is efficient, and Rust handles memory management automatically.

To illustrate the distinction and conversion between String and &str, consider the following example:

```
fn main() {
    let s1 = "hello";
    let s2 = s1.to_string(); // &str to String
    let s3: &str = &s2; // String to &str
    println!("s1: {}, s2: {}, s3: {}", s1, s2, s3);
}
```

In the above code, s1 is a string slice &str, and s2 is a String obtained by calling the to_string method on s1. The conversion from String back to &str is achieved by borrowing, which is facilitated using the & operator.

String manipulation often necessitates iteration over characters, substrings, or bytes. Rust's extensive iterator trait implementations make it straightforward to perform these operations:

```
fn main() {
    let s = String::from("Rust");
    for c in s.chars() {
        print!("{} ", c); // Outputs: R u s t
    }
    println!();

    for b in s.bytes() {
        print!("{} ", b); // Outputs: 82 117 115 116
    }
}
```

The chars method returns an iterator over the characters of a String, while the bytes method returns an iterator over its bytes. These iterators allow for various transformations and filtering operations.

Substrings can be accessed using slicing notation:

```
fn main() {
    let s = String::from("hello");
    let slice1 = &s[0..2]; // "he"
    let slice2 = &s[1..]; // "ello"
    println!("slice1: {}, slice2: {}", slice1, slice2);
}
```

Rust ensures slices are valid UTF-8, preventing slicing that results in invalid characters. Attempting to create an invalid slice will cause the program to panic at runtime.

Concatenation of strings in Rust can be achieved using the + operator or the format! macro. The + operator requires one operand to be a String and the other a &str:

```
fn main() {
    let s1 = String::from("Hello, ");
    let s2 = String::from("world!");
    let s3 = s1 + &s2; // s1 is moved and cannot be used anymore
    println!("{}", s3); // Outputs: Hello, world!
}
```

Alternatively, the format! macro provides a more flexible and convenient approach without requiring ownership transfer:

```
fn main() {
    let s1 = String::from("tic");
    let s2 = String::from("tac");
    let s3 = String::from("toe");
    let s = format!("{}-{}-{}", s1, s2, s3); // s1, s2, and s3 are not moved
    println!("{}", s); // Outputs: tic-tac-toe
}
```

Efficient string manipulation also considers performance implications. Functions such as replace, split, and trim are optimized to guarantee optimal performance:

```
fn main() {
    let s = String::from(" hello rust ");
    let trimmed = s.trim();
    let replaced = s.replace("rust", "world");
    let parts: Vec<&str> = s.split_whitespace().collect();

    println!("Trimmed: '{}', Replaced: '{}', Parts: {:?}", trimmed, replaced, parts);
}
```

The trim method removes leading and trailing whitespace. The replace method substitutes all occurrences of a substring with another, and split_whitespace splits the string based on whitespace, collecting the results into a Vec.

Understanding these fundamental operations and methods on strings enables efficient and effective string management in Rust, contributing significantly to robust application development.

8.4 HashMaps: Key-Value Storage

HashMaps in Rust provide a highly efficient mechanism for storing and retrieving key-value pairs. Utilizing a hashing algorithm, they allow for average-time complexity of $O(1)$ for insertions, deletions, and lookups. This efficiency makes HashMaps ideal for a variety of applications where rapid data retrieval is crucial.

To utilize HashMaps in Rust, it is necessary to include the std::collections::HashMap in your scope. The following example demonstrates the fundamental operations of a HashMap, including creation, insertion, access, and removal of elements.

```
use std::collections::HashMap;

fn main() {
    // Create a new HashMap
    let mut scores = HashMap::new();

    // Insert key-value pairs into the HashMap
    scores.insert(String::from("Blue"), 10);
    scores.insert(String::from("Yellow"), 50);

    // Access value associated with a key
    let team_name = String::from("Blue");
    match scores.get(&team_name) {
        Some(&score) => println!("The score for {} is {}", team_name, score),
        None => println!("{} team not found", team_name),
    }

    // Remove a key-value pair
    scores.remove(&team_name);

    // Iterate over all key-value pairs
    for (key, value) in &scores {
        println!("{}: {}", key, value);
    }
}
```

The insert method adds key-value pairs to the HashMap. Rust ensures type safety by requiring that all keys be of the same type, and all values be of another same type, typically specified during the HashMap's creation. If duplicate keys are inserted, the HashMap will update the value associated with the existing key.

To retrieve the value associated with a specific key, use the get method, which returns an Option<&V>. This means the returned value is either

Some(&value) if the key exists, or None if the key is not found. Pattern matching is used to handle these cases.

The remove method takes a reference to the key for the entry to be removed, efficiently eliminating the key-value pair from the map.

HashMaps can also be iterated over. In the example above, a for-loop iterates over all key-value pairs in the HashMap. The & symbol is used to destructure each tuple into its key and value components, allowing us to perform actions on each.

The keys in HashMap must be hashable and comparable for equality. The Hash and Eq traits from the standard library make this possible. Rust's standard implementation uses the SipHash algorithm, providing a strong trade-off between performance and resistance to trivial collision attacks. While default settings can be sufficient, customization is possible through the use of the Hash and BuildHasher traits.

Consider an advanced use case where the HashMap needs to store more complex types or utilize specialized hashing algorithms. Here's an example where a custom hash function is implemented:

```
use std::collections::HashMap;
use std::collections::hash_map::RandomState;
use std::hash::{BuildHasher, Hash, Hasher};

struct CustomHasher {
    state: u64,
}

impl Hasher for CustomHasher {
    fn finish(&self) -> u64 {
        self.state
    }

    fn write(&mut self, bytes: &[u8]) {
        for &b in bytes {
            self.state = self.state.wrapping_mul(31).wrapping_add(b as u64);
        }
    }
}

struct CustomBuildHasher;

impl BuildHasher for CustomBuildHasher {
    type Hasher = CustomHasher;

    fn build_hasher(&self) -> CustomHasher {
        CustomHasher { state: 0 }
    }
}

fn main() {
    let custom_hasher = CustomBuildHasher{};
    let mut map: HashMap<_, _, CustomBuildHasher> = HashMap::with_hasher(
            custom_hasher);
```

```
    map.insert("Alice", 10);
    map.insert("Bob", 11);

    for (key, value) in &map {
        println!("{}: {}", key, value);
    }
}
```

This example customizes the hashing process. CustomHasher provides a basic hashing approach and is part of a custom BuildHasher, which in turn, is utilized in the creation of the HashMap. Such flexibility proves invaluable for specialized needs or optimizing specific scenarios.

Through performant data handling, constant-time complexity, and flexible usage, HashMap stands as a powerful and reliable tool in Rust's collection arsenal. Understanding its mechanics and potential customizations allows for refined control over key-value storage operations, directly contributing to the efficiency and robustness of software solutions.

8.5 HashSets: Unordered Collections of Unique Items

A HashSet in Rust is a collection that represents an unordered group of unique items. This makes HashSet particularly useful for ensuring that a set of elements does not contain duplicates. The underlying mechanism of HashSet is implemented using a hash table, which offers average-case complexity of $O(1)$ for insertion, deletion, and membership operations. The Rust standard library provides the HashSet struct as part of the std::collections module.

To use HashSet, it must be imported first:

```
use std::collections::HashSet;
```

Creating a HashSet

A HashSet can be created using the new method or the with_capacity method if a specific capacity is desired:

```
let mut set = HashSet::new(); // Create an empty HashSet
let mut set_with_capacity = HashSet::with_capacity(10); // Create a HashSet with
    capacity for 10 elements
```

Adding and Removing Elements

To add elements to a HashSet, the insert method is used. This method returns a boolean indicating whether the value was inserted ('true' if it did not previously exist in the set):

```
let mut fruits = HashSet::new();
fruits.insert("Apple");
fruits.insert("Banana");
fruits.insert("Orange");
```

The remove method is used to delete elements from the set, returning 'true' if the value was present and removed:

```
let removed = fruits.remove("Banana");
// 'removed' is true since "Banana" was in the set and has been removed
```

Checking for Membership

To check if an element is present in the HashSet, the contains method is used:

```
if fruits.contains("Apple") {
    println!("The set contains Apple.");
}
```

Iterating Over a HashSet

Although HashSet is unordered, we can iterate over the items it contains. This can be done using a 'for' loop:

```
for fruit in &fruits {
    println!("{}", fruit);
}
```

Set Operations

HashSet supports mathematical set operations such as union, intersection, difference, and symmetric difference. These operations can be computationally efficient due to the hash table backing.

- Union: Combines two sets, including all unique elements from both.

```
let set1: HashSet<_> = ["Apple", "Banana"].iter().cloned().collect();
let set2: HashSet<_> = ["Banana", "Orange"].iter().cloned().collect();
let union_set: HashSet<_> = set1.union(&set2).cloned().collect();
```

- Intersection: Finds common elements between two sets.

```
let intersection_set: HashSet<_> = set1.intersection(&set2).cloned().collect();
```

- Difference: Finds elements present in the first set but not in the second.

```
let difference_set: HashSet<_> = set1.difference(&set2).cloned().collect();
```

- Symmetric Difference: Finds elements in either set but not in both.

```
let symmetric_difference_set: HashSet<_> = set1.symmetric_difference(&set2).cloned
    ().collect();
```

Hashing and Custom Types

For a type to be stored in a HashSet, it must implement the Eq and Hash traits. Rust's primitive types and standard library types already implement these traits. To store a custom type in a HashSet, traits must be implemented explicitly:

```
use std::collections::HashSet;
use std::hash::{Hash, Hasher};

#[derive(Debug, Eq)]
struct CustomType {
    id: u32,
    name: String,
}

impl Hash for CustomType {
    fn hash<H: Hasher>(&self, state: &mut H) {
        self.id.hash(state);
        self.name.hash(state);
    }
}

impl PartialEq for CustomType {
    fn eq(&self, other: &Self) -> bool {
        self.id == other.id && self.name == other.name
    }
}

let mut custom_set = HashSet::new();
custom_set.insert(CustomType { id: 1, name: String::from("Item1") });
custom_set.insert(CustomType { id: 2, name: String::from("Item2") });
```

In scenarios where performance is critical and the distribution characteristics of the data are well understood, custom hashers can be used. By default, Rust uses a cryptographic hash function (SipHash) ensuring resistance to collision attacks. However, for some cases, a faster but potentially less secure hasher can be employed.

Performance Considerations

HashSet is generally performant with constant time complexity $O(1)$ for basic operations under average conditions. The size of the set, the load factor, and the quality of the hash function contribute to the performance characteristics. Rust's HashSet dynamically resizes to maintain an optimal load factor, thereby balancing memory usage and speed. If the exact number of items that will be stored is known ahead of time, initializing the set with with_capacity can avoid frequent reallocations, improving performance.

Effectively choosing and implementing appropriate hash functions for custom types can also influence performance. In high-stake applications, profiling and benchmarking using Rust's cargo bench can provide insights necessary for optimization.

8.6 Iterating Over Collections

Iterating over collections in Rust is a fundamental feature that enables efficient data manipulation and retrieval. The Iterator trait in Rust defines the functionality required for creating and using iterators.

An iterator in Rust is any type that implements the Iterator trait, which provides a way to sequentially access elements in a collection. The Iterator trait is defined in the standard library ('std::iter') and has two required methods: next and size_hint.

The next method returns an Option<T>. When called, next attempts to return the next item in the sequence. If iteration is complete, it returns None.

```
pub trait Iterator {
    type Item;

    // Advances the iterator and returns the next value.
    fn next(&mut self) -> Option<Self::Item>;

    // Provides an (lower, upper) bound on the remaining length of the iterator.
    fn size_hint(&self) -> (usize, Option<usize>) {
        (0, None)
    }
}
```

To iterate over a collection, Rust provides a variety of methods that create iterators. Common collections like vectors, strings, hash maps, and hash sets have built-in methods to produce iterators.

Iterating Over Vectors

Vectors in Rust provide several methods to create iterators. The primary method is iter, which returns an iterator over the references to the elements of the vector. For mutable access, iter_mut provides a similar function but returns mutable references.

```
let v = vec![1, 2, 3, 4];

// Iterating over references
for item in v.iter() {
    println!("{}", item);
}

// Iterating with mutable references
let mut v = vec![1, 2, 3, 4];
for item in v.iter_mut() {
    *item += 1;
}

// Iterating and taking ownership
for item in v.into_iter() {
    println!("{}", item);
}
```

Iterating Over Strings

Strings in Rust can be iterated over in several ways. The chars method returns an iterator over the characters of a string. The bytes method yields an iterator over the individual bytes.

```
let s = String::from("hello");

// Iterating over characters
for c in s.chars() {
    println!("{}", c);
}

// Iterating over bytes
for b in s.bytes() {
    println!("{}", b);
}
```

Iterating Over HashMaps and HashSets

Hash maps and hash sets provide iterators to access their elements. For hash maps, the iter method returns an iterator over key-value pairs. For hash sets, iter gives an iterator over the set's values.

```
use std::collections::HashMap;

let mut map = HashMap::new();
map.insert("a", 1);
map.insert("b", 2);

// Iterating over key-value pairs
for (key, value) in map.iter() {
```

```
    println!("{}: {}", key, value);
}

use std::collections::HashSet;

let mut set = HashSet::new();
set.insert(1);
set.insert(2);

// Iterating over values
for value in set.iter() {
    println!("{}", value);
}
```

Common Iteration Patterns

Several common patterns and methods often accompany iteration in Rust. The while let construct, for loops, and various iterator adaptors enhance the control and functionality of iteration.

While Let Loops:

```
let v = vec![1, 2, 3, 4];
let mut iter = v.iter();

while let Some(item) = iter.next() {
    println!("{}", item);
}
```

Using Filter and Map:

```
let v = vec![1, 2, 3, 4];

// Filtering elements
let filtered: Vec<_> = v.iter()
    .filter(|&&x| x % 2 == 0)
    .collect();

println!("{:?}", filtered);

// Mapping values
let mapped: Vec<_> = v.iter()
    .map(|&x| x * 2)
    .collect();

println!("{:?}", mapped);
```

Enumerate: The enumerate method adds an index to each element of the iterator.

```
let v = vec!["a", "b", "c"];

for (index, value) in v.iter().enumerate() {
    println!("Index: {}, Value: {}", index, value);
}
```

Iterators allow for concise, readable, and efficient processing of collections. Various methods and patterns, like iter, iter_mut, into_iter, and intricate adaptors like filtering, mapping, and enumerating, facilitate powerful iteration capabilities within Rust, ensuring flexibility while maintaining performance.

8.7 Using Iterators

Iterators in Rust provide a powerful and flexible way to traverse collections. They offer a systematic approach for accessing elements sequentially without exposing the underlying structure. Rust's iterator trait and methods enable developers to write efficient, readable, and idiomatic code when dealing with collections.

The Iterator trait in Rust defines methods that are used to iterate over elements. The most fundamental method is next(), which advances the iterator and returns the next value. When the iterator is exhausted, next() returns None. The Iterator trait is defined as follows:

```
// Simplified definition of the Iterator trait
pub trait Iterator {
    type Item;
    fn next(&mut self) -> Option<Self::Item>;
}
```

To illustrate the use of iterators, consider a vector of integers. We can obtain an iterator for this vector and use the next() method to traverse its elements:

```
let v = vec![1, 2, 3, 4, 5];
let mut iter = v.iter();

while let Some(element) = iter.next() {
    println!("{}", element);
}
```

```
1
2
3
4
5
```

The iter() method returns an iterator over immutable references to the vector's elements. It is also possible to create an iterator that yields mutable references using the iter_mut() method, as shown:

```
let mut v = vec![1, 2, 3, 4, 5];
let mut iter = v.iter_mut();
```

```
while let Some(element) = iter.next() {
    *element *= 2;
}
println!("{:?}", v);
```

```
[2, 4, 6, 8, 10]
```

Alternatively, the into_iter() method consumes the collection and returns an iterator that takes ownership of the collection's elements. This can be useful when you no longer need to use the collection after iteration:

```
let v = vec![1, 2, 3, 4, 5];
let iter = v.into_iter();

for element in iter {
    println!("{}", element);
}
```

```
1
2
3
4
5
```

Rust's iterator trait also provides many convenient methods to manipulate and process data. Some commonly used methods include map(), filter(), collect(), fold(), and any(). Below, we demonstrate their usage with examples.

The map() method allows the application of a function to each element of an iterator, producing a new iterator:

```
let v = vec![1, 2, 3, 4, 5];
let double_iter = v.iter().map(|x| x * 2);

for element in double_iter {
    println!("{}", element);
}
```

```
2
4
6
8
10
```

The filter() method filters elements based on a predicate function, generating a new iterator that only contains elements satisfying the predicate:

```
let v = vec![1, 2, 3, 4, 5];
let even_iter = v.iter().filter(|&&x| x % 2 == 0);

for element in even_iter {
```

```
    println!("{}", element);
}
```

2
4

The collect() method is used to transform an iterator into a collection, such as a vector, hash map, or other data structure. This method consumes the iterator:

```
let v = vec![1, 2, 3, 4, 5];
let doubled: Vec<_> = v.iter().map(|x| x * 2).collect();

println!("{:?}", doubled);
```

[2, 4, 6, 8, 10]

The fold() method reduces an iterator into a single value by repeatedly applying a combining function, starting with an initial value:

```
let v = vec![1, 2, 3, 4, 5];
let sum = v.iter().fold(0, |acc, &x| acc + x);

println!("{}", sum);
```

15

The any() method checks if any elements in the iterator satisfy a given predicate, returning a boolean:

```
let v = vec![1, 2, 3, 4, 5];
let has_even = v.iter().any(|&x| x % 2 == 0);

println!("{}", has_even);
```

true

Rust's iterators provide a powerful abstraction for working with sequences of elements, enabling the composition of complex operations with simple and readable code. Through the iterator methods, developers can easily transform, filter, and collect data, helping to write efficient and idiomatic Rust programs.

8.8 Creating Custom Iterators

In Rust, creating custom iterators provides a powerful way to traverse through data structures and perform sophisticated iteration patterns, particularly when built-in iterators do not suffice. This section will elucidate the process of designing and implementing custom iterators by leveraging Rust's traits and language constructs, while ensuring safety and efficiency.

To create a custom iterator, one must implement the Iterator trait for a struct. The Iterator trait requires the definition of the next method, which specifies how to produce each element of the sequence until it is exhausted.

Consider an example where we create a custom iterator to iterate over a range of even numbers. The following steps outline the process:

1. **Define the Iterator Struct:** We start by defining a struct to hold the iterator state.

```
// Define a struct to represent the EvenNumbers iterator.
struct EvenNumbers {
    current: usize,
    max: usize,
}
```

2. **Implement the Iterator Trait:** The Iterator trait must be implemented for the struct, requiring the definition of the next method which returns an Option type. None signals the end of the iteration, while Some(T) yields the next value.

```
impl Iterator for EvenNumbers {
    type Item = usize;

    fn next(&mut self) -> Option<Self::Item> {
        if self.current > self.max {
            None
        } else {
            let next_value = self.current;
            self.current += 2;
            Some(next_value)
        }
    }
}
```

3. **Implement a Constructor:** It is customary to provide an associated function to initialize the iterator with the appropriate state.

```
// Implement an associated function to create a new instance of EvenNumbers.
impl EvenNumbers {
    fn new(max: usize) -> EvenNumbers {
        EvenNumbers { current: 0, max }
    }
}
```

4. **Using the Custom Iterator:** By implementing the Iterator trait, the custom iterator can now be used in the same way as built-in iterators.

```
// Create and use the custom iterator.
fn main() {
```

```
    let even_numbers = EvenNumbers::new(10);
    for number in even_numbers {
        println!("{}", number);
    }
}
```

The output would be:

```
0
2
4
6
8
10
```

Creating an iterator that consumes another iterator is another common pattern. This requires wrapping an existing iterator and extending its functionality. For example, suppose we want an iterator that provides the running average of another iterator over a specified window size.

1. **Define the Struct:** Define a struct to hold the state, including the inner iterator, window size, and a buffer to keep track of elements within the window.

```
// Define struct to represent the RunningAverage iterator.
struct RunningAverage<I> where I: Iterator {
    iter: I,
    window_size: usize,
    window: Vec<I::Item>,
}

impl<I> RunningAverage<I>
where
    I: Iterator,
    I::Item: Copy + std::ops::Add<Output = I::Item> + From<u8> + std::ops::Div<
        Output = I::Item> {
    fn new(iter: I, window_size: usize) -> RunningAverage<I> {
        RunningAverage {
            iter,
            window_size,
            window: Vec::with_capacity(window_size),
        }
    }
}
```

2. **Implement the Iterator Trait:** Implement the Iterator trait for the struct, calculating the running average within the next method.

```
// Implement the Iterator trait for RunningAverage.
impl<I> Iterator for RunningAverage<I>
where
    I: Iterator,
    I::Item: Copy + std::ops::Add<Output = I::Item> + From<u8> + std::ops::Div<
        Output = I::Item> {
    type Item = I::Item;

    fn next(&mut self) -> Option<Self::Item> {
        if let Some(value) = self.iter.next() {
```

```
            self.window.push(value);
            if self.window.len() > self.window_size {
                self.window.remove(0);
            }
            let sum: I::Item = self.window.iter().copied().fold(0.into(), |a, b| a + b);
            Some(sum / (self.window.len() as u8).into())
        } else {
            None
        }
    }
}
```

3. **Using the RunningAverage Iterator:**

```
// Create and use the RunningAverage iterator.
fn main() {
    let numbers = vec![1, 2, 3, 4, 5, 6, 7, 8, 9];
    let running_avg = RunningAverage::new(numbers.into_iter(), 3);

    for avg in running_avg {
        println!("{}", avg);
    }
}
```

The output would depend on the running averages for the provided window size:

```
1
1
2
3
4
5
6
7
8
```

This section elucidates the design of custom iterators in Rust with practical examples, providing a foundation to create efficient and safe iteration mechanisms tailored to specific needs.

8.9 Consuming Adaptors on Iterators

Consuming adaptors are crucial components in Rust's iterator framework, enabling the transformation of iterators to produce new forms of data or to finalize operations on a collection. These adaptors modify the iterator in a fundamental way, often resulting in the consumption of the iterator—rendering it unusable after the operation. Understanding how to use these adaptors effectively is essential for leveraging the full power and flexibility of Rust's iterator system.

A common example of a consuming adaptor is the sum function. The sum function, when invoked on an iterator, consumes the iterator and returns the total sum of its elements. Consider the following Rust code:

```
let numbers = vec![1, 2, 3, 4, 5];
let total: i32 = numbers.iter().sum();
println!("The sum is: {}", total);
```

In this example, the sum consuming adaptor iterates through each element in the vector and produces a single integer representing the sum of all the elements. Here, numbers.iter() returns an iterator over the elements of numbers. Once sum() is called, the iterator is consumed and can no longer be used.

Another frequently used consuming adaptor is collect. Unlike sum, which reduces the iterator to a single value, collect transforms the elements of an iterator into a collection. This operation is very flexible because collect can be used to gather the elements into various data structures, including vectors, hash maps, and others. Here's how collect works:

```
let numbers = vec![1, 2, 3, 4, 5];
let doubled_numbers: Vec<i32> = numbers.iter().map(|&x| x * 2).collect();
println!("Doubled numbers: {:?}", doubled_numbers);
```

In this example, the map adaptor applies a function that doubles each element before collect converts the results back into a vector. Note that map itself is another adaptor which transforms the elements of an iterator but does not consume the iterator; it is collect that finalizes the operation by consuming the iterator.

For more advanced use-cases, consuming adaptors like fold and reduce offer powerful mechanisms to aggregate data. The fold function, for instance, takes an initial accumulator and a closure to combine each element with the accumulator. Here is an example:

```
let numbers = vec![1, 2, 3, 4, 5];
let product: i32 = numbers.iter().fold(1, |acc, &x| acc * x);
println!("The product is: {}", product);
```

In this example, fold starts with an initial value of 1 and multiplies it by each element of the vector, resulting in the product of all elements.

The reduce function is similar to fold but does not require an initial accumulator value. It assumes that the first element is the initial value and then combines it with the remaining elements using the provided closure:

```
let numbers = vec![1, 2, 3, 4, 5];
let product: Option<i32> = numbers.iter().reduce(|acc, &x| acc * x);
```

```
if let Some(prod) = product {
    println!("The product is: {}", prod);
}
```

The result of reduce is wrapped in an Option because it is possible that the iterator is empty, in which case None is returned.

Additionally, the for_each function iterates through an iterator and applies a closure to each element. This is useful for side-effects rather than data aggregation. Consider the following example:

```
let numbers = vec![1, 2, 3, 4, 5];
numbers.iter().for_each(|&x| println!("Number: {}", x));
```

Here, for_each consumes the iterator and applies the closure, which prints each element.

Employing these consuming adaptors not only makes the code more concise and readable but also enforces Rust's safety mechanisms by guaranteeing that an iterator is not used after consumption. Understanding and mastering consuming adaptors is essential for efficient data processing and iteration in Rust.

8.10 Chaining Operations on Iterators

Chaining operations on iterators can greatly enhance code readability and efficiency by enabling a series of transformations and computations to be performed in a concise, functional style. In Rust, iterators are a powerful abstraction that allow developers to compose complex operations in a fluent manner. This section examines the multitude of ways to chain iterator methods to achieve efficient data processing.

Consider a scenario where we have a vector of integers, and we wish to filter for even numbers, map each number to its square, and then collect the result into a new vector. We can achieve this using Rust's iterator chaining capabilities.

```
fn main() {
    let numbers = vec![1, 2, 3, 4, 5, 6, 7, 8, 9, 10];
    let even_squares: Vec<i32> = numbers.iter()
                                        .filter(|&&x| x % 2 == 0)
                                        .map(|&x| x * x)
                                        .collect();

    println!("{:?}", even_squares);
}
```

```
[4, 16, 36, 64, 100]
```

In this example, the iter() method creates an iterator over references to the elements of the vector. The filter() method retains only the elements for which the provided closure returns true, and the map() method transforms each element using the given closure. Finally, the collect() method gathers the results into a Vec<i32>.

filter() and map() are part of the iterator adaptor methods. Iterator adaptors take an iterator and return another iterator. This allows multiple calls to be chained together:

- filter_map(): combines filtering and mapping into a single operation.
- enumerate(): pairs each element with its index.
- peekable(): allows peeking at the next element without consuming it.
- skip(): skips a specified number of elements.
- take(): only allows a specified number of elements to be taken.

For instance, chaining skip() and take():

```
fn main() {
    let numbers = vec![1, 2, 3, 4, 5, 6, 7, 8, 9, 10];
    let result: Vec<i32> = numbers.iter()
                            .skip(2)
                            .take(5)
                            .cloned()
                            .collect();

    println!("{:?}", result);
}
```

```
[3, 4, 5, 6, 7]
```

In this instance, skip(2) starts iteration from the third element (index 2, corresponding to value 3), and take(5) results in a new iterator over the next five values. The cloned() method is used to convert the &i32 references to owned i32 values before collecting them into a vector.

Chaining operations can also integrate inspect() to debug intermediate steps without consuming the iterator:

```
fn main() {
    let numbers = vec![1, 2, 3, 4, 5, 6, 7, 8, 9, 10];
    let even_squares: Vec<i32> = numbers.iter()
                                  .filter(|&&x| x % 2 == 0)
```

```
        .inspect(|&x| println!("Even number: {}", x))
        .map(|&x| x * x)
        .collect();

    println!("{:?}", even_squares);
}
```

```
Even number: 2
Even number: 4
Even number: 6
Even number: 8
Even number: 10
[4, 16, 36, 64, 100]
```

inspect() is particularly useful for inserting log statements or performing side-effect operations at intermediate stages.

Additionally, iterators can be chained for more complex operations, such as using zip() to combine two iterators into pairs of values from each:

```
fn main() {
    let a = vec![1, 2, 3];
    let b = vec![4, 5, 6];
    let pairs: Vec<(i32, i32)> = a.iter().zip(b.iter()).collect();
    println!("{:?}", pairs);
}
```

```
[(1, 4), (2, 5), (3, 6)]
```

The zip() method facilitates operations across multiple iterators, making it indispensable in scenarios involving parallel processing of collections.

Advanced usage might involve nested iterators combined with flat_map(), which flattens an iterator of iterators into a single iterator of values:

```
fn main() {
    let nested = vec![vec![1, 2, 3], vec![4, 5, 6], vec![7, 8, 9]];
    let flattened: Vec<i32> = nested.into_iter().flat_map(|v| v.into_iter()).collect();
    println!("{:?}", flattened);
}
```

```
[1, 2, 3, 4, 5, 6, 7, 8, 9]
```

flat_map() allows applying a transformation that generates iterators and then flattens these into a single continuous sequence of elements.

Robust chaining of operations on iterators in Rust offers rich functional programming capabilities within a highly performant systems programming language. Practicing these techniques leads to more concise, readable, and efficient code.

8.11 Performance Considerations with Collections and Iterators

When working with collections and iterators in Rust, performance considerations play a critical role in the efficiency and responsiveness of your software. Understanding these considerations helps developers write more optimized and scalable Rust code.

Rust's collections such as Vec<T>, String, HashMap<K, V>, and HashSet<T> are designed with performance in mind. However, their performance characteristics differ based on factors such as memory layout, growth strategies, and underlying implementation details.

The Vec<T> collection, for instance, dynamically allocates memory as elements are added. This involves a potential reallocation and copying of elements when the current capacity is exceeded. Therefore, if the intended number of elements is known in advance, it is beneficial to use the with_capacity method to preallocate sufficient space, minimizing the need for reallocation.

```
let mut vec: Vec<i32> = Vec::with_capacity(100);
for i in 0..100 {
    vec.push(i);
}
```

The String type is a specialized form of Vec<u8>, and similar principles regarding capacity and reallocation apply. When appending to a String, using the push_str method is efficient, but if concatenating multiple strings, using the format! macro or String::from_utf8 with precalculated capacity is preferable.

HashMap<K, V> and HashSet<T> use hash tables under the hood. The performance of these collections highly depends on the quality of the hash function and the distribution of hash values. Higher load factors (number of elements to buckets) can lead to more frequent collisions and slower lookup times. Balancing load factor through proper capacity management and understanding hash performance are essential for optimizing these collections. Rust's standard library defaults to using SipHash, which provides good security at the cost of slight performance overhead.

```
use std::collections::HashMap;

let mut map = HashMap::with_capacity(50);
for i in 0..50 {
    map.insert(i, i.to_string());
}
```

Iterators, both built-in and custom, offer elegant solutions for traversing and manipulating collections. However, considerations such as iterator method chaining and unoptimized closures can introduce overhead. Rust ensures zero-cost abstractions for iterators through aggressive inlining and loop unrolling, but this is contingent on the complexity of the iteration logic.

The use of .iter() versus .into_iter() versus .iter_mut() is also significant:

- .iter() borrows the collection, allowing read-only access and iteration.
- .into_iter() consumes the collection, transferring ownership and enabling transformation into iterators.
- .iter_mut() provides mutable references, allowing modifications.

```
let v = vec![1, 2, 3];

for &x in v.iter() {
    println!("{}", x);
}

for x in v.into_iter() {
    println!("{}", x);
}

let mut v2 = vec![1, 2, 3];
for x in v2.iter_mut() {
    *x += 1;
}
```

Advanced iterator techniques such as consuming adaptors (e.g., sum(), collect()) and chaining operations (e.g., filter(), map()) should be carefully evaluated. While they enable concise and expressive code, the trade-off between readability and performance must be examined, especially in performance-critical paths.

```
let v = vec![1, 2, 3, 4, 5];
let processed: Vec<i32> = v.into_iter()
    .filter(|&x| x % 2 == 0)
    .map(|x| x * x)
    .collect();
```

Using functional-style iterator chains can be highly performant due to compiler optimizations. However, it is crucial to understand that the intermediate operations generate different kinds of iterators, and unnecessary allocations can be avoided by using iterator adaptors efficiently.

Profiling and benchmarking using tools like cargo-bench and criterion enable empirical analysis of performance characteristics, identifying bottlenecks and quantifying the impact of optimizations.

In practice, focusing on algorithmic complexity and minimizing expensive operations help in striking a balance between maintainability and performance. Employing profiling tools to identify hot paths and optimizing those sections can lead to substantial performance gains without premature optimization of non-critical code paths.

Chapter 9

Concurrency in Rust

This chapter explores concurrency in Rust, distinguishing it from parallelism and highlighting the language's focus on safe concurrent programming. It covers the creation and management of threads, shared data handling via the Send and Sync traits, and the use of Mutex types for safe data sharing. The chapter also addresses atomic operations, message passing with channels, and asynchronous programming. Common concurrency pitfalls and best practices are discussed to ensure robust and efficient multi-threaded Rust applications.

9.1 Introduction to Concurrency

Concurrency in programming refers to the ability of a program to make progress on more than one task at the same time. It is a fundamental concept that enables efficient utilization of hardware and the execution of multiple tasks in overlapping time periods.

A critical aspect of understanding concurrency is distinguishing it from parallelism. While concurrency is about dealing with multiple tasks at once (potentially not simultaneously), parallelism specifically refers to performing multiple tasks at the exact same time. Rust, as a systems programming language, provides robust tools and constructs that facilitate concurrent execution in a safe and efficient manner.

Concurrency is essential in modern applications where performance and responsiveness are paramount. It can be leveraged to handle I/O-bound operations, optimize computational workload distribution, and create responsive user interfaces. In Rust, concurrency is achieved through several mechanisms, each designed to ensure safe and predictable behavior, which is vital in a language that prioritizes safety.

To begin exploring concurrency in Rust, one must first acknowledge the conceptual foundation laid by threads. Threads are the basic unit of execution within a program. Rust's approach to threads embodies its ethos of safety and concurrency.

```
use std::thread;

fn main() {
    let handle = thread::spawn(|| {
        for i in 1..10 {
            println!("Spawned thread: {}", i);
        }
    });

    for i in 1..10 {
        println!("Main thread: {}", i);
    }

    handle.join().unwrap();
}
```

In this example, two threads are created: the main thread and a spawned thread. The thread::spawn function takes a closure, spawning a new thread of execution. Both threads run concurrently, each printing numbers in their sequence. The handle.join().unwrap() ensures the main thread waits for the spawned thread to complete its execution, demonstrating simple yet effective concurrency in Rust.

Concurrency involves shared data handling, a complex topic made manageable by Rust through the Send and Sync traits. These traits ensure data is shared across threads safely without falling prey to common concurrency pitfalls such as data races.

Send allows types to be transferred across thread boundaries. Types that implement this trait can be safely sent from one thread to another.

```
use std::sync::mpsc;
use std::thread;

let (tx, rx) = mpsc::channel();

thread::spawn(move || {
    tx.send(String::from("Hello, world!")).unwrap();
});

println!("{}", rx.recv().unwrap());
```

In this code, a message-passing channel (mpsc) is used to transfer a String between threads, highlighting the Send trait's role.

Sync, on the other hand, ensures it is safe for multiple threads to reference (but not necessarily mutate) a type concurrently. Data types that implement this trait can be shared between threads.

```
use std::sync::Arc;
use std::thread;

let numbers = Arc::new(vec![1, 2, 3, 4, 5]);
let mut handles = vec![];

for i in 0..5 {
    let numbers = Arc::clone(&numbers);
    let handle = thread::spawn(move || {
        println!("Thread {}: {:?}", i, numbers[i]);
    });
    handles.push(handle);
}

for handle in handles {
    handle.join().unwrap();
}
```

Here, Arc (atomic reference counting) is used to enable safe shared access to a vector across multiple threads, illustrating the Sync trait's significance.

Rust also tackles concurrency with different strategies beyond threads and traits. Message passing, for instance, enables threads to communicate without sharing memory, significantly reducing the risks of concurrent execution. This paradigm ensures that each thread operates on independent data, sending messages to each other as necessary.

Furthermore, Rust offers sophisticated concurrency primitives like Mutex and atomic types (for example, AtomicBool, AtomicIsize) to handle shared mutable state safely. The Mutex type allows access to shared data by multiple threads while preventing simultaneous data mutation, thus providing a fail-safe mechanism against data races and ensuring data integrity.

Lastly, Rust's async/await syntax introduces a high-level abstraction for managing asynchronous operations, enhancing the expressiveness and efficiency of concurrent code.

Understanding these foundational elements is essential to mastering concurrency in Rust. Each tool and construct plays a specific role in facilitating safe concurrent execution, aligning with Rust's overarching goal of ensuring memory safety and preventing data races without compromising performance.

9.2 Concurrency vs Parallelism

Concurrency and parallelism, though often interchanged in casual conversation, are distinct concepts in the realm of computer science and programming. Understanding the differences between them is crucial for leveraging Rust's capabilities in the most efficient manner.

Concurrency involves the composition of independently executing processes. It focuses on managing multiple tasks at once but does not necessarily mean executing them simultaneously. For instance, in an operating system, multiple applications may appear to run concurrently, but the processor switches between them rapidly. This interleaving gives the illusion of simultaneous execution. Concurrency is primarily concerned with the coordination and correctness of tasks without them necessarily being performed at the same instant.

Parallelism, on the other hand, involves performing multiple tasks simultaneously, aiming to execute computations concurrently on different processors or cores. Parallelism can lead to significant performance improvements by distributing workload across multiple processing units. Unlike concurrency, parallelism explicitly deals with simultaneous execution, addressing computational speed and efficiency.

Below is a simple example to illustrate the distinction between concurrency and parallelism using Rust:

```
use std::thread;
use std::time::Duration;

fn concurrent_tasks() {
    let handle1 = thread::spawn(|| {
        for i in 1..5 {
            println!("Task1: {}", i);
            thread::sleep(Duration::from_millis(50));
        }
    });

    let handle2 = thread::spawn(|| {
        for i in 1..5 {
            println!("Task2: {}", i);
            thread::sleep(Duration::from_millis(50));
        }
    });

    handle1.join().unwrap();
    handle2.join().unwrap();
}

fn main() {
    concurrent_tasks();
}
```

The above Rust code demonstrates concurrency through the use of threads. Although the tasks are logically running concurrently, they may be executed in an interleaved manner, depending on the system scheduler, as shown in a possible output below:

```
Task1: 1
Task2: 1
Task1: 2
Task2: 2
Task1: 3
Task2: 3
Task1: 4
Task2: 4
```

This interleaving does not guarantee that both tasks are running exactly at the same time, just that they are being managed concurrently.

In contrast, consider the following example which might be adapted to exemplify parallelism via Rust using the Rayon's parallel iterator, provided that the underlying hardware supports multiple processing units:

```
extern crate rayon;
use rayon::prelude::*;

fn parallel_tasks() {
    let data = vec![1, 2, 3, 4, 5, 6, 7, 8];

    data.par_iter().for_each(|item| {
        println!("Processing item: {}", item);
    });
}

fn main() {
    parallel_tasks();
}
```

Utilizing Rayon's par_iter converts the sequential iterator into a parallel iterator, efficiently distributing the task across multiple threads if available. This execution can occur simultaneously on multiple cores, potentially resulting in a performance gain. A possible output emphasizing parallel execution:

```
Processing item: 1
Processing item: 2
Processing item: 3
Processing item: 4
Processing item: 5
Processing item: 6
Processing item: 7
Processing item: 8
```

Here, each item is processed concurrently across different threads, ideally running in parallel and taking full advantage of multi-core architectures.

The critical distinction lies in the execution model: * Concurrency is about structure and can be maintained with a single-core processor by context switching and time slicing. * Parallelism, however, is fundamentally about utilizing multiple cores or processors to achieve true simultaneous execution.

Rust's strong emphasis on memory safety with its ownership model significantly aids in managing concurrency without data races and other common pitfalls.

In implementing concurrent and parallel systems using Rust, understanding these nuances helps to choose appropriate abstractions and libraries that align with specific performance goals and safety requirements.

Understanding these distinctions is fundamental for constructing robust and efficient concurrent applications in Rust.

9.3 Using Threads in Rust

In Rust, threads are the primary abstraction by which we execute concurrent code. Rust provides a rich API for thread management, emphasizing both efficiency and safety.

To create a new thread in Rust, the std::thread module offers the spawn function. This function takes a closure or a function and executes it in a separate thread. The following example demonstrates a basic usage of thread::spawn.

```
use std::thread;

fn main() {
    let handle = thread::spawn(|| {
        for i in 1..10 {
            println!("Hello from the spawned thread: {}", i);
            // Simulate some work by sleeping for 1 millisecond.
            thread::sleep(std::time::Duration::from_millis(1));
        }
    });

    for i in 1..5 {
        println!("Hello from the main thread: {}", i);
        thread::sleep(std::time::Duration::from_millis(1));
    }

    // Wait for the spawned thread to finish
    handle.join().unwrap();
}
```

When executed, the above code produces the following interleaved output:

```
Hello from the main thread: 1
Hello from the main thread: 2
Hello from the spawned thread: 1
Hello from the main thread: 3
Hello from the spawned thread: 2
Hello from the main thread: 4
Hello from the spawned thread: 3
Hello from the spawned thread: 4
Hello from the spawned thread: 5
Hello from the spawned thread: 6
Hello from the spawned thread: 7
Hello from the spawned thread: 8
Hello from the spawned thread: 9
```

thread::spawn returns a JoinHandle, which is used to manage the spawned thread. Calling join on the JoinHandle blocks the thread that called it until the spawned thread terminates.

A significant aspect of using threads in Rust is ensuring data safety. Rust's ownership system ensures that data races are avoided. For instance, when moving data into a thread, the ownership of that data must be transferred to the thread, ensuring exclusive access.

Consider a scenario where multiple threads need access to shared data. Rust provides mechanisms like Mutex and atomic types for secure sharing. Here is an example showing how to share data across threads using Arc (Atomic Reference Counting) and Mutex.

```
use std::sync::{Arc, Mutex};
use std::thread;

fn main() {
    let counter = Arc::new(Mutex::new(0));
    let mut handles = vec![];

    for _ in 0..10 {
        let counter = Arc::clone(&counter);
        let handle = thread::spawn(move || {
            let mut num = counter.lock().unwrap();
            *num += 1;
        });
        handles.push(handle);
    }

    for handle in handles {
        handle.join().unwrap();
    }

    println!("Result: {}", *counter.lock().unwrap());
}
```

This program creates 10 threads, each incrementing the same counter. We use Arc to provide multiple ownerships and Mutex to ensure that only one thread updates the counter at one time. The output should be:

```
Result: 10
```

In Rust, thread creation is lightweight, but excessive numbers of threads may lead to increased overhead and potential performance degradation. Therefore, Rust also supports higher-level abstractions like thread pools, where a fixed number of threads can execute multiple tasks.

A simple thread pool implementation might look like this:

```
use std::sync::{mpsc, Arc, Mutex};
use std::thread;

pub struct ThreadPool {
    workers: Vec<Worker>,
    sender: mpsc::Sender<Job>,
}

type Job = Box<dyn FnOnce() + Send + 'static>;

impl ThreadPool {
    pub fn new(size: usize) -> ThreadPool {
        assert!(size > 0);

        let (sender, receiver) = mpsc::channel();
        let receiver = Arc::new(Mutex::new(receiver));
        let mut workers = Vec::with_capacity(size);

        for id in 0..size {
            workers.push(Worker::new(id, Arc::clone(&receiver)));
        }

        ThreadPool { workers, sender }
    }

    pub fn execute<F>(&self, f: F)
    where
        F: FnOnce() + Send + 'static,
    {
        let job = Box::new(f);
        self.sender.send(job).unwrap();
    }
}

struct Worker {
    id: usize,
    thread: Option<thread::JoinHandle<()>>,
}

impl Worker {
    fn new(id: usize, receiver: Arc<Mutex<mpsc::Receiver<Job>>>) -> Worker {
        let thread = thread::spawn(move || loop {
            let job = receiver.lock().unwrap().recv().unwrap();
            println!("Worker {} got a job; executing.", id);
            job();
        });

        Worker {
```

```
            id,
            thread: Some(thread),
        }
    }
}
```

This thread pool allows submitting jobs that will be executed by a fixed number of threads. The type alias Job represents the work to be done, and each worker thread waits for a job, executes it, and repeats the process.

By implementing threads efficiently and safely, Rust ensures that concurrent programming is both powerful and reliable.

9.4 Sharing Data Between Threads

Sharing data between threads in Rust necessitates a sound understanding of the language's ownership rules and concurrency primitives. Rust enforces memory safety through its strict ownership model, which gets particularly challenging when data is shared among concurrently executing threads. This section delves into the methodology and best practices for safely sharing data between threads in Rust, focusing on key abstractions and types that facilitate this process.

The Role of Arc

The Arc (Atomic Reference Counted) type is pivotal when multiple threads need read access to shared data. An Arc is a thread-safe reference-counting pointer that enables multiple ownership of the same data. It functions similarly to Rc<T>, but it's designed for concurrent environments by leveraging atomic operations to ensure thread-safe reference counting.

To create an Arc, you use the Arc::new method. Consider the following example, which demonstrates the creation of an Arc:

```
use std::sync::Arc;
use std::thread;

let data = Arc::new(vec![1, 2, 3]);

for _ in 0..3 {
    let data_ref = Arc::clone(&data);
    thread::spawn(move || {
        println!("{:?}", data_ref);
    });
}
```

In the example above, Arc::clone is used to create new references to the same Arc instance, incrementing the reference count atomically. Each thread receives a reference and can safely read the underlying vector concurrently.

The Use of Mutex

When there is a need for both read and write access to shared data, threading must ensure exclusive access to prevent data races. Rust provides the Mutex (mutual exclusion) type for this purpose. A Mutex wraps the data and ensures that only one thread can access the data at any given time by enforcing a locking mechanism.

Here is an example of using a Mutex in conjunction with Arc:

```
use std::sync::{Arc, Mutex};
use std::thread;

let data = Arc::new(Mutex::new(vec![1, 2, 3]));

for _ in 0..3 {
    let data_ref = Arc::clone(&data);
    thread::spawn(move || {
        let mut data = data_ref.lock().unwrap();
        data.push(4);
        println!("{:?}", data);
    });
}
```

In this snippet, Arc ensures that the Mutex can be shared among the threads, while Mutex::lock ensures that only one thread can modify the vector at a time. The unwrap call is used to handle the Result returned by lock, which can fail if another thread holding the lock panics.

Combining Arc and RwLock

In some cases, it's beneficial to allow multiple readers or a single writer. Rust's RwLock (read-write lock) accomplishes this. Similar to Mutex, RwLock provides interior mutability, but it distinguishes between read and write locks. Multiple read locks can be held simultaneously, but a write lock excludes all other locks.

An example of using RwLock with Arc:

```
use std::sync::{Arc, RwLock};
use std::thread;

let data = Arc::new(RwLock::new(vec![1, 2, 3]));

for _ in 0..3 {
    let data_ref = Arc::clone(&data);
    thread::spawn(move || {
        {
            let data = data_ref.read().unwrap();
```

```
            println!("Read data: {:?}", data);
        }

        {
            let mut data = data_ref.write().unwrap();
            data.push(4);
            println!("Modified data: {:?}", data);
        }
    });
}
```

In this case, the read lock and write lock are acquired using read and write, respectively, ensuring that reading can occur concurrently while writing remains exclusive.

Using Atomic Types

For simpler data types where more granular control is desired, Rust provides atomic types like AtomicBool, AtomicIsize, AtomicUsize, and AtomicPtr. These types allow safe concurrent modification of simple values without locking mechanisms, relying instead on atomic operations.

Consider an example using AtomicUsize:

```
use std::sync::atomic::{AtomicUsize, Ordering};
use std::sync::Arc;
use std::thread;

let counter = Arc::new(AtomicUsize::new(0));

for _ in 0..10 {
    let counter_ref = Arc::clone(&counter);
    thread::spawn(move || {
        counter_ref.fetch_add(1, Ordering::SeqCst);
    });
}

// Allow some time for threads to run
thread::sleep(std::time::Duration::from_millis(50));

println!("Final counter value: {}", counter.load(Ordering::SeqCst));
```

This example demonstrates how AtomicUsize allows multiple threads to increment a shared counter safely. The fetch_add method performs an atomic addition, and Ordering::SeqCst specifies the memory ordering, ensuring changes are properly synchronized across threads.

By understanding and employing these concurrency primitives, you can share data across threads in Rust safely and efficiently, adhering to the language's principles of safety and performance.

9.5 The Send and Sync Traits

In Rust, concurrency is approached with the principles of safety and expressiveness at its core. This is achieved through the use of traits, such as Send and Sync, which form the foundation of safe data sharing and manipulation across threads. Understanding these traits is essential for harnessing the full potential of Rust's concurrency model.

The Send trait allows ownership of types to be transferred between threads. If a type implements the Send trait, it indicates that it is safe to send it to another thread. Most primitive types and standard library types implement Send by default. For example, Vec<T>, Box<T>, and String are all Send. However, types that contain non-thread-safe internal mutability, such as Rc<T> or RefCell<T>, do not implement Send because transferring them between threads can lead to undefined behavior.

The Sync trait, on the other hand, allows types to be referenced from multiple threads. If a type implements the Sync trait, it indicates that it is safe for its references to be shared between threads. In simpler terms, a type T is Sync if &T (an immutable reference to T) is Send. This is crucial for types that require multiple threads to access the same data concurrently. Most primitive types are Sync. For example, i32 and &i32 are both Sync. However, interior mutability types like Cell<T> and RefCell<T> are not Sync because their internal mutability is not protected against concurrent access.

Consider the following illustrative code that demonstrates the Send and Sync traits:

```
use std::rc::Rc;
use std::sync::Arc;
use std::cell::RefCell;
use std::thread;

fn main() {
    let x = Rc::new(5);

    let handle = thread::spawn(move || {
        println!("{}", x);
    });

    handle.join().unwrap(); // This will not compile because Rc<T> is not Send
}
```

In the code above, attempting to move an Rc<T> to another thread results in a compile-time error because Rc<T> does not implement Send. To fix this, we can use Arc<T>, which is a thread-safe reference-counted pointer and implements both Send and Sync.

```
use std::sync::Arc;
use std::thread;

fn main() {
    let x = Arc::new(5);

    let x1 = Arc::clone(&x);
    let handle = thread::spawn(move || {
        println!("{}", x1);
    });

    handle.join().unwrap();
}
```

In the revised code, Arc<T> is used instead of Rc<T>, allowing us to safely share the ownership of T across multiple threads.

Let's also demonstrate a scenario where Sync is crucial. Consider the following code snippet:

```
use std::sync::{Mutex, Arc};
use std::thread;

fn main() {
    let data = Arc::new(Mutex::new(0));

    let mut handles = vec![];

    for _ in 0..10 {
        let data = Arc::clone(&data);
        let handle = thread::spawn(move || {
            let mut num = data.lock().unwrap();
            *num += 1;
        });
        handles.push(handle);
    }

    for handle in handles {
        handle.join().unwrap();
    }

    println!("Result: {}", *data.lock().unwrap());
}
```

In this example, Arc<Mutex<i32» is employed to ensure both safe shared mutability and thread-safe access to the i32 value. The Mutex type ensures that only one thread can modify the i32 value at a time, while Arc enables safe ownership sharing across threads. The Mutex itself is Sync, making it permissible for the multiple references to it to be sent across threads using Arc.

Together, Send and Sync traits play a pivotal role in the Rust concurrency model by providing compile-time guarantees that ensure thread safety. These traits prevent data races and other concurrency pitfalls, ensuring safe and efficient concurrent programming.

9.6 Message Passing

Message passing is a concurrency pattern where threads or tasks communicate by sending messages to each other. This approach can help avoid some common pitfalls associated with shared memory concurrency, such as race conditions and deadlocks. In Rust, message passing is primarily implemented using channels provided by the std::sync::mpsc module, where mpsc stands for multiple producer, single consumer. This section will delve into the mechanisms of message passing, how to set up channels, send and receive messages, and handle typical issues that may arise when using this pattern.

The most basic form of a channel in Rust consists of a transmitter (Sender) and a receiver (Receiver). The transmitter is used to send messages, while the receiver is used to receive them. Here is a simplistic example of creating a channel and using it to send a message between threads:

```
use std::sync::mpsc;
use std::thread;

fn main() {
    // Create a channel
    let (tx, rx) = mpsc::channel();

    // Spawn a new thread and move the transmitter into it
    thread::spawn(move || {
        let message = String::from("Hello, Rust!");
        tx.send(message).unwrap();
    });

    // Receive the message
    let received = rx.recv().unwrap();
    println!("Received: {}", received);
}
```

In this example, the mpsc::channel function creates a channel, returning a tuple of Sender and Receiver. The transmitter, tx, is moved into the newly spawned thread using the move keyword, which ensures that the closure takes ownership of tx. The send method on the transmitter sends a message through the channel, and the recv method on the receiver blocks the main thread until a message is received, at which point it unwraps the result and prints it.

Rust's ownership system ensures that sending types over channels is safe because the system enforces that the type fully moves from the sender to the receiver, preventing concurrency issues. However, to leverage message passing effectively, it's essential to understand various advanced patterns and error handling techniques.

An important aspect to consider in channels is the handling of multiple producers. Rust's mpsc module supports cloning the transmitter to allow multiple threads to send messages over the same channel, facilitating fan-in channels where many producers send messages to a single consumer.

```
use std::sync::mpsc;
use std::thread;
use std::time::Duration;

fn main() {
    let (tx, rx) = mpsc::channel();

    for i in 0..5 {
        let tx_clone = tx.clone();
        thread::spawn(move || {
            let message = format!("Hello from thread {}", i);
            tx_clone.send(message).unwrap();
            thread::sleep(Duration::from_millis(50));
        });
    }

    drop(tx); // Close the original transmitter

    for received in rx {
        println!("Received: {}", received);
    }
}
```

In this example, the original transmitter tx is cloned for each thread using tx.clone(), allowing multiple threads to send messages to the same receiver. After spawning the threads, the original transmitter tx is dropped, which is necessary to close the channel correctly. The receiver uses a loop to process all incoming messages. The iterator over rx automatically stops when all senders are dropped.

Handling communication channels also involves dealing with potential errors. For instance, the send method returns a Result indicating whether the message was successfully sent. Similarly, the recv method can return an error if the channel is closed. Proper error handling ensures robust concurrent applications:

```
use std::sync::mpsc;
use std::thread;

fn main() {
    let (tx, rx) = mpsc::channel();

    let handle = thread::spawn(move || {
        for i in 0..3 {
```

```
        if tx.send(i).is_err() {
            println!("Receiver has dropped");
            return;
        }
    }
});

for received in rx {
    println!("Got: {}", received);
}

handle.join().unwrap();
}
```

In this code, we include error handling for the send method. If the receiver is dropped (e.g., by exiting the loop prematurely), the send method returns an error, detected by the is_err() call. Similarly, the receiver handles the potential closure of the channel by using an iterator, which gracefully ends when no more messages are sent.

For more complex scenarios, Rust's mpsc module supports sending various data structures, such as tuples or custom struct types, across channels. This flexibility allows structuring inter-thread communication efficiently:

```
use std::sync::mpsc;
use std::thread;

struct Data {
    id: u32,
    value: String,
}

fn main() {
    let (tx, rx) = mpsc::channel();

    let handle = thread::spawn(move || {
        let data = Data {
            id: 1,
            value: String::from("Complex Data"),
        };
        tx.send(data).unwrap();
    });

    let received = rx.recv().unwrap();
    println!("Received: id={}, value={}", received.id, received.value);

    handle.join().unwrap();
}
```

Here, we define a struct Data and send an instance of it from one thread to another. This demonstrates Rust's capacity to handle more advanced data types in its concurrency model, maintaining the benefits of safe and efficient message passing.

By understanding and utilizing channels in Rust, developers can implement safe and effective concurrent applications. Through message passing, threads can communicate in a controlled manner, reducing the risks associated with shared memory and ensuring consistent application behavior.

9.7 The Mutex Type for Safe Sharing

In Rust, ensuring safe access to shared data in concurrent programming is achieved through various mechanisms. One of the primary tools provided by Rust for this purpose is the Mutex type. A Mutex (short for mutual exclusion) is a synchronization primitive that provides safe, exclusive access to the data it guards, allowing only one thread to access the data at a time.

The Basics of Using Mutex

To use a Mutex, you need to wrap the shared data in a Mutex instance. The Mutex type is defined in Rust's standard library within the std::sync module, so it must be brought into scope:

```
use std::sync::Mutex;
```

Creating a Mutex that guards a data type, for example, an integer:

```
let m = Mutex::new(5);
```

This example initializes a Mutex instance that wraps the integer value 5. The mutex provides interior mutability, allowing the data to be modified even if the outer type (in this case, the Mutex) is immutable.

Locking and Accessing Data

To access and manipulate the data inside the Mutex, you must lock it first. Locking a Mutex ensures that only one thread at a time can access the data. The lock method is used to acquire the lock. It returns a Result<MutexGuard<T>, PoisonError<MutexGuard<T»>, which means it needs to be handled properly to ensure safety:

```
let mut num = m.lock().unwrap();
*num += 1;
```

In this case, calling lock on the Mutex instance m returns a MutexGuard. This guard is a smart pointer that automatically releases the lock when it goes out of scope, ensuring the mutex is unlocked. The unwrap method is used to handle the Result, panicking if the lock could not be acquired. The guard can then be dereferenced to access the underlying data.

Handling Poisoned Locks

A Mutex can get into a poisoned state if a thread holding the lock panics. When this happens, subsequent calls to lock will return a PoisonError. This ensures that other threads are notified of the abnormal situation and can take appropriate action:

```
match m.lock() {
    Ok(mut num) => *num += 1,
    Err(poisoned) => {
        let mut num = poisoned.into_inner();
        *num += 1;
    }
}
```

Here, if the mutex is poisoned, we extract the data using into_inner and continue the operation. This pattern ensures that we handle poisoned locks gracefully.

Using Mutex with Multiple Threads

To effectively use Mutex across multiple threads, Arc (an atomic reference-counted type) is often used. This allows safe sharing of the Mutex instance across threads without violating ownership rules.

```
use std::sync::{Arc, Mutex};
use std::thread;

let counter = Arc::new(Mutex::new(0));
let mut handles = vec![];

for _ in 0..10 {
    let counter = Arc::clone(&counter);
    let handle = thread::spawn(move || {
        let mut num = counter.lock().unwrap();
        *num += 1;
    });
    handles.push(handle);
}

for handle in handles {
    handle.join().unwrap();
}
```

```
println!("Result: {}", *counter.lock().unwrap());
```

In this example, an Arc<Mutex<i32» is created to manage a counter. The Arc::clone method is used to share ownership of the Arc across threads. Each thread locks the mutex, increments the number, and then releases the lock. The join method ensures that all threads complete before printing the final counter value. This example highlights how Arc and Mutex work together to provide thread-safe access to shared data.

Common Pitfalls and Best Practices

When using Mutex, several pitfalls should be avoided for robust concurrent programming:

- **Deadlocks**: Occur when two or more threads are waiting indefinitely for each other to release their locks. To avoid deadlocks, acquire multiple locks in a predefined order and within a single thread context if possible.
- **Lock Contention**: Excessive locking and unlocking, especially in highly concurrent programs, can lead to performance degradation. Strive to minimize the critical section (the part of the code where the mutex is locked).
- **Poisoning**: Handle poisoned locks to ensure your program can recover gracefully. Use proper error handling to manage PoisonError.

Understanding and correctly using Mutex in Rust is central to writing safe concurrency code. It ensures exclusive access to shared data, protecting against data races while providing the necessary tools to handle exceptional situations like poisoned locks.

9.8 Atomic Types and Operations

In concurrent programming, atomic operations are essential to ensure data consistency and prevent race conditions. An atomic operation is one that completes without interruption, making it indivisible. In Rust, atomic types and operations ensure that these indivisible transactions occur across multiple threads, allowing programs to safely manipulate shared data.

Rust's std::sync::atomic module provides primitives for atomic operations on integral types. These atomic types include AtomicBool, AtomicIsize, AtomicUsize, AtomicI8, AtomicU8, AtomicI16, AtomicU16, AtomicI32, AtomicU32, AtomicI64, and AtomicU64. Each atomic type supports operations that are safe to use across threads and prevent data races.

The common atomic operations provided by these types include:

- load: Atomically loads a value.
- store: Atomically stores a value.
- swap: Atomically swaps the current value with a new value.
- compare_and_swap (CAS): Compares the current value with a specified value and, if they are equal, sets a new value.
- fetch_add and fetch_sub: Atomically adds to or subtracts from the current value, respectively.
- fetch_and, fetch_or, and fetch_xor: Atomically performs bitwise AND, OR, and XOR operations, respectively.

To illustrate the use of atomic types and operations, consider the following examples:

```
use std::sync::atomic::{AtomicUsize, Ordering};
use std::sync::Arc;
use std::thread;

fn main() {
    let counter = Arc::new(AtomicUsize::new(0));

    let mut handles = vec![];

    for _ in 0..10 {
        let counter = Arc::clone(&counter);
        let handle = thread::spawn(move || {
            for _ in 0..1000 {
                counter.fetch_add(1, Ordering::Relaxed);
            }
        });
        handles.push(handle);
    }

    for handle in handles {
        handle.join().expect("Thread panicked");
    }
```

```
    println!("Result: {}", counter.load(Ordering::Relaxed));
}
```

In this example, an AtomicUsize is used to count the number of increments performed by multiple threads concurrently. Each thread adds 1000 to the counter using fetch_add. The Ordering::Relaxed parameter specifies that no synchronization or ordering constraints are enforced on these operations, which is appropriate when only counting.

Different ordering constraints can be specified, including:

- Ordering::Relaxed: No ordering constraints, only atomicity is guaranteed.
- Ordering::Acquire: Ensures that subsequent operations are not reordered before the load or store operation.
- Ordering::Release: Ensures that preceding operations are not reordered after the load or store operation.
- Ordering::AcqRel: Provides both acquire and release semantics, preventing reordering of operations before and after it.

Atomic operations are an essential tool in concurrent programming to achieve lock-free synchronization. However, choosing the appropriate ordering constraint is crucial to avoid subtle bugs and performance issues.

For situations requiring more sophisticated coordination between threads, atomic operations might not suffice. Rust provides higher-level synchronization primitives like Mutex or RwLock as discussed in other sections. Atomic operations are low-level tools that are best suited for scenarios where minimal overhead and maximal performance are desired.

To summarize, understanding and effectively utilizing atomic types and operations is fundamental for writing safe concurrent programs in Rust. By mastering these atomic primitives, developers can implement efficient and robust multi-threaded applications without falling into common concurrency pitfalls.

9.9 Using Channels for Communication

Channels in Rust provide a robust mechanism for thread communication, aligning with the language's guarantees of memory safety and freedom from data races. Channels operate on a sender-receiver model, ensuring that once a value has been sent from one thread, it can be reliably received by another, thereby facilitating safe data transfer across threads.

To leverage channels, we need to use the std::sync::mpsc module, which stands for multiple producer, single consumer. This model implies that while multiple threads can send messages into the channel, only one thread can receive messages from it.

```
use std::sync::mpsc;
use std::thread;

fn main() {
    // Create a channel
    let (tx, rx) = mpsc::channel();

    // Spawn a new thread
    thread::spawn(move || {
        let val = String::from("hello");
        tx.send(val).unwrap();
        // val is moved here and can no longer be used
    });

    // Receiving the value in the main thread
    let received = rx.recv().unwrap();
    println!("Got: {}", received);
}
```

In this example, we start by importing the mpsc module and the thread module. We create a channel using the mpsc::channel() function, which returns a tuple with a transmitter (tx) and a receiver (rx). We then spawn a new thread that sends a string message "hello" through the channel using the send method on the transmitter. The send method will return a Result type, which is unwrapped to handle any potential errors.

Back in the main thread, the receiver calls recv to block and wait for a message to be sent through the channel. The recv method also returns a Result, which we unwrap to obtain the sent message and print it.

Channels also support non-blocking receives through the try_recv method. This method allows the program to continue execution immediately if no message is available.

```
use std::sync::mpsc;
use std::thread;
use std::time::Duration;
```

```
fn main() {
    let (tx, rx) = mpsc::channel();

    thread::spawn(move || {
        let val = String::from("hello");
        thread::sleep(Duration::from_secs(1));
        tx.send(val).unwrap();
    });

    loop {
        match rx.try_recv() {
            Ok(received) => {
                println!("Got: {}", received);
                break; // Exit the loop once the message is received
            }
            Err(_) => {
                println!("No message received yet");
                thread::sleep(Duration::from_millis(100));
            }
        }
    }
}
```

In this example, the spawned thread sleeps for one second before sending the message. Meanwhile, the main thread uses try_recv in a loop, which immediately returns a result indicating whether a message is available. If no message is present, the loop prints a message and the thread sleeps briefly before checking again. This non-blocking approach can be used for polling while performing other tasks.

Channels can also facilitate communication from multiple threads to a single receiver. This is possible since the transmitter (tx) can be cloned, allowing multiple independent threads to send messages to the same receiver.

```
use std::sync::mpsc;
use std::thread;
use std::time::Duration;

fn main() {
    let (tx, rx) = mpsc::channel();

    for i in 0..5 {
        let tx_clone = tx.clone();
        thread::spawn(move || {
            let message = format!("Message from thread {}", i);
            tx_clone.send(message).unwrap();
            thread::sleep(Duration::from_secs(1));
        });
    }

    for received in rx.iter().take(5) {
        println!("Received: {}", received);
    }
}
```

Here, tx.clone() is used to create independent transmitters in each thread, allowing them to send messages to the single receiver that iterates and collects messages as they arrive. The rx.iter().take(5) call ensures that the receiver will only process five messages, which matches the number of spawned threads.

By handling message passing with channels, Rust ensures safe and effective communication between threads, avoiding the complexities and pitfalls associated with direct data sharing. This approach reinforces Rust's commitment to safe concurrency and predictable, bug-free multithreading environments.

9.10 Async Programming in Rust

Asynchronous programming in Rust allows handling operations, such as I/O tasks or timers, without blocking a thread. This facilitates efficient task management, particularly in I/O-bound applications, by enabling concurrent task execution within a single thread. Rust's async ecosystem is built upon a foundation of zero-cost abstractions, ensuring minimal overhead.

Rust provides the async and await keywords, supplemented by the Future trait, to facilitate writing asynchronous code. An async function returns a Future, which is a value that represents an operation that has not yet completed. The await keyword allows a program to yield control until the Future completes, at which point the program resumes execution.

```
use std::time::Duration;
use tokio::time::sleep;

async fn perform_task() {
    println!("Task started");
    sleep(Duration::from_secs(2)).await;
    println!("Task completed");
}
```

In the example above, the perform_task function is declared as async, making it return a Future. Inside this function, the sleep function from the tokio runtime is called, which pauses for two seconds asynchronously. The await keyword ensures that the function yields control during this waiting period, allowing other asynchronous tasks to progress.

To execute asynchronous functions, a runtime is essential. The tokio and async-std are two popular asynchronous runtimes in the Rust ecosystem. These runtimes provide an execution context for asynchronous tasks, managing task scheduling and execution.

```
#[tokio::main]
async fn main() {
    perform_task().await;
    println!("All tasks completed");
}
```

In a tokio runtime, the #{tokio::main} attribute macro is used to define the entry point of the program. The main function is also declared as async, allowing it to call perform_task with await, ensuring that the task completes before proceeding.

Asynchronous programming heavily relies on the Future trait, which represents a value that may not be immediately available. The poll method on a Future is used by the runtime to check the status of the computation.

```
use std::pin::Pin;
use std::task::{Context, Poll};
use std::future::Future;

struct MyFuture;

impl Future for MyFuture {
    type Output = u32;

    fn poll(self: Pin<&mut Self>, cx: &mut Context<'_>) -> Poll<Self::Output> {
        Poll::Ready(42)
    }
}
```

In this example, MyFuture implements the Future trait. The poll method returns Poll::Ready with a value of 42, signifying that the future has already completed.

Complex tasks often require composing multiple futures. Combinators like join! and select! from the futures crate enable running multiple futures concurrently or selecting the first future that completes.

```
use futures::join;
use tokio::time::sleep;
use std::time::Duration;

async fn task1() {
    println!("Task 1 started");
    sleep(Duration::from_secs(1)).await;
    println!("Task 1 completed");
}

async fn task2() {
    println!("Task 2 started");
    sleep(Duration::from_secs(2)).await;
    println!("Task 2 completed");
```

```
}

async fn run_tasks() {
    join!(task1(), task2());
    println!("Both tasks completed");
}
```

The run_tasks function concurrently executes task1 and task2 using the join! macro. Both tasks start nearly simultaneously, optimizing the overall runtime.

For high-level task management, creating custom Executors and Spawners allows fine-grained control over task scheduling and execution. Executors handle the execution of futures, while spawners submit futures to be executed.

Rust's async ecosystem supports the .await syntax for improved readability. Combining async capabilities with robust error handling using Result types ensures more predictable and safer asynchronous code.

Using channels for communication in asynchronous tasks facilitates inter-task communication without shared memory. The tokio crate provides mpsc (multiple-producer, single-consumer) channels as a primary communication mechanism.

```
use tokio::sync::mpsc;

async fn producer(tx: mpsc::Sender<i32>) {
    for i in 1..=5 {
        tx.send(i).await.unwrap();
    }
}

async fn consumer(mut rx: mpsc::Receiver<i32>) {
    while let Some(value) = rx.recv().await {
        println!("Received: {}", value);
    }
}

#[tokio::main]
async fn main() {
    let (tx, rx) = mpsc::channel(32);
    tokio::spawn(producer(tx));
    consumer(rx).await;
}
```

This example illustrates creating a channel and launching a producer and consumer asynchronously. The producer sends values through the channel, which the consumer receives and processes.

Rust's async programming model ensures memory safety and prevents data races, aligning with the language's core principles. By leveraging async functions, futures, and appropriate runtimes, developers can write highly efficient and responsive Rust applications.

9.11 Handling Concurrency Pitfalls

Concurrency introduces a realm of potential pitfalls that can compromise program integrity and efficiency. This section delves into the most prevalent concurrency issues and elucidates best practices for circumventing them within Rust's paradigms.

Deadlocks occur when two or more threads are waiting indefinitely for resources held by each other. Consider a scenario with two threads, A and B, and two resources, $R1$ and $R2$. If A acquires $R1$ and waits for $R2$, while B acquires $R2$ and waits for $R1$, neither thread can proceed.

```
use std::sync::{Mutex, Arc};
use std::thread;

let resource1 = Arc::new(Mutex::new(0));
let resource2 = Arc::new(Mutex::new(0));

let res1_clone = Arc::clone(&resource1);
let res2_clone = Arc::clone(&resource2);

let handle1 = thread::spawn(move || {
    let _lock1 = res1_clone.lock().unwrap();
    thread::sleep(std::time::Duration::from_millis(50));
    let _lock2 = res2_clone.lock().unwrap();
});

let handle2 = thread::spawn(move || {
    let _lock1 = res2_clone.lock().unwrap();
    thread::sleep(std::time::Duration::from_millis(50));
    let _lock2 = res1_clone.lock().unwrap();
});

handle1.join().unwrap();
handle2.join().unwrap();
```

The above code illustrates a classic deadlock scenario. Both threads lock their respective resources and wait for the other, precipitating a deadlock. To avoid deadlocks, a consistent lock acquisition order can be employed, ensuring all threads acquire locks in the same sequence.

Data races are another critical pitfall where two threads simultaneously access the same data, and at least one access is a write. Rust's ownership model, enforced by strict borrowing rules, significantly mitigates data races. Below, we illustrate a data race scenario:

```
use std::sync::{Arc, Mutex};
use std::thread;
```

```
let counter = Arc::new(Mutex::new(0));

let mut handles = vec![];

for _ in 0..10 {
    let counter_clone = Arc::clone(&counter);
    let handle = thread::spawn(move || {
        for _ in 0..1000 {
            let mut num = counter_clone.lock().unwrap();
            *num += 1;
        }
    });
    handles.push(handle);
}

for handle in handles {
    handle.join().unwrap();
}

println!("Result: {}", *counter.lock().unwrap());
```

In this Rust code, the Mutex type enforces exclusive access, effectively preventing data races. Each thread locks the Mutex before modifying the counter, ensuring thread-safe increments.

Livelocks, though less common, occur when threads continuously change their state in response to each other without making progress. Unlike deadlocks, livelocked threads remain active; however, they fail to perform useful work. Implementing exponential backoff or introducing randomness in retry mechanisms can help prevent livelocks.

Memory leaks in concurrent applications, though not exclusive to concurrency, can be exacerbated by improper handling of resources shared among threads. Rust's ownership and borrowing principles alleviate many memory leak issues, but care must be taken with complex data structures such as cyclical references. Utilizing Rc and Weak references helps prevent reference cycles.

Arc should be used over Rc for atomic reference counting, ensuring safe concurrency. Consider the following code, demonstrating a memory-safe, concurrent counter:

```
use std::sync::{Arc, Mutex};
use std::thread;

let counter = Arc::new(Mutex::new(0));
let mut handles = vec![];

for _ in 0..10 {
    let counter_clone = Arc::clone(&counter);
    let handle = thread::spawn(move || {
        for _ in 0..1000 {
            let mut num = counter_clone.lock().unwrap();
            *num += 1;
        }
```

```
    });
    handles.push(handle);
}

for handle in handles {
    handle.join().unwrap();
}

println!("Counter result: {}", *counter.lock().unwrap());
```

Handling shared state correctly is pivotal. Mutex, coupled with Arc, facilitates safe mutable state sharing, ensuring consistent data manipulation across threads. Best practices involve minimizing lock scopes to reduce contention, avoid holding locks longer than necessary, and prefer message passing when feasible for isolating thread-specific data.

Race conditions can occur even without explicit data races, typically where the sequence of execution affects the program's outcome. Rust prevents many race conditions through compile-time checks, but logical errors in algorithm design can still introduce them. Employing rigorous testing, formal verification methods, and tools like loom for concurrent systems can identify and resolve potential race conditions.

Promptly addressing panics in multithreaded contexts is crucial. A panicking thread in Rust unwinds the stack without affecting other threads; however, shared resources might remain in inconsistent states. Using catch_unwind can capture panics, allowing for graceful handling and resource cleanup:

```
use std::panic;
use std::sync::{Arc, Mutex};
use std::thread;

let counter = Arc::new(Mutex::new(0));

let handle = thread::spawn({
    let counter_clone = Arc::clone(&counter);
    move || {
        let result = panic::catch_unwind(|| {
            let mut num = counter_clone.lock().unwrap();
            *num += 1;
            panic!("Panicking in thread!");
        });

        if let Err(_) = result {
            println!("Thread panicked, but state is consistent.");
        }
    }
});

handle.join().unwrap();
println!("Counter result: {}", *counter.lock().unwrap());
```

By capturing the panic, the code above maintains control over the execution flow, ensuring resources remain in a consistent state. Employing these practices can significantly enhance the robustness of concurrent Rust applications, mitigating common concurrency pitfalls effectively.

Chapter 10

Smart Pointers and Memory Management

This chapter delves into Rust's smart pointers and memory management strategies. It introduces various types of smart pointers, including Box<T> for heap allocation, Rc<T> for reference counting, and RefCell<T> for interior mutability. The chapter also covers Arc<T> for atomic reference counting and Weak<T> to prevent reference cycles. Key traits like Deref and Drop are explained, along with custom smart pointers. Issues such as memory leaks are examined, and best practices for effective memory management in Rust are provided through case studies.

10.1 Introduction to Smart Pointers

Smart pointers in Rust provide a method to handle memory safely and efficiently, integrating ownership and borrowing principles with additional functionalities. Unlike regular pointers, smart pointers not only hold the address of heap-allocated memory but also encapsulate ownership semantics, reference counting, interior mutability, and other safe memory management techniques. These features collectively minimize common issues like double-free errors, data races, and memory leaks.

To understand smart pointers comprehensively, we will examine their basic properties and behavior. Smart pointers in Rust are mainly defined through structs, and they implement the Deref and Drop traits to manage dereferencing and cleanup, respectively. By conforming to these traits, smart pointers enable seamless integration with Rust's ownership model and automatic memory management.

Box<T>, for instance, is one of the simplest and most commonly used smart pointers in Rust. It allocates objects on the heap and ensures that the allocated memory is properly freed when the Box goes out of scope. Here's a basic example demonstrating the usage of Box<T>:

```
fn main() {
    let x = 5;
    let y = Box::new(x); // ‘y‘ is now a Box containing ‘x‘
    println!("x: {}, y: {}", x, *y);
}
```

When executed, this program outputs:

```
x: 5, y: 5
```

In this example, x is an integer allocated on the stack, while y is a Box that allocates an integer on the heap. The derefencing operator * is used to access the value inside the Box. This encapsulation ensures that the heap-allocated memory is automatically deallocated when y goes out of scope, preventing memory leaks.

Another widely used smart pointer is **Rc<T>**, which stands for reference counting. Rc<T> is useful in scenarios where multiple parts of a program need to own a value. It keeps track of the number of references to data on the heap, ensuring that the data is only released once there are no more references. However, Rc<T> is not thread-safe.

Here's an example of Rc<T>:

```
use std::rc::Rc;

fn main() {
    let a = Rc::new(5);
    let b = Rc::clone(&a); // Cloning the Rc increases the reference count
    println!("a: {}, b: {}", a, b);
    println!("Count: {}", Rc::strong_count(&a)); // Reference count is 2
}
```

When executed, this program outputs:

```
a: 5, b: 5
Count: 2
```

In this case, a and b are two references to the same heap-allocated value 5. The reference count is incremented by cloning Rc. When both a and b go out of scope, the count drops to zero, and the heap-allocated memory is deallocated.

For thread-safe reference counting, Rust provides **Arc<T>**, where Arc stands for atomic reference counting. Arc<T> behaves similarly to Rc<T> but is designed for concurrent environments. Each operation on Arc<T> uses atomic operations to ensure thread safety at the cost of some performance overhead compared to Rc<T>.

An example of using Arc<T> in a multi-threaded context:

```
use std::sync::Arc;
use std::thread;

fn main() {
    let x = Arc::new(5);
    let y = Arc::clone(&x);

    let handle = thread::spawn(move || {
        println!("y from thread: {}", y);
    });

    println!("x from main: {}", x);
    handle.join().unwrap();
}
```

When executed, this program outputs:

```
x from main: 5
y from thread: 5
```

In this example, both the main thread and the spawned thread have ownership of the same heap-allocated value. Arc<T> ensures that reference counting is performed safely across threads, preventing data races.

Rust also includes smart pointers such as **RefCell<T>** and **Cell<T>** for enabling interior mutability. This feature allows immutable data to be modified, breaking Rust's typical mutability rules but guaranteeing safety via runtime checks. RefCell<T> enforces borrowing rules at runtime instead of compile-time, allowing for mutable borrows even when the value is immutable.

An example of RefCell<T>:

```
use std::cell::RefCell;

fn main() {
    let a = RefCell::new(5);
    *a.borrow_mut() += 1;
    println!("a: {}", a.borrow());
}
```

When executed, this program outputs:

a: 6

Here, a is an immutable RefCell containing an integer. By using borrow_mut, we are able to mutate the value inside the RefCell. This pattern is particularly useful in situations where Rust's static borrow checker is too restrictive for dynamically checked borrowing at runtime.

These introductory concepts establish a solid foundation for understanding the various types of smart pointers offered by Rust. Each smart pointer type, through traits and specific functionality, facilitates safe and efficient memory management, empowering developers to write robust and concurrent software.

10.2 Box<T>: Heap Allocation

Box<T> is a smart pointer in Rust that provides heap allocation. It allows developers to allocate values on the heap rather than the stack, which can be essential for managing large amounts of data or for data that needs to live beyond the scope of a single function. By default, Rust allocates variables on the stack, which is suitable for most data types due to the stack's fast access. However, the stack has limited size, making it unsuitable for large data sets. Heap allocation, on the other hand, allows for dynamic memory management, enabling the storage of larger data structures.

One of the primary uses of Box<T> is to move data off the stack and onto the heap. This can be particularly useful for types whose size is not known at compile time or when working with recursive data structures. The following example illustrates the use of Box<T>:

```
fn main() {
    let b = Box::new(5);
    println!("b = {}", b);
}
```

In this example, the integer value 5 is allocated on the heap, and b is a smart pointer to this heap-allocated value. The Box::new function is used to create the heap allocation.

Notably, Box<T> is primarily used in scenarios involving complex or large data structures like linked lists, trees, and other recursive types. Consider a simple example of a recursive type representing a linked list:

```
enum List {
```

```
    Cons(i32, Box<List>),
    Nil
}

use List::{Cons, Nil};

fn main() {
    let list = Cons(1, Box::new(Cons(2, Box::new(Cons(3, Box::new(Nil))))));
}
```

In this example, List is a recursive type. The Cons variant contains two elements: an i32 value and a Box<List>. By using Box<T>, we ensure that each list element is allocated on the heap, allowing the construction of large or complex lists without running into stack overflow issues.

To further understand the memory layout when using Box<T>, consider the following steps: - When a value is stored inside a Box, its memory is allocated on the heap. - The Box itself is a pointer to this heap-allocated memory. - The memory on the heap is automatically deallocated when the Box goes out of scope.

Let's examine how Box<T> achieves this through the Deref and Drop traits:

- Deref: Enables Box<T> to behave like a reference to the contained value. We can use the dereference operator (*) to access the value inside the Box. This allows for seamless interaction with the value without knowing it is heap-allocated.

  ```
  let x = 5;
  let y = Box::new(x);

  assert_eq!(5, x);
  assert_eq!(5, *y);
  ```

  In this code, *y dereferences the Box to access the value inside.

- Drop: Provides a way to customize the behavior when a Box<T> goes out of scope. The Drop trait's drop method is responsible for deallocating the heap memory.

  ```
  struct CustomSmartPointer {
      data: String,
  }

  impl Drop for CustomSmartPointer {
      fn drop(&mut self) {
          println!("Dropping CustomSmartPointer with data '{}'!", self.data);
      }
  }
  ```

```
fn main() {
    let c = CustomSmartPointer { data: String::from("my stuff") };
    let d = CustomSmartPointer { data: String::from("other stuff") };
    println!("CustomSmartPointers created.");
}
```

When c and d go out of scope, Rust calls their drop methods, cleaning up the heap-allocated memory.

Understanding the interaction between Box<T>, Deref, and Drop is essential for effectively using Box in Rust. Implementing these traits ensures that Rust's ownership and borrowing rules are adhered to, maintaining memory safety and preventing leaks.

10.3 Rc<T>: Reference Counting

The Rc<T> (Reference Counted) smart pointer provides a mechanism for enabling multiple ownership of data by tracking the number of references to it. This is particularly useful in situations where immutable data needs to be shared across different parts of a program. Rc<T> ensures that data is deallocated only when there are no references left pointing to it, thereby preventing premature deallocation and providing a form of memory safety.

To begin with, importing Rc from the standard library is necessary:

```
use std::rc::Rc;
```

Creating a new instance of Rc<T> is straightforward using the Rc::new function. This function takes ownership of the data and returns an Rc<T> instance that can be cloned to create multiple references.

```
// Creating a new Rc<T> instance
let data = Rc::new(vec![1, 2, 3]);
```

The Rc::clone method increments the reference count and provides a new Rc<T> instance pointing to the same allocation. Importantly, it does not perform a deep copy of the data, making this operation efficient.

```
// Cloning the Rc<T> instance
let data_clone = Rc::clone(&data);
```

The strong count maintained by Rc<T> increases with each clone and decreases when an Rc<T> instance goes out of scope. The

Rc::strong_count function can be used to fetch the current reference count.

```
// Checking the strong count
println!("Reference Count: {}", Rc::strong_count(&data)); // Output: 2
```

Given Rc<T> is aimed at enabling shared ownership of immutable data, it does not allow mutability of the underlying value. However, having access to the RefCell<T> interior mutability pattern in combination with Rc<T> can help bypass this limitation. Consider this example:

```
use std::cell::RefCell;

// Creating an Rc<RefCell<T>> instance for interior mutability
let data = Rc::new(RefCell::new(vec![1, 2, 3]));

// Cloning the Rc<RefCell<T>> instance
let data_clone = Rc::clone(&data);

// Mutating the underlying data
data_clone.borrow_mut().push(4);

println!("{:?}", data.borrow()); // Output: [1, 2, 3, 4]
```

It's important to understand that Rc<T> is not thread-safe as it does not implement synchronization primitives. For scenarios involving concurrent access, the atomic counterpart Arc<T> should be used instead. When multiple threads need to share ownership of data, Arc<T> provides atomic reference counting:

```
use std::sync::Arc;

// Creating a new Arc<T> instance for thread-safe reference counting
let data = Arc::new(vec![1, 2, 3]);

// Cloning the Arc<T> instance for shared data in multiple threads
let data_clone = Arc::clone(&data);
```

By focusing on single-threaded use-cases, Rc<T> eliminates the performance overhead associated with thread-safety, making it more efficient when shared between components within the same thread.

Moving forward, let's consider an illustrative example that employs Rc<T> in a simple data structure. This Rust program models a graph where each node can point to multiple other nodes.

```
use std::rc::Rc;
use std::cell::RefCell;

struct Node {
    value: i32,
    edges: RefCell<Vec<Rc<Node>>>,
}
```

```
impl Node {
    fn new(value: i32) -> Rc<Node> {
        Rc::new(Node { value, edges: RefCell::new(vec![]) })
    }

    fn add_edge(from: &Rc<Node>, to: Rc<Node>) {
        from.edges.borrow_mut().push(to);
    }
}

let node1 = Node::new(1);
let node2 = Node::new(2);
let node3 = Node::new(3);

Node::add_edge(&node1, node2.clone());
Node::add_edge(&node1, node3.clone());
```

In this example, the graph nodes are represented using Rc<Node> instances, enabling shared ownership through reference counting. The RefCell<Vec<Rc<Node»> within each node allows mutability of the edges vector despite each node being wrapped in an Rc<T>.

It is essential to understand the trade-offs associated with using Rc<T>. While facilitating shared ownership, developers must be cautious of potential reference cycles, which can create memory leaks where objects are not properly deallocated because references to each other keep their reference counts non-zero. Employing the Weak<T> type, discussed in the subsequent section, helps to mitigate such risks by providing non-owning references.

Combining multiple smart pointers effectively, Rc<T> can be a powerful tool in Rust's memory management arsenal, enabling complex data structures and efficient resource sharing while maintaining safety guarantees.

10.4 RefCell<T>: Interior Mutability

The RefCell<T> type is part of Rust's standard library and provides a mechanism to achieve interior mutability. Interior mutability is a design pattern in Rust that allows you to mutate data even when there exist immutable references to that data. This is particularly useful in scenarios where you need to mutate data within enums, or when employing functional patterns that require immutable data structures while performing changes to the data.

In Rust, traditional mutability rules require that you have mutable access to a variable in order to modify it. The RefCell<T> type can be used to bypass this restriction by providing runtime-checked borrowing. This means that even though you might have immutable references to a variable, RefCell<T> allows inner mutability through runtime borrow checking, which is less restrictive than compile-time checking but introduces runtime overhead.

Creating a RefCell: To create a RefCell, you simply instantiate it with the data type you wish to mutate. An example of creating and using a RefCell is shown below:

```
use std::cell::RefCell;

let data = RefCell::new(5); // Creates a RefCell containing the value 5
```

Borrowing and Mutating RefCell: RefCell<T> provides two key methods borrow() and borrow_mut() for immutable and mutable borrowing, respectively. When these methods are called, they return smart pointers Ref and RefMut which provide access to the contents of the RefCell. It's important to note that:

- Multiple immutable borrows (borrow()) are allowed.
- Only a single mutable borrow (borrow_mut()) is allowed.
- Mutable and immutable borrows cannot coexist.

Example demonstrating borrowing and mutating:

```
let data = RefCell::new(5);

{
    let mut value = data.borrow_mut(); // Mutable borrow
    *value += 1; // Modify the value
} // Mutable borrow ends here

println!("Updated value: {}", data.borrow()); // Immutable borrow for reading
```

Output: Updated value: 6

When using RefCell, it is critical to handle potential borrowing errors. If a borrow violation occurs, e.g., attempting to create a mutable borrow while an immutable borrow is active, Rust will panic and terminate the program. This runtime validation ensures the borrow rules are upheld dynamically.

Use Cases: RefCell is particularly useful in the following scenarios:

- Graph data structures: In graph data structures or trees where edges/vertices need to be updated without having to use mutable references everywhere.

- Enums: Altering data inside enums that are referenced immutably elsewhere.

- Functional Programming: When adhering to principles of functional programming where data is often immutable, but some controlled mutability is needed internally.

Performance Considerations: The use of RefCell introduces a slight runtime overhead due to borrow checking at runtime as opposed to compile-time. Hence, it should be used judiciously in performance-critical code paths. Reference cycles also need to be managed carefully, as inappropriate use of RefCell in combination with other types like Rc<T> can lead to memory leaks.

Combining with Rc<T>: A common use case for RefCell<T> is together with Rc<T>, Rust's reference counting smart pointer. This combination allows multiple ownership of mutable data. Example:

```
use std::cell::RefCell;
use std::rc::Rc;

let shared_data = Rc::new(RefCell::new(5));

let shared_data_clone = Rc::clone(&shared_data);
{
    let mut value = shared_data_clone.borrow_mut(); // Mutable borrow
    *value += 5;
}

println!("Value in shared_data: {}", shared_data.borrow()); // Immutable borrow for
    reading
```

Output: Value in shared_data: 10

In this situation, Rc provides reference counting, while RefCell enables interior mutability. Both these types together facilitate scenarios where you have shared, mutable state across different parts of the program.

Given the meaningful advantages and careful considerations needed, RefCell<T> remains a powerful tool for enabling interior mutability in Rust. Utilizing it correctly means balancing its flexibility with mindful awareness of its runtime cost and potential borrowing pitfalls.

10.5 Arc<T>: Atomic Reference Counting

In concurrent programming, you often need to share data between threads safely and efficiently. Rust's standard library provides Arc<T>

(Atomic Reference Counting) to achieve this. Arc<T> is a thread-safe reference-counting pointer, meaning you can share a piece of data among multiple threads with minimal impact on performance and without the need for complex synchronization code.

The primary distinction between Rc<T> and Arc<T> is that Arc<T> employs atomic operations to manage the reference count. This characteristic allows Arc<T> to be safely shared among threads, unlike Rc<T>, which is limited to single-threaded scenarios. To provide a detailed understanding, we will examine several aspects of Arc<T> including its creation, usage, and atomic operations.

```
use std::sync::Arc;
use std::thread;

fn main() {
    // Create an Arc<T> from a String
    let shared_string = Arc::new(String::from("Rust Essentials"));

    // Clone the Arc<T> to create a new reference
    let cloned_string = Arc::clone(&shared_string);

    println!("Original: {:?}", shared_string);
    println!("Clone: {:?}", cloned_string);
}
```

When you create an Arc<T>, it allocates memory on the heap for the data and initializes the atomic reference count. Cloning an Arc<T> increments the reference count by one, allowing multiple Arc<T> instances to own the same data. The reference count is decremented when an Arc<T> goes out of scope, and the data is deallocated once the count reaches zero.

The Arc::clone function is significant because it provides the means to safely share data across threads. This procedure involves atomic operations ensuring the reference count is correctly maintained even when multiple threads attempt to modify it simultaneously.

```
use std::sync::Arc;
use std::thread;

fn main() {
    let shared_vector = Arc::new(vec![1, 2, 3]);

    let handles: Vec<_> = (0..3).map(|i| {
        let cloned_vector = Arc::clone(&shared_vector);
        thread::spawn(move || {
            println!("Thread {}: {:?}", i, cloned_vector);
        })
    }).collect();

    for handle in handles {
        handle.join().unwrap();
```

```
    }
}
```

In this example, a vector wrapped in an Arc<T> is shared among multiple threads. Each thread receives a clone of the original Arc<T>, ensuring the reference count is properly managed. The atomic operations within Arc<T> guarantee that each thread correctly increments and decrements the reference count, preventing race conditions.

The Arc::clone function is specifically designed to be light-weight. Internally, it performs an atomic increment operation on the reference count, which is efficient but ensures thread safety. This atomic increment can be implemented using processor-specific instructions, such as lock inc on x86 architectures, which prevent race conditions at the hardware level.

```
Thread 0: [1, 2, 3]
Thread 1: [1, 2, 3]
Thread 2: [1, 2, 3]
```

Sharing Arc<T> promotes safe concurrency; however, it is important to note that Arc<T> itself does not provide mutability. Rust's ownership model ensures safety by enforcing rules at compile time, but in situations where multiple threads need to mutate the shared data, a combination of Arc<T> and Mutex<T> (or other synchronization primitives) might be necessary.

```
use std::sync::{Arc, Mutex};
use std::thread;

fn main() {
    let shared_counter = Arc::new(Mutex::new(0));

    let handles: Vec<_> = (0..10).map(|_| {
        let cloned_counter = Arc::clone(&shared_counter);
        thread::spawn(move || {
            let mut num = cloned_counter.lock().unwrap();
            *num += 1;
        })
    }).collect();

    for handle in handles {
        handle.join().unwrap();
    }

    println!("Counter: {:?}", *shared_counter.lock().unwrap());
}
```

Here, Arc<T> is combined with Mutex<T> to allow concurrent mutations. Each thread locks the Mutex<T> before updating the counter to ensure exclusive access, demonstrating how Rust's standard library facilitates safe concurrency patterns.

Atomic reference counting is a powerful abstraction for concurrent programming, and Arc<T> encapsulates this concept in a highly usable form. By leveraging its safety and efficiency guarantees, you can manage shared state across threads with ease, harnessing the full potential of modern multicore processors while avoiding common pitfalls of concurrent programming.

10.6 Weak<T>: Preventing Reference Cycles

In Rust, managing memory efficiently and safely is crucial. One of the significant hazards in systems programming is the potential for creating reference cycles, which can lead to memory leaks even with smart pointers like Rc<T>. To mitigate this issue, Rust provides the Weak<T> type, which offers a way to reference Rc<T> managed data without incrementing the strong reference count. This assists in breaking reference cycles while still allowing shared access to the data.

The Weak<T> type in Rust is essentially a non-owning reference to the data managed by Rc<T>. This means that a Weak<T> pointer doesn't affect the reference count of the Rc<T>, thereby not contributing to the cycle.

```
use std::rc::{Rc, Weak};
use std::cell::RefCell;

struct Node {
    value: i32,
    parent: RefCell<Weak<Node>>,
    children: RefCell<Vec<Rc<Node>>>,
}

let leaf = Rc::new(
    Node {
        value: 3,
        parent: RefCell::new(Weak::new()),
        children: RefCell::new(vec![]),
    }
);

let branch = Rc::new(
    Node {
        value: 5,
        parent: RefCell::new(Weak::new()),
        children: RefCell::new(vec![Rc::clone(&leaf)]),
    }
);
```

```
*leaf.parent.borrow_mut() = Rc::downgrade(&branch);
```

In the example, we define a Node structure holding a value and references to its parent and children. The parent field uses Weak<Node> to refer to its parent efficiently, preventing a reference cycle.

Understanding Rc<T> and Weak<T> counts

The Rc<T> type maintains two counts:

- strong_count: the number of Rc<T> instances.
- weak_count: the number of Weak<T> instances.

When the strong_count drops to zero, the data is deallocated. However, weak_count does not affect deallocation directly. This way, Weak<T> can point to data that is no longer valid if all the Rc<T> instances have been dropped.

```
println!("leaf strong = {}, weak = {}", Rc::strong_count(&leaf), Rc::weak_count(&leaf
    ));
println!("branch strong = {}, weak = {}", Rc::strong_count(&branch), Rc::
    weak_count(&branch));
```

This code snippet reveals the reference counts for the leaf and branch objects.

Upgrading Weak<T> to Rc<T>

A Weak<T> can be upgraded to a Rc<T> by calling the upgrade method, which returns an Option<Rc<T»․ If the Rc<T> instance still exists, the method returns Some(Rc<T>), otherwise it returns None.

```
if let Some(parent) = leaf.parent.borrow().upgrade() {
    println!("Leaf has a parent with value: {}", parent.value);
} else {
    println!("Leaf's parent has been dropped");
}
```

This snippet demonstrates checking if a Weak<T> reference (i.e., parent) can be upgraded to a strong Rc<T> reference. Upgrading helps ensure that the referenced data is still valid and accessible.

Breaking Reference Cycles with Human-Readable Output

Breaking reference cycles can be verified by inspecting counts before and after upgrades.

```
let leaf_clone = Rc::clone(&leaf);
*leaf_clone.parent.borrow_mut() = Weak::new();
println!("After breaking the cycle:");
```

```
println!("leaf strong = {}, weak = {}", Rc::strong_count(&leaf_clone), Rc::
    weak_count(&leaf_clone));
```

The above snippet illustrates how to break a reference cycle by setting the Weak<T> reference in leaf_clone to a new, empty Weak. This minimizes the risk of memory leaks.

Rust's ability to utilize Weak<T> effectively helps programmers avoid cyclical references that could lead to memory leakage, thus promoting efficient memory management. Leveraging Weak<T> in design patterns involving parent-child relationships ensures mutual references are handled safely.

This detail-oriented exploration of Weak<T> within Rc<T> environments helps developers grasp the essentials of reference counting and cycle avoidance, aligning with Rust's philosophy of safe and efficient systems programming.

10.7 Smart Pointer Traits: Deref and Drop

In Rust, smart pointers are more than just wrappers around heap-allocated data; they implement specific traits that offer additional functionality. Two of the most crucial traits in the context of smart pointers are Deref and Drop. Understanding these traits is essential for leveraging Rust's smart pointers effectively.

The Deref trait allows an instance of a smart pointer to behave like a reference to the pointed-to value. This trait is particularly useful for operator overloading and seamless interaction with standard references. When you implement the Deref trait, you enable your smart pointer to be used in places where a reference would be expected.

```
use std::ops::Deref;

struct MySmartPointer<T> {
    data: T,
}

impl<T> MySmartPointer<T> {
    fn new(data: T) -> MySmartPointer<T> {
        MySmartPointer { data }
    }
}

impl<T> Deref for MySmartPointer<T> {
    type Target = T;

    fn deref(&self) -> &Self::Target {
```

```
        &self.data
    }
}

fn main() {
    let x = 5;
    let y = MySmartPointer::new(x);

    assert_eq!(5, *y);
}
```

In this example, MySmartPointer<T> contains a single element of type T. The Deref trait is implemented to allow MySmartPointer<T> to dereference to a reference of T.

Within the impl block for Deref, the deref method is defined to return a reference to the data field. The burden of using this method is alleviated by Rust's automatic dereferencing through the * operator, enabling a natural and ergonomic interaction with the smart pointer.

The Drop trait provides a mechanism to customize the destructor behavior for types. When an object goes out of scope, Rust automatically calls the drop method to clean up any resources held by the object. Implementing the Drop trait on a smart pointer can facilitate complex resource management, such as deallocating heap memory or releasing file handles.

```
struct MySmartPointer<T> {
    data: T,
}

impl<T> MySmartPointer<T> {
    fn new(data: T) -> MySmartPointer<T> {
        MySmartPointer { data }
    }
}

impl<T> Drop for MySmartPointer<T> {
    fn drop(&mut self) {
        println!("Dropping MySmartPointer with data: {:?}", self.data);
    }
}

fn main() {
    let _x = MySmartPointer::new(42);
    // Dropping MySmartPointer will automatically call the drop method
}
```

The Drop trait implementation shown above ensures that a message is printed to the console when the MySmartPointer goes out of scope. The drop method takes a mutable reference to self and is invoked automatically by the Rust runtime, ensuring safe cleanup of resources while avoiding double free errors.

Together, the Deref and Drop traits provide foundational capabilities for designing custom smart pointers, integrating them smoothly into Rust's type system, and ensuring proper resource management. These traits empower smart pointer types to behave in a manner consistent with built-in references, making custom implementations more flexible and powerful.

10.8 Using Custom Smart Pointers

In Rust, custom smart pointers can be created to extend or alter the default behavior provided by the standard library smart pointers. A custom smart pointer is often defined by implementing the Deref and Drop traits. This allows precise control over dereferencing behavior and destructor actions, respectively.

To illustrate creating a custom smart pointer, consider designing a smart pointer that logs a message when it is created and when it is dropped. This example will show how one can manage resources and implement the Deref and Drop traits to mimic pointer behavior while adding additional functionality.

```
use std::ops::Deref;

struct MySmartPointer<T> {
    data: T,
}

impl<T> MySmartPointer<T> {
    fn new(data: T) -> MySmartPointer<T> {
        MySmartPointer { data }
    }
}

impl<T> Deref for MySmartPointer<T> {
    type Target = T;

    fn deref(&self) -> &T {
        &self.data
    }
}

impl<T> Drop for MySmartPointer<T> {
    fn drop(&mut self) {
        println!("Dropping MySmartPointer with data: {:?}", self.data);
    }
}
```

The custom smart pointer MySmartPointer is defined with a single field data of generic type T. The implementation of new allows for the creation of a new instance of MySmartPointer. The Deref trait is then implemented so that instances of MySmartPointer can be dereferenced to access the underlying data. The Drop trait is implemented to log a message when an instance of MySmartPointer goes out of scope.

To demonstrate how this custom smart pointer functions, consider the following example usage:

```
fn main() {
    let x = 5;
    let my_pointer = MySmartPointer::new(x);

    println!("MySmartPointer points to: {}", *my_pointer);
}
```

```
MySmartPointer points to: 5
Dropping MySmartPointer with data: 5
```

When the main function ends, my_pointer goes out of scope, triggering the Drop implementation and logging the message.

Another critical aspect of custom smart pointers is handling memory safety and borrowing correctly. Rust's ownership model ensures memory safety, but custom implementations must adhere to these rules to avoid potential pitfalls. Consider a variation where the custom smart pointer manages a heap-allocated resource.

```
use std::ops::Deref;
use std::mem::drop;

struct MyBox<T> {
    data: Box<T>,
}

impl<T> MyBox<T> {
    fn new(data: T) -> MyBox<T> {
        MyBox { data: Box::new(data) }
    }
}

impl<T> Deref for MyBox<T> {
    type Target = T;

    fn deref(&self) -> &T {
        &self.data
    }
}

impl<T> Drop for MyBox<T> {
    fn drop(&mut self) {
        println!("Dropping MyBox with data");
        // The Box<T> will be dropped automatically, deallocating the heap memory.
    }
}
```

In MyBox, the data is wrapped in Rust's standard Box<T>, which handles heap allocation and deallocation. Implementing the Deref and Drop traits ensures the custom pointer integrates seamlessly with Rust's borrowing system.

```
fn main() {
    let my_box = MyBox::new(10);

    println!("MyBox points to: {}", *my_box);
}
```

```
MyBox points to: 10
Dropping MyBox with data
```

Creating complex smart pointers often involves managing multiple resource ownership and lifetimes scenarios. For instance, implementing a reference-counted smart pointer could further illustrate advanced usage of Rust's features.

The flexibility of Rust's system allows the design of custom smart pointers tailored to specific requirements. Understanding and utilizing the Deref and Drop traits is essential for safe and efficient memory management. Developing these custom pointers refines control over resource management while adhering to Rust's strict safety guarantees.

10.9 Memory Leaks and How to Avoid Them

Memory leaks occur when a program allocates memory but fails to release it back to the system, leading to wasted memory resources. Although Rust aims to prevent memory leaks through its ownership model and automatic memory management, there are still scenarios where leaks can occur. This section examines common causes of memory leaks in Rust and strategies to avoid them.

Memory leaks can occur in Rust when reference cycles are unintentionally created. Reference cycles prevent the memory from being freed even though it is no longer accessible.

Example of a Reference Cycle:

Consider the following example where two objects reference each other, creating a cycle:

```
use std::rc::Rc;
use std::cell::RefCell;

struct Node {
    value: i32,
    next: Option<Rc<RefCell<Node>>>,
}
```

```
let a = Rc::new(RefCell::new(Node { value: 1, next: None }));
let b = Rc::new(RefCell::new(Node { value: 2, next: Some(a.clone()) }));

a.borrow_mut().next = Some(b.clone());
```

In this example, a references b and b references a, forming a cycle. Consequently, neither a nor b can be dropped once they are no longer needed because their reference counts never reach zero.

To avoid this issue, we can use Weak<T>, which is a counterpart to Rc<T> that does not increment the strong reference count. This allows the creation of non-owning references that do not prevent the values they reference from being dropped.

Corrected Example Using Weak<T>*:*

```
use std::rc::{Rc, Weak};
use std::cell::RefCell;

struct Node {
    value: i32,
    next: Option<Rc<RefCell<Node>>>,
    prev: Option<Weak<RefCell<Node>>>,
}

let a = Rc::new(RefCell::new(Node { value: 1, next: None, prev: None }));
let b = Rc::new(RefCell::new(Node { value: 2, next: Some(a.clone()), prev: None }));

a.borrow_mut().next = Some(b.clone());
b.borrow_mut().prev = Some(Rc::downgrade(&a));
```

In this revised example, b's prev field uses Weak, breaking the cycle and allowing the memory to be properly freed.

Another scenario where memory leaks can happen is when global allocation patterns are misused. For instance, keeping persistent data structures that grow indefinitely can result in memory exhaustion. One common strategy to avoid this is implementing suitable data structure management techniques such as trimming unused elements or periodically clearing caches.

Example of Clearing Caches:

```
use std::collections::HashMap;

struct Cache {
    data: HashMap<String, String>,
}

impl Cache {
    fn new() -> Self {
        Cache { data: HashMap::new() }
    }

    fn store(&mut self, key: String, value: String) {
```

```
        self.data.insert(key, value);
    }

    fn clear(&mut self) {
        self.data.clear();
    }
}

let mut cache = Cache::new();
cache.store("key1".to_string(), "value1".to_string());
cache.store("key2".to_string(), "value2".to_string());

// Clear the cache to free memory
cache.clear();
```

Applying such techniques ensures that memory allocated for temporary purposes is adequately freed, thereby avoiding unintentional memory leaks. Additionally, thorough testing and profiling enjoy a critical role in identifying and mitigating memory leaks.

Furthermore, the integration of automated tools like Valgrind or cargo geiger can be utilized to detect memory-related issues explicitly. These tools analyze the program execution to identify memory leaks by tracking the memory allocation and deallocation patterns.

Example of Using Valgrind:

Compile the Rust program with debugging information:

```
cargo build --debug
```

Run the program under Valgrind to detect memory leaks:

```
valgrind --leak-check=full target/debug/program_name
```

The output will provide detailed information on any memory leaks detected, enabling the developer to trace and rectify the issues.

Another essential aspect of memory management to avoid leaks is correctly implementing the Drop trait for custom smart pointers or structures that handle resource allocation. The Drop trait allows the execution of custom deallocation logic when an object goes out of scope.

Example of Implementing Drop *Trait:*

```
struct CustomSmartPointer {
    data: String,
}

impl Drop for CustomSmartPointer {
    fn drop(&mut self) {
        println!("Dropping CustomSmartPointer with data: {}", self.data);
    }
}
```

```
{
    let c = CustomSmartPointer { data: String::from("my data") };
} // CustomSmartPointer's drop method is called here
```

In this example, when c goes out of scope, its drop method is automatically called to handle any necessary cleanup.

Lastly, adopting best practices, such as limiting the scope of variables and preferring stack allocation where feasible, further reduces the likelihood of memory leaks. Encapsulating complex ownership patterns within well-defined lifetimes also aids in the systematic management of memory resources, ensuring that memory is efficiently allocated and deallocated.

By understanding and implementing these strategies, developers can effectively mitigate the risk of memory leaks and ensure robust and efficient memory management in their Rust programs.

10.10 Best Practices for Memory Management

Effective memory management is critical for ensuring that applications are both efficient and free from errors such as memory leaks or undefined behaviors. Rust provides a range of tools and idioms to handle memory safely and efficiently. Here, we will discuss best practices that can help in achieving optimal memory management in Rust.

- **Understanding the Ownership Model:**

  Grasping the ownership model is fundamental to effective memory management in Rust. Ownership rules ensure that each value has a single owner at any given time, which automatically deallocates memory when the owner goes out of scope. When passing ownership, explicitly think about whether you need to move, borrow, or clone the data:

  ```
  // Moving ownership
  let x = String::from("hello");
  let y = x; // x is now invalid

  // Borrowing ownership
  let s = String::from("world");
  let len = calculate_length(&s); // s is still valid
  ```

- **Prefer Using Smart Pointers When Necessary:**

  Although Rust's ownership model handles most cases, smart pointers are indispensable when shared ownership or interior mutability is required. Use Box<T> for heap allocation, Rc<T> and Arc<T> for shared ownership, and RefCell<T> for interior mutability.

```
use std::rc::Rc;

let a = Rc::new(5);
let b = Rc::clone(&a);
```

- **Avoid Reference Cycles:**

  Reference counting smart pointers such as Rc<T> can create reference cycles causing memory leaks. Use Weak<T> to prevent such cycles.

```
use std::rc::{Rc, Weak};
use std::cell::RefCell;

struct Node {
    value: i32,
    parent: RefCell<Weak<Node>>,
    children: RefCell<Vec<Rc<Node>>>,
}

let leaf = Rc::new(Node {
    value: 3,
    parent: RefCell::new(Weak::new()),
    children: RefCell::new(vec![]),
});
```

- **Use Scoped Threads:**

  When working with concurrency, prefer using scoped threads to ensure that all data accessed by the thread remains valid throughout its execution.

```
use std::thread;

let vec = vec![1, 2, 3];
thread::scope(|s| {
    s.spawn(|| {
        println!("{:?}", vec);
    });
});
```

- **Minimize Clone Calls:**

  Cloning data can be expensive in terms of both performance and memory. Instead of cloning, try to use references or smart pointers to share data.

```
let x = Rc::new(vec![1, 2, 3]);
let y = Rc::clone(&x); // Instead of x.clone()
```

- **RAII for Resource Management:**

  Utilize the RAII (Resource Acquisition Is Initialization) pattern to manage resources. Rust's Drop trait allows automatic cleanup when resources go out of scope.

```
use std::fs::File;

fn main() {
    let file = File::open("foo.txt").unwrap();
    // file is automatically closed when it goes out of scope
}
```

- **Be Explicit with Lifetimes:**

  Lifetimes prevent dangling references by explicitly specifying the scope a reference must be valid for. Make sure to use lifetimes to inform the compiler of these relationships.

```
fn longest<'a>(x: &'a str, y: &'a str) -> &'a str {
    if x.len() > y.len() {
        x
    } else {
        y
    }
}
```

- **Handle Panics Gracefully:**

  Panics can cause memory leaks if not handled properly. Use std::panic::catch_unwind to handle panics and ensure cleanup.

```
use std::panic;

let result = panic::catch_unwind(|| {
    // code that might panic
});

if let Err(error) = result {
    println!("Handled panic: {:?}", error);
}
```

- **Leverage Rust Tools and Linters:**

  Use tools like clippy and rustfmt to identify memory management issues. These tools can offer suggestions for improving code quality.

```
$ cargo clippy
$ cargo fmt
```

Applying these best practices facilitates robust and efficient memory management in Rust applications. Through rigorous adherence to the ownership model, strategic use of smart pointers, and thoughtful programming patterns, memory-related issues can be minimized, leading to safer and more reliable software.

10.11 Case Studies in Smart Pointers

To consolidate our understanding of smart pointers in Rust, we examine several practical use cases. These case studies illustrate how different smart pointers are utilized in real-world applications and provide insights into efficient memory management practices.

Case Study 1: Implementing a Linked List

A linked list is an ideal example for demonstrating the use of Box<T>. Below is an implementation of a singly linked list using Box<T>.

```
enum List {
    Cons(i32, Box<List>),
    Nil,
}

use List::{Cons, Nil};

fn main() {
    let list = Cons(1, Box::new(Cons(2, Box::new(Cons(3, Box::new(Nil))))));
}
```

In this example, Box<T> allows the nodes to be allocated on the heap, enabling a recursive data structure. Each node in the list contains an integer and owns the next node via a Box<List> until the list ends with Nil.

Case Study 2: Reference Counting with Rc<T>

A tree data structure is well-suited for showcasing Rc<T>, which enables multiple ownership. Below is an example of a simple tree with Rc<T>.

```
use std::rc::Rc;

enum Tree {
    Node(i32, Rc<Tree>, Rc<Tree>),
    Nil,
}

use Tree::{Node, Nil};

fn main() {
```

```
    let left_child = Rc::new(Node(2, Rc::new(Nil), Rc::new(Nil)));
    let right_child = Rc::new(Node(3, Rc::new(Nil), Rc::new(Nil)));
    let root = Rc::new(Node(1, left_child.clone(), right_child.clone()));

    println!("Root count: {}", Rc::strong_count(&root));
    println!("Left child count: {}", Rc::strong_count(&left_child));
    println!("Right child count: {}", Rc::strong_count(&right_child));
}
```

The Rc::clone method increments the reference count, ensuring memory is managed safely by the Rust compiler. This example demonstrates shared ownership and reference counting in a tree structure, printing out the reference counts of each node.

Case Study 3: Interior Mutability with RefCell<T>

The RefCell<T> type is used for mutability inside immutable structures. Below, we apply RefCell<T> in a scenario where we need to mutate data inside an Rc<T>.

```
use std::rc::Rc;
use std::cell::RefCell;

#[derive(Debug)]
struct Node {
    value: i32,
    next: Option<Rc<RefCell<Node>>>,
}

fn main() {
    let first = Rc::new(RefCell::new(Node { value: 1, next: None }));
    let second = Rc::new(RefCell::new(Node { value: 2, next: None }));

    // Link first node to second node
    first.borrow_mut().next = Some(second.clone());

    // Modify second node's value
    second.borrow_mut().value = 3;

    println!("{:?}", first);
}
```

The usage of RefCell<T> allows mutable access to the inner value while still enforcing borrow rules at runtime. This feature enables data modification within immutable structures, which isn't permitted with Box<T> or Rc<T> alone.

Case Study 4: Atomic Reference Counting with Arc<T>

Multithreaded applications often require shared ownership with thread safety. The Arc<T> smart pointer is particularly useful in this context. Consider the following example where multiple threads access a shared data structure:

```
use std::sync::{Arc, Mutex};
```

```
use std::thread;

fn main() {
    let data = Arc::new(Mutex::new(0));

    let mut handles = vec![];
    for _ in 0..10 {
        let data = Arc::clone(&data);
        let handle = thread::spawn(move || {
            let mut num = data.lock().unwrap();
            *num += 1;
        });
        handles.push(handle);
    }

    for handle in handles {
        handle.join().unwrap();
    }

    println!("Result: {}", *data.lock().unwrap());
}
```

The Arc<T> type ensures data shared across threads is reference counted and safely accessible. The Mutex<T> is used here to enforce mutual exclusion, preventing data races.

Case Study 5: Preventing Reference Cycles with Weak<T>

To prevent reference cycles, which lead to memory leaks, Weak<T> can be employed. Here, we modify a tree structure to use Weak<T> for parent pointers:

```
use std::rc::{Rc, Weak};
use std::cell::RefCell;

#[derive(Debug)]
struct Node {
    value: i32,
    parent: RefCell<Weak<Node>>,
    children: RefCell<Vec<Rc<Node>>>,
}

fn main() {
    let leaf = Rc::new(Node {
        value: 3,
        parent: RefCell::new(Weak::new()),
        children: RefCell::new(vec![]),
    });

    let branch = Rc::new(Node {
        value: 5,
        parent: RefCell::new(Weak::new()),
        children: RefCell::new(vec![leaf.clone()]),
    });

    *leaf.parent.borrow_mut() = Rc::downgrade(&branch);

    println!("Branch: {:?}", branch);
    println!("Leaf: {:?}", leaf);
```

```
    println!("Leaf parent: {:?}", leaf.parent.borrow().upgrade());
}
```

This structure enables circular references between parent and child nodes without creating memory leaks. The Rc::downgrade method converts an Rc<T> to a Weak<T>, and Weak<T>::upgrade() returns an Option<Rc<T»>.

These case studies illustrate the versatility and safety of Rust's smart pointers in various practical scenarios. By employing smart pointers like Box<T>, Rc<T>, RefCell<T>, Arc<T>, and Weak<T>, developers can manage memory effectively while ensuring safety and performance across single and multithreaded environments.

Made in the USA
Monee, IL
04 November 2026

67387598R00164